CROP CIRCLES
AND
CLIMATE CHANGE

Jerry Lesac

PRESS

Dear Harald.
Thank you for
your friendship
and for opening your
home to me. God
will surely richly reward
you.
Your help made this
book a reality!!
In Christ's love
Jerry

DEDICATION

To the Lord Eternal, and His Son Christ Jesus, who are and remain ever faithful. Without them I could do nothing.

To my earthly father, Petar Lesac who sadly did not live to see this book come to fruition may he forgive me.

To that dear Pastor and friend Ross Fox bless his memory who was used mightily by His Majesty to teach and instruct me on what the Christian life is really all about. Your motto Ross -Life Is Relationships was never truer especially when it comes to our Blessed Lord and Savior.

To Les Johnson who helped me immensely by editing and correcting my many mistakes. To him I owe a debt of gratitude.

And lastly but not least to those many dear friends of whom I cannot list here, you know who you are, who have prayed immensely on my behalf. Believe me when I say, I have felt your prayers. Thank you! Thank you! Thank you!!!

INTRODUCTION

There is perhaps no topic of greater concern today than the topic of our weather and what is happening to it. For as one can see one cannot open a newspaper or watch a televised news broadcast without coming across almost daily now reports of everything from severe droughts, to flooding, windstorms, hurricanes, tornado's, ice storms, and even hailstones the size of small melons occurring somewhere on this planet of ours. It's actually becoming such now that even the high north is beginning to experience unusually warm weather, a matter which is raising alarm bells among the Eskimos given the melting effect it is having on the polar ice caps. Then next to all of this we also have the phenomena of crop circles. There are some really strange and inexplicable things taking place throughout the entire world? As a result, many studies have therefore been conducted and scientific papers written with most, if not all of them, placing the blame for it all {the weather anyway} on industrial pollution. The many debates and arguments being that the earth can no longer cope with the enormous amount of heat and gas that we pour into it everyday. Heat and gas that is causing our planet to experience something akin to what a greenhouse experiences wherein that the heat that is produced doesn't dissipate but rather becomes trapped, as it were, in the upper atmosphere which causes the production of moisture. The experts refer to it as global warming- an explanation which certainly sounds logical enough to accept and believe. As the scientific data continues to mount, however, there has come to light some surprising information that has quite perplexed the experts; for as it turns out climate change is really not something unique to just our own day and age. Rather, climate change, it has now been observed, has been an ongoing phenomenon throughout mankind's entire history. So much so in fact that many past societies were found to have actually collapsed under the weight of it all. A rather startlingly discovery that has so stirred the halls of academia with many questions and concerns for it was always believed that the collapse of such societies in the past was the result of social, political, and or economic factors. That however is no longer the case with this new data now bringing to light how a changing climate was responsible for why many past civilizations collapsed under everything from severe flooding, to windstorms, tornados, thunderstorms, hail and quite incredibly to droughts that were observed to have lasted for as long as 200 hundred years! Observations that have quite shocked and dismayed the experts leaving them to question why would that happen and why during a time in our planet's history where nothing that man created would be responsible for the weather to have acted in such ways? It has actually become quite the enigma, leading many within the field of meteorological science to the assumption that either weather is not as stable as originally thought or there has to be something else going on here. A matter which ultimately is leading many scientists to now look into other areas of knowledge and understanding like astronomy for example with a particular emphasis on the sun itself. They are going about looking into practically every area and avenue of knowledge except for the one area of knowledge that seldom gets any attention at all-religion. A subject that apparently has got a great deal to say like for example...

"Rain will come in torrents, and I will send hailstones hurtling down and violent winds will burst forth... In my wrath I will unleash a violent wind, and in my anger hailstones and torrents of rain will fall with destructive fury." {Ezekiel 13: 8-13}

"When He thunders, the waters in the heavens roar; He makes clouds rise from the ends of the earth. He sends lightning with the rain and brings out the wind from His storehouses." {Jeremiah 51:16}

"The Lord will cause men to hear His majestic voice and will make them see His arm coming down with raging anger and consuming fire, with cloudburst, thunderstorm and hail." {Isaiah 30:30}

It appears that by way of these words there is something altogether different going on with our weather systems. What could it actually be possible that present day climate change could have something to do with the story of Noah? That there could actually be a religious explanation for what we see happening? Well apparently yes that is precisely the case as we shall see in this utterly fascinating study of ours.

TABLE OF CONTENTS

CHAPTER ONE

THE STORY OF
NOAH - GLOBAL WARMINGS
TRUE BEGINNINGS

If the study of climate change begins anywhere it would certainly have to be in the story of Noah. A story that if one remembers one's Sunday school lessons revolves around how the world was at one time completely destroyed by a climate change that was of such enormous proportions that it literally submerged the entire planet under water, and why was this? Well the reason we are told was because God the Creator of all life chose the weather as the means by which He communicated His anger and ultimately His judgment upon a world gone insane with living in wickedness. A life of wickedness that had reached the point of such total and complete depravity that as God said to Noah, *'every inclination of the thoughts of their hearts was only evil all of the time.'* {Genesis 6:5} The issue of sin which is lawlessness had apparently become such that the people of Noah's generation had succumbed to everything where it was concerned and imagine how incredibly terrible that must have been with vices like lust, greed, malice, deceit, envy, slander, arrogance, theft, murder, adultery, and sexual immorality all going completely unchecked in a society. In fact what would all of that ultimately have led to? Well, no doubt to anarchy and that on a scale beyond anything anyone could possibly imagine which left God with but one choice and that was to bring that generation to an end. An end that ultimately came by a flood of rain that occurred over a period of 40 days and 40 nights that was of such enormous proportions that it submerged the entire planet under water thereby effectively killing off everything. Except that is of course for the man named Noah and his immediate family, who being found faithful and righteous and were saved out of it by the building of an enormous boat of which God commanded and taught him how to build so that he could save himself, his immediate family and a pair of a certain number of animals whom God chose and brought into the ark. Life would begin anew under a new age and by a covenant whereby God would never again destroy all life by such a worldwide flood of rain.

"Then God said to Noah and to his sons with him: "*I now establish my covenant with you and with your descendants after you and with every living creature that was with you-the birds, the livestock and all the wild animals, all those that came out of the ark with you-every living creature on earth. Never again will all life be cut off by the waters of a flood; never again will there be a flood to destroy the Earth.*" And God said, This is the covenant I am making between me and you and every living creature with you, a covenant for all generations to come: I have set my rainbow in the clouds, and it will be a sign of the covenant between me and the earth. Whenever I bring clouds over the earth and the rainbow appears in the clouds, I will remember my covenant between me and you and all living creatures of every kind. Never again will the waters become a flood to destroy all life. Whenever the rainbow appears in the clouds, I will remember the everlasting covenant between God and all living creatures of every kind on the earth. So God said to Noah, This is the sign of the covenant I have established between me and all life on the earth.*" {Genesis 9: 8-17}

This is where it all began, a biblical history which explains to us that pollution ultimately is not something that just comes from industrial sources but rather by way of that which comes out of the human heart and character of mankind. That invariable poison of the human character that manifests itself by way of a lawlessness involving every-thing from cursing to lying, stealing, adultery, greed, pride and murder, the seven great pillars of the worst of human conduct and behavior that has for countless generations been responsible for an immeasurable amount of pain and suffering. The reasons behind so much bloodshed and the very existence of which one would think would be seen and received as more than enough proof that what the bible testifies to is true in its entirety. Surely one need only look at our daily headlines to see the incredible enormity of it all by way of everything from huge financial scandals involving major international corporations, government mismanagement on a scale beyond belief and judicial system's rocked by enormous corruption. Far too many proud and greedy people lying, stealing, killing and committing so many forms of adultery now that it is hard to imagine. It's in fact becoming such now that where the issue of adultery is concerned not even our children are being spared the experience of it all with and get this- a society actually having to implement an Amber Alert program because of it. Our children if you can imagine are actually ending up being abducted by unscrupulous people for the purposes of satisfying their many perverted lusts. One recent example of which was portrayed in a most unbelievable and unimaginable manner with the abduction of 10 year old Holly Jones of Toronto who was raped and then murdered in a most horrific way. Or yet to that most infamous of all crimes that took place in the country of Belgium some 10 years ago where law enforcement officials found in the basement of a man's home two abducted children who were found to have starved to death inside a steel cage.

Arlon, Belgium
   "Convicted pedophile Marc Dutroux was jailed for life yesterday for kidnapping, raping and killing girls as young as eight, closing a case that has transfixed Belgium for nearly 8 years.

After hours of deliberation, the court also jailed Dutroux's former wife and two other people at the end of a legal saga that led to widespread but unproven suspicions that a top-level pedophile ring was protecting the country's most hated man.

"Marc Dutroux you have been condemned to the maximum sentence," said Judge Stephane Goux after reading out the prison terms to a hushed courtroom in this eastern Belgian town.

"I believe that you still come out a bit better than most of the victims, who are no longer among the living."

"The crimes had haunted Belgian since Dutroux's arrest in 1996. Many came to believe he worked under the protection of a secret pedophile ring whose members included police, politicians and other influential figures."

"In blunders that enraged the public, police bungled the search for the victims, some of whom had been missing for more than a year. During a court visit after his arrest, Dutroux managed to briefly escape custody."

"The jury blamed Martin for causing the death of Julie Lejeune and Melissa Russo, both 8, who came to represent the horror of the Child murders across the global media."

"The two friends apparently starved to death in the couples "dungeon" while Dutroux was imprisoned for other crimes. Martin fed the dogs guarding the dungeon but claimed she was too frightened to go into the secret cellar in the slums of Charleroi, fearing the "little beasts" would attack her."

"The bodies of An Marchal and Eefje Lambrecks were dug up next to the house after his arrest. They had been drugged, gagged and buried alive."

"An Marchal's father, Paul, standing outside the courthouse where white flowers were attached to railings in memory of the victims, said "I am a bit disappointed that the [co-defendants] didn't get the maximum sentence."

"Prosecutors had sought 30 to 35 years for Martin, 30 years for Lelievre and a minimum of 10 years for Nihoul." {By Francois Lenoir Reuters with files from The Daily Telegraph}

It is rather unbelievable and this is not just some rare case but rather is actually becoming a worldwide phenomenon. Imagine we actually have people who are taking delight in using preteens and even children this way now and this in many cases even by ones own parents? Yes parents; for as has been discovered by law enforcement officials there are parents who are actually providing their own children for such purposes especially where the Internet is concerned. That electronic medium of exchange that has the producers of such smut looking to get away with practically anything they can while actually hoping to remain anonymous in the process. Anything and everything for money these days:

'Internet service providers face a crackdown over child pornography police warn'

Toronto- "Police have a warning for Canada's Internet service providers in the wake of the horrifying sex slaying of 10 year old Holly Jones: It's just a matter of time before they'll face a major crackdown as investigators battle a scourge of child pornography.

Providers have failed to voluntarily police themselves and only aggressive law enforcement will now work, said Detective Sgt. Paul Gillespie of Toronto police's sex crimes unit.

"There is absolutely no will in Canada in the service provider industry and it's very, very frustrating to us," Gillespie said Friday.

"They don't think they're responsible for anything that occurs in their domain. Rather than helping us they all stand behind their lawyers and privacy issues."

The issue of Internet kiddie porn and violence against children was brought into stark focus Thursday when a 36-year-old software programmer pleaded guilty to Holly's abduction, rape, murder and dismemberment.

Michael Briere, who had no criminal record but won't have sexual interest in children, told police he had been viewing child pornography on the Internet just before he took the streets in May 2003 and snatched Holly at random.

"This is the fuel that drives their engines," said Gillespie. "This fuels their fantasy and unfortunately in some circumstances, like this latest case in Toronto this drove this fellow into a frenzy.

Bell Canada, operators of Sympatico, one of the country's largest Internet access providers, said it's not its job to patrol the Internet.

"It is the role of law enforcement to police or monitor content," said Bell spokesman Mohammed Nakhooda.

But he added Bell does take immediate action when asked "explicitly" to do so by the authorities.

American law enforcement officials say at least one of the three men arrested for possession of child porn has had contact offenses against kids.

Still, Dr. Peter Collins, a forensic psychiatrist said it's difficult to state categorically that viewing child pornography causes pedophiles to act out their fantasies.

Nevertheless, he said, it makes little difference. "Each and every pornographic image [of a child] is a permanent depiction of their sexual abuse," said Collins, an assistant professor at the University of Toronto. "So the mere demand for child pornography on the Internet is creating victims."

Numbers are difficult to come by but police estimate there are more than 100,000 kitty porn websites that contain hundreds of thousands of vile images, including the rapes of babies still in their diapers.

Police say industry co-operation would go a long way toward freeing up resources needed to track down those who actually produce the material." (Canadian Press Sunday, June 20, 2004 The Province)

Pornography and pornographers are popping up everywhere with many of them trying to cash in on what has become a billion dollar business and industry with many of these pornographers actually trying to legalize it going so far as to even turn it into a political issue by campaigning. Look at the windfall of taxes it would generate. Apparently they have all but forgotten that sex was meant to be an important bonding between two people for the purposes of one's own children. What they've decided to do instead though is to treat it as more of a recreational activity. A sport if you will that has both men and women taking on so many multiple partners now that it defies description even going so far as to lust after their own kind. Activities of which will and surely are leading to destruction of the family unit altogether, a matter which one would think would be of the gravest of concern for every nation. Surely it shouldn't take much to see and understand that given how the family unit no longer consists of two parents but rather has increasingly more to do with single parenthood. It's like a new kind of widowhood where abandoned mothers and now increasingly fathers as well, who along with their orphaned children are desperately left looking to the governments for their welfare. This is what we are fast coming to in our societies today and if this wasn't troubling enough what surely has to be the most inexplicable matter of all is how this is leading to a Brady Bunch type of family situation to occur. Unlike the sitcom of the 1970's though where the family consisted of divorcee's each coming into some new relationship with three children of their own, the father with three sons and the mother with three daughters, what we have today is something altogether different. For today what we have is this Brady Bunch consisting more and more of a single man arriving with three sons who are the products of three other mothers and the single woman arriving with three daughters who are the products of three other fathers. A truly bizarre and unbelievable situation which quite literally is becoming that much worse and deplorable a predicament seeing how the bedrooms come equipped with keyholes or rather video feeds. Now just an exaggeration you may be saying? Hardly as one look at such TV programs as Maury or Jerry Springer will reveal and you will find such daily talk show headlines as 'Lovers Misbehaving' or 'Which of 27 Men is the Father of my Child' or yet 'Please Don't Cheat on me with My Mother.' A truly unbelievable spectacle and do you know what has to be the crowning achievement of all is how abortion has become the great problem solver! A great problem solver because sex sometimes creates mistakes and mistakes because the act is not an intimate loving act between two partners for the purpose of bonding and creating one's own children but rather becoming something of a recreational activity. A sport if you will that has turned itself upon children no less! Unbelievable and to think that if all of this wasn't enough try to understand this...

KASSEL, Germany - "In chilling tones, a self-declared cannibal told a German court yesterday how he killed and ate a man he says consented to be dissected and consumed in front of a video camera. Armin Miewes explained in four hours of graphic testimony that his fantasy about cannibalism began during a lonely childhood and later escalated into an obsession. It climaxed on the night of March 10, 2001, when he killed and ate a fellow human being he had met over the Internet.

"I kissed him again, I prayed, I prayed for forgiveness for him and for me, and then I did it," he told the hushed court. I had the fantasy, and in the end I fulfilled it."

Meiwes, a 42 year old computer technician, said he had also had the chance to feast on other apparently willing victims, claiming there are hundreds and thousands out there looking to be eaten," but they were not the right type.

The macabre case is unprecedented in German legal history, arousing intense and horrified interest.

Since cannibalism is not technically a crime in Germany, prosecutors have charged Meiwes with murder for the purposes of sexual satisfaction and 'disturbing the peace of the dead' for carving up the corpse.

Meiwes says he regrets what he did but insists it was not murder because he was doing what he had been asked.

He denied killing his victim, Bernd Juergen Brandes, a 43 year old Berlin engineer, for sexual pleasure, saying that although they had sex a few hours before, his satisfaction was in seeing their friendship fulfilled to the ultimate." (France-Presse, December 4, 2003 The Vancouver Province)

Now talk about something truly unbelievable! What an abomination and to think and find that if this is what is happening today then what Noah must have been faced with must have been that much more worse if things could get any worse? Wow if something hasn't gone wrong with society!? If something hasn't gone terribly, terribly wrong with our societies today and to find and think that here we are a people choosing to reject the bible as just a book of man made ideas is unbelievable to say the least. Scandalous actually! Does not it and it alone provide the knowledge necessary to understand what these kinds of bizarre behaviors are a result of and what needs to be done to prevent it from occurring? Of course most certainly it does, but no, mankind today has instead bought into the lie from science that tells them that when it comes to religion and faith and the existence of God it's all just a matter of conjecture. What did we really just pop out of nothing one day and lo and behold here we are to live life and that by way of trial and error and that through war and misery no less with the fittest among us lording it over everyone else? In fact imagine it this way if you will, you as a parent trying to go through life explaining to a son or daughter, well I really have no idea why we are here or what the purpose of it all is. All I know is your mother and I created you and that was a rather strange kind of thing for we had to wait some 9 months before you were completed. So here take this Petri-dish and this microscope and look and try to find out for yourselves what it is all about. Isn't that a rather dumb thing? Moreover to find and think that here we are a people capable of communicating with each other like this with language and speech and not have someone who can communicate the why and what for of our own existence has to be the most incredible if not absurd matter of all. Especially from the perspective of a Creator! For what kind of a Creator would a Creator be if after having planned, designed and then creating this magnificent world He just decided to up and leave, leaving what He created to just fend for itself. Would that not be a rather absurd and ridiculous kind of thing to do if not outright cruel? In fact, imagine doing that to ones own children and then turning around and having someone say to a son or daughter to just believe they have a mother and a father. What kind of utter nonsense and stupidity is that? Accordingly what we should really be asking ourselves then is not the what, where and how did we come to exist on this planet, but rather who, where and how does the communicating occur. Surely that should be the important and vital question to ask ourselves and do we have an answer? Well of course we most certainly do and though it comes by way of a book called the bible it by no means ends there. This idea that people have of God and faith being communicated just by way of some preacher preaching his own particular brand or version of biblical interpretation is utter nonsense. There is a great deal more, much, much more to the work of Almighty God than that and just one of the ways in which that occurs is called *Climate Change*.

You see when it comes right down to it what people have failed to look at and understand is that what happened to Noah and his generation did not end with him alone. Rather he was only the first in a long line of individuals and societies who lived to experience climate change although of course not to the extant of what they had experienced. Rather what began to occur was how God began to us the weather as a kind of communication tool whereby He communicates either His love or anger depending upon the circumstances of human conduct and behavior. The history of it is really quite astounding as we shall see with perhaps the book of Job being the one book in the entire bible that lays the foundation and basis for understanding it all. Actually if Job isn't the premier meteorologist of the entire bible for unlike Noah who only gives us climate change as a historical act with Job we have someone who goes much further by providing us with some invaluable insights into the work of Almighty God. Not only that but we also have some important insights into the very nature of the human character and how it needs to be changed and purified ultimately. Climate change is not about industrial pollution but rather has far more to do with another kind of pollution that the bible calls sin and my how utterly frightening this pollution is getting now. Indeed to the degree that unlike Noah's generation which had nothing to do with scientific investigation and knowledge we however today are quite literally opening up what will surely be a Pandora's Box of horrors. Just take as an example the medical community and this utterly shocking report:

'The sale of dead body parts has become big business'

"Although such macabre commerce is technically illegal, there is evidence that it is now a common and highly profitable-practice.

A U.S. organization called Life Dynamics Inc. has documented and recently published the chilling details of how this new commercial enterprise has opened up the gates of profit by selling tissues and organs from aborted babies.

Essentially, abortuaries are compensated by tissue collection companies through a "site fee," whereby a technician is given space in the abortuary and access to the bodies of the dead babies. The technician then removes the tissues/organs that have been specifically requested by a "third party" and sends them off as a donation.

The third-party {i.e. medical researchers} gratefully accepts the donation and then pays the company, what is referred to as a "handling retrieval fee."

Typically "handling fees" are $999 for a brain {with a 30 percent discount if there is significant fragmentation}, $325 for a spinal cord and $550 for gonads. Limbs are about 150$ and skin is offered for a rock bottom, this week-only price of $100."

Are you offended? Shocked? Disgusted? You should be.

This is the reality of what our culture of death has come to. Human life no longer has any intrinsic value. Our willingness to abort children for our own convenience has eliminated that thought from our mindset. But commercial enterprises has now upped the ante-life has no value as long as it is alive. Once death comes, a tiny baby suddenly has value-commercial value.

Some say that the piecemeal sell-off of body parts is a positive development that makes the best of a bad situation since fetal tissue provides the raw material for medical research that could, at some point, create a cure for our ailments.

Fetal brain cells have been transplanted into the brains of individuals suffering from Parkinson's disease and Alzheimer's. Pancreatic tissue has been transferred into diabetics to help patients to make their own insulin; liver cells have been transplanted into malfunctioning livers.

Fetal tissue is in hot demand for such experiments because of the presence of large amounts of stem cells- young, undifferentiated cells that can easily be cultured and "tricked" into developing whatever specialized cells are required. Because the cells are young, they're less likely to be rejected by the recipient's immune system." {by Susan Martinuk pg. A22 The Vancouver Province Wednesday, October 27/1999}

Wow, what we have become capable of today it's almost godlike isn't it and to think that if a God does indeed exist then what He must be feeling and thinking watching all of this? For this particular writer there is only one word that could possibly come to mind ABOMINABLE! ABSOLUTELY ABOMINABLE! Accordingly may God have mercy, may He help us all!

CHAPTER TWO

THE STORY OF JOB-THE WORLDS PREIMINENT METEOROLOGIST

Now in what has to be one of the most unlikely of places to find an explanation for present day climate change and it would certainly have to be in the book of Job from the Old Testament of the bible. A book that most people receive as a study on suffering something of which upon closer analysis is not what the book is actually all about. Rather it is a book that deals with the important issues of faith and character, two all-important issues that in the life of mankind is of enormous importance to God. The suffering that we see experienced by the main character was only meant to be the means by which God and that nemesis of His and ours namely Satan could determine what this man Job was actually made of and how severe was this suffering of Job's. A suffering that from his perspective was most unfair and even unjust given his life of righteousness and faithfulness to God, a matter of which he actually prided himself upon. For he lived his life always being careful to obey all of God's Commandments and tried to make sure that his family did as well. When God it seemed turned against him though and allowed such suffering to come upon him that he ended up literally on a dust heap having lost everything he was a man devastated. Devastated by the thought that here was a man who had lived to uphold all of God's Commandments and one who took great pride to do exactly that and now was being singled out by God for a punishment that not even the wicked had ever experienced. It was something that he could not understand and after a time of great reflection it led him to lament his entire existence and wishes that he would have died from the moment of his birth rather than to live to see this come upon him and his family. {Job 3:1-26} It is a rather strange story, one in which brings us to the question of why would such a thing happen to such a faithful man and why would any of it have anything to do with climate change?

Now to begin with what we are faced with right off in this biography of Job is a man whose character and faith had

30

to be proved; for the charge against God concerning him was that his faith was not really genuine. That is his faith was based solely upon what he was getting in return from God. That is a life full of all kinds of wealth free from any kind of suffering and a protection from his enemies. The charge therefore against God was that if God were to remove some of that protection and allow suffering to come upon Job he would learn quickly enough what Job's true motives and character really was...

> "Then the Lord said to Satan, *Have you consid-ered my servant Job? There is no one on earth like him; he is blameless and upright, a man who fears God and shuns evil.*"
> "Does Job fear God for nothing? Satan replied. Have you not put a hedge around him and his house-hold and everything he has? You have blessed the work of his hands, so that his flocks and herds are spread throughout the land. But stretch out your hand and strike everything he has, and he will surely curse you to your face." {Job: 1:8-11}

Satan didn't think much of God's acclaim of Job and what a bold if not an altogether foolish move for a mere created being to do bringing into question, as he was, the Creator's own judgment of a human being. In fact what audacity! What is even more astonishing though is God's response to Satan, for instead of crushing this mere insect of a creature for having the insolence to both question and contradict its Creator instead allows this Satan to afflict Job to see whether its accusations are really true and not just once but twice.

> "Then the Lord said to Satan, *Have you consid-ered my servant Job? There is no one on earth like him; he is blameless and upright, a man who fears*

God and shuns evil. And he still maintains his integrity, though you incited me against him to ruin him without reason."

"Skin for skin!" "Satan replied. A man will give all he has for his life. But stretch out your hand and strike his flesh and bones and he will surely curse you to your face."

"The Lord said to Satan, "*Very well, then, he is in your hands; but you must spare his life.*" "So Satan went out from the presence of the Lord and afflicted Job with painful sores from the soles of his feet to the top of his head." {Job 2:3-7}

It is a rather surprising response from the Creator for surely He doesn't need anyone to instruct Him about what mankind is actually about. Furthermore and perhaps more importantly than this is how God in His reputation and character of righteousness and holiness would never have gone into a relationship to bless a man as He did Job originally without surely knowing full well in advance what that man was actually made of. For God would never have allowed Himself to be put into the position of having His own reputation and character brought into question and this especially by such a pathetic created creature as this Satan. {See chapter 6 for a detailed account of what and who Satan is} Something of which would surely have occurred if Job proved out to be the kind of superficial man that Satan thought he was and if that comes as a surprise to you at how God's own character could be brought into question, just consider, is that not exactly what would happen if God were to bless us in some way and then finds us living immoral and unfaithful lives? Of course most certainly it would and it would in turn give enemies of His and ours like this Satan an inroad into stealing away His glory and to the profaning of His name. So what was at stake here then was more than just Job's life but God's glory as well; and that accordingly is why God allowed suffering to come upon Job but with an *__important difference!__* For though it was Satan's desire to all but destroy this man of God and in the process prove God wrong thereby causing a very long shadow to be cast upon God and His character, God had a more important purpose. A purpose that we find is explained to us by these words from the book of the prophet Isaiah:

> *"See I have refined you, though not as silver; I have tested you in the furnace of affliction. For my own sake I do this. How can I let myself be defamed? I will not yield my glory to another." {48: 10-11}*

You see this is what was at the heart of what was actually happening to Job and it should come as no surprise that it would occur this way. For as is so often the case where mankind is concerned nothing really says more about us than when we are afflicted in some way with some measure of suffering. For what usually happens when we are afflicted with some measure of suffering is that we will most often take matters into our own hands and because of our sinful/evil nature we will do things or say things that brings out and reflect our true nature and character. How we respond under suffering and affliction therefore is with God of enormous importance for when combined with having faith in Him. What it says is that our faith in God is not really genuine and that in turn reflects upon God and in such a way that if He were to bless us with great wealth and then finds us living morally bankrupt lives would defame Him and that He takes *with extreme seriousness*. So serious in fact, that when it comes to the work of His Son Christ Jesus upon the cross of Calvary can lead to some extremely grave consequences in the life of the believer. For as the scriptures make it abundantly clear it is His Majesty who often goes about being disgraced in the eyes of the world and this because His followers choose to dabble in the ways of the world:

"It is impossible for those who have once been enlightened, who have tasted the heavenly gift, who have shared in the Holy Spirit, who have tasted the goodness of the word of God and the powers of the coming age, if they fall away, to be brought back to repentance, because to their loss they are crucifying the Son of God all over again and subjecting Him to public disgrace." {Hebrews 6: 4-6}

His reputation literally takes a hit because what He died for in effect becomes more or less for nothing. Surely it doesn't or shouldn't take much to see and understand that; especially by way of all of the scandals that have plagued the North American Church recently involving leaders like Jim Bakker, Jimmy Swaggart and a whole host of others now. Like for further example what has and is being reported in the media and in courtrooms across the nation with quite a number of Catholic priests and their victimization of children. Or yet to those who in the name of Almighty God think it is proper and even holy to live as polygamists and that with mere children no less and to make matters worse we are even seeing now those who are actually looking to ordain people of gay lifestyles into the priesthood. My word what courage people have to commit sins all the while claiming to represent and even invoking the name of Almighty God into it all. The most blatant and dangerous of which is surely occurring now with factions of Islam and their use of violence in the name of and for Almighty God. Don't people understand that by doing such things they are quite literally placing Almighty God into an unfavorable light where His glory and reputation is concerned. Again it shouldn't take much to see and understand that especially by way of an article like this pulled from the local newspaper:

Deity 'discredited'

If Watson and Crick are once again making waves among the devout, it is not a new phenomenon. In 1961, Crick resigned as a fellow of Churchill College, Cambridge, after it was proposed building a chapel.

When Sir Winston Churchill wrote to him pointing out that "none need enter the chapel unless they wish," Crick replied that on those grounds, the college should build a brothel, and enclosed a check for 10 guineas.

"My hope is that eventually it will be possible to build permanent accommodation within the college to house a carefully chosen selection of young ladies in the charge of a suitable madam who, once the institution has become traditional, will doubtless be provided, without offense, with dining rites at the high table," he wrote.

Watson described how he gave up attending Mass at the start of the Second World War. "I came to the conclusion that the Church was just a bunch of fascists that supported Franco. I stopped going on Sunday mornings and watched the birds with my father instead." (Highfield The Vancouver Sun 2003)

You see what we have here is a classic example of the harm done to one's reputation and though these scientists might argue that what was said was not an attack against Christ Himself it nevertheless is:

"As it is written: God's name is blasphemed among the Gentiles because of you." {Romans 2:24}

"Many will follow their shameful ways and bring the way of truth into disrepute." {2 Peter 2:24}

So the seriousness of this can't be emphasized enough and whether the church {Universal} is truly guilty or not is of course a matter for God to judge, something of which unbeknown it seems to practically everyone does in fact happen:

"If we deliberately keep on sinning after we have received the knowledge of the truth, no sacrifice for sins is left, but only a fearful expectation of judgment and of raging fire that will consume the enemies of God. Anyone who rejected the Law of Moses died without mercy on the testimony of two or three witnesses. How much more severely do you think a man deserves to be punished who has trampled the Son of God under foot, who has treated as an unholy thing the blood of the covenant that sanctified him, and who has insulted the Spirit of grace? For we know Him who said "It is mine to avenge; I will repay, and again, The Lord will judge His people." {Hebrews 10: 26- 30}

The issue of forgiveness may very well be the principle work of Almighty God but one should never think or be of the opinion that it is the be all and end all of everything where God is concerned. Grace may be sufficient but don't ever think that God suffers fools easily especially when it comes to the issue of communion:

"For I received from the Lord what I also passed on to you: The Lord Jesus, on the night he was betrayed, took bread, and when he had given thanks, he broke it and said, "This is my body, which is broken for you; do this in remembrance of me. " In the same way, after supper he took the cup, saying, "This cup is the new covenant in my blood; do this, whenever you drink it in remembrance of me." For whenever you eat this bread and drink this cup, you proclaim the Lord's death until he comes. *Therefore, whoever eats the bread or drinks the cup of the Lord in an unworthy manner will be guilty of sinning against the body and blood of the Lord. A man ought to examine himself before he eats of the bread and drinks of the cup. For anyone who eats and drinks without recognizing the body of the Lord eats and drinks judgment on himself. That is why many among you are weak and sick, and a number of you have fallen asleep. But if we judged ourselves, we would not come under judgment. When we are judged by the Lord, we are being disciplined so that we will not be condemned with the world."* {1Corinthians 11: 23-32}

It's not just about forgiveness as though that was the be all and end all of God's work with humankind. There is the issue of discipline and yes even judgment! A discipline that goes far beyond just scolding us when we do something wrong as our parents did, but rather a discipline that entails a work of refining our characters so that we can become the kind of people worthy of sharing in His holiness and are found faithful to Him in everything that happens. Children who are not arrogant and rebellious but who are submissive and loving to a father that cares and loves them enormously. This is essentially what it is all about and according to the book of Hebrews it is this kind of discipline that will <u>prove</u> <u>out in the end whether we are truly God's children or not</u>:

> "And you have forgotten that word of encouragement that addresses you as sons: 'My son, do not make light of the Lord's discipline, and do not lose heart when He rebukes you, ***because the Lord disciplines those He loves, and He punishes everyone He accepts as a son.'***
> Endure hardship as discipline; God is testing you as sons. For what son is not disciplined by his father? If you are not disciplined {and everyone undergoes discipline}, then you are illegitimate children and not true sons. Moreover, we have all had human fathers who disciplined us and we respected them for it. How much more should we submit to the Father of our spirits and live! Our fathers disciplined us for a little while as they thought best; but God disciplines us for our good, that we may share in His holiness. No discipline seems pleasant at the time, but painful. Later on, however, it produces a harvest of righteousness and peace for those who have been trained by it." {Hebrews 12:5-11}

So God accordingly is not finished with anyone of us. An important work of refining is still to be done and that was the case with Job and how did he fare through it all? Well we find that Job did quite well with the first remarkable thing that he did was to prove Satan wrong in his accusation of him by holding firm to his faith in God even going so far as to rebuke his wife when she did the unthinkable by telling him to simply curse God and die.

> "His wife said to him, 'Are you still holding on to your integrity?' 'Curse God and die!' "He replied,

'You are talking like one of the foolish woman.'
'Shall we accept good from God, and not trouble?"
{Job 2:10}

Job was no fool, proving right from the outset of his trial
that he was a wise and faithful individual. He understood
enough about life and God to understand that ones life does
not consist in ones material possessions. However, that being
said Job was having a difficult time reconciling how he a
man of faith and good morals, could suffer such loss when so
many others around him who had and were living immoral
lives were living peaceful and even prosperous lives. It all
becomes rather unbelievable for him and with his experience
and knowledge of life it is a deeply perplexing and inexplicable matter. He looks about him in utter disbelief and when
his three friends {Eliphaz, Bildad, and Zophar} joined him
in his sufferings to try and console him begin to question
him as to this predicament of his going so far as to bring into
question his integrity thinking he must have done something
wrong to deserve all this was too much for Job. For now his
pride was being affected and that was not something that he
was going to let go without a fight. Accordingly he strikes
back with many long speeches about his life of faith and
service to God and even deals them a blow of sarcasm as
well! Questions are thrown back and forth in defense and
anger until after having exhausted practically every avenue
of understanding finds Job contending with Almighty God to
the extent of wanting a court of law to be convened with His
Creator. Just listen to these words of his:

"But I desire to speak to the Almighty and to argue
my case with God." {13:3}

"Even today my complaint is bitter; His hand is heavy
in spite of my groaning. If only I knew where to find

Him; if only I could go to His dwelling! I would state my case before Him and fill my mouth with arguments. I would find out what he would answer me, and consider what he would say."{23:1-5}

"Oh that I had someone to hear me! I sign now my defense-let the Almighty answer me; let my accuser put his indictment in writing." {31:35}

Now can you imagine something like this! Wow what a courageous or perhaps foolish thing for a mere mortal of a man to do demanding as he is a court of law to be convened with the Divine! God certainly must have found this quite incredible if not unbelievable how a mere created work of sand and water would dare to presume to question Him regarding His own actions on his own planet! Most certainly Almighty God does not sit in a docket to be judged by what He created, rather He sits as Sovereign over the affairs of mankind and we are the ones who become accountable to Him and what does God do with this? Well contrary to what some might think God does not strike Job with any kind of further affliction or punishment but rather looks to question Job himself, something of which quite remarkably begins with a youngster by the name of Elihu who apparently is full of more wisdom and understanding than these men. An arbiter who being inspired by God begins to harangue Job and these three men for their apparent lack of knowledge and understanding of everything called religion and God. Through him God begins a series of long and eloquent speeches and in the process reveals some interesting issues about Job's character the first of which is his self-righteousness.

"But you have said in my hearing- I heard the very words- I am pure and without sin; I am clean and free from guilt. Yet God has found fault with me;

40

he considers me his enemy. He fastens my feet in the shackles; he keeps close watch on all my paths." {Job 33: 8-11}

Elihu knew and understood that this was a confession that no mere mortal man should ever be found to make, one that both shocked and angered him. Then if that wasn't enough what further comes to light is how rebellious Job became towards God something of which leads Elihu to exclaim that because of it Job needs to be tested to an even higher degree.

"Men of understanding declare, wise men who hear me say to me, Job speaks without knowledge; his words lack insight. Oh that Job might be tested to the utmost for answering like a wicked man! To his sin he adds rebellion; scornfully he claps his hands among us and multiplies his words against God." {Job 34:34-37}

Rather interesting isn't it. The cream was certainly rising to the top, so to speak, and what was being discovered was not very becoming for a man of Job's position and to think that he needed to be tested even further because of it is rather staggering. Opening one's mouth can truly get a person into some hot water. For Job though to have the kind of courage to defend him-self the way he was certainly speaks volumes about the kind of man Job was. For no man would either be able or even dare for that matter to do what Job was doing and that is maintaining his integrity the way he was and this before Almighty God! Righteousness was important to this man and interestingly enough God took note of it! {Job 2:3 & 13:16} However, that being said when the time came for God to speak to him; God has some very important issues to vent with this man beginning with:

"Who is this that darkens my counsel with words without knowledge? Brace yourself like a man; I will question you, and you shall answer me." {38:2-3}

God after finally hearing enough of Job's diatribe begins to interestingly enough question Job himself and that with some 70 questions interspersed with some remarkable knowledge dealing with practically every matter of life beginning with the asking of where exactly he was when the earth was created! Imagine God the very Creator of everything actually looks to this mere mortal of a man to explain by sarcasm no less the scientific underpinnings of how everything that exists on this planet works. From the laying of the earth's foundation, to the way in which the heavens exist the way they do, to the rivers and oceans, to the animals, and to the way in which the birds of the air can fly. It's a magnificent speech that opens Job to a whole new world and by it points out to him in no uncertain terms exactly with whom he is dealing. A response that quite literally takes Job down a very painful road by having him see himself for what exactly he is in the grand scope of things. A response that even has Almighty God asking this mere mortal of a man these astounding questions:

"Will the one who contends with the Almighty correct Him? Let him who accuses God answer him!" {Job 40:2}

"Would you discredit my justice? Would you condemn me to justify yourself? {Job 40: 7-8}

The hearing of which by Job must have surely caused him to gasp in horror and tremble in fear. Imagine what an incredible response for a divine being of unquestionable character, power, and holiness to actually give a mere created mortal of a man. A response that just goes to show and prove yet again just how merciful and long-suffering Almighty God truly is with mankind. For surely with Job's attitude and self-righteous nature he was more than deserving of a punishment rather than the receiving of an answer by God and perhaps he would have been punished if he had not done the honorable thing by quickly repenting for his words and actions:

"Then Job answered the Lord:

I am unworthy-how can I reply to you? I put my hand over my mouth. I spoke once, but I have no answer-twice, but I will say no more." {40:3-5}

"I know that you can do all things; no plan of yours can be thwarted. You asked, 'Who is this that obscures my counsel without knowledge?' Surely I spoke of things I did not understand, things to wonderful for me to know. You said, 'Listen now, and I will speak; I will question you, and you shall answer me.' My ears had heard of you but now my eyes have seen you. Therefore I despise myself and repent in dust and ashes." {42:1-6}

To lie in the dust on one's face before the Creator is certainly the correct and proper position for mankind to be in. Job did the right thing at precisely the right time before Almighty God, and by doing so comes to find himself in God's good graces again. In fact, after this and after all is finally said and done Job finds himself being accepted by God to the extent that God would only accept his prayers and not those of his three friends who as it turns out came near to the place of judgment. God turned His anger against them and how strange that is for were they not on God's side throughout the whole ordeal?

"After the Lord had said these things to Job, he said to Eliphaz the Temanite, *I am angry with you and your two friends, because you have not spoken of me what is right, as my servant Job has. So now take seven bulls and seven rams and go to my servant Job and sacrifice a burnt offering for yourselves. My servant Job will pray for you, and I will accept his pray and not deal with you according to your folly. You have not spoken of me what is right as my servant Job has.* So Eliphaz the Temanite, Bildad the Shuhite and Zofar the Naamathite did what the Lord told them; and the Lord accepted Job's prayer." {Job 42: 7-9}

Most certainly they were but as it turned out they ended up in serious trouble and why of course is because they unlike Job failed to repent and that was a most serious offense given how they ended up more or less condemning an innocent man. For as the arbiter Elihu had pointed out, 'they had found no way to refute Job and yet had condemned him.' {Job 32:3} To have done that while acting as a kind of defense team on God's behalf was a most serious offense one in which His Majesty would not and indeed could not in any way allow to go unpunished. For it quite literally ended up placing God into an unfavorable light where His reputation and character was concerned. Accordingly that is why we find a payment of blood being made in the sum of seven bulls and seven rams, which at that time was the method of reparation for one's transgressions. {Job 42:8}

So as we see this is how things turned out for Job and what a remarkable turn of events it was, one that surely must have placed a very large smile on his heart. Job ends up being vindicated and that by God Himself no less and for his faithfulness Job receives from God a special place of importance and is blessed by Him beyond his wildest dreams. In fact, not only was everything that was stolen from him returned but he receives 10 times as much as he ever had before. He becomes a man blessed beyond measure but more importantly than any of that was his reinstatement as a just and righteous man in the eyes of his community which to Job was extremely important. Moreover he also lives to such a ripe old age that he sees his children and grandchildren to the fourth generation. This is how it all ended for Job and this because he remained faithful to God to the end and what a truly amazing feat that was to accomplish. Of far greater importance than any of that though was the change that took place in Job. A change that certainly turned out for the better and how Satan must have hated this man to the extent that given the opportunity, he would have certainly killed him. For practically everything Job did only proved Satan out to be a liar for Job was not a superficial man. He more than proved out to be a man of integrity and character just as God said although Job did need an attitude adjustment. That and perhaps being the proud man that he was he was in need of some humility and how interesting and important it is to find him making a confession that is similar to the one we saw in that earlier statement from Isaiah regarding this very issue of the refining of the human character:

"But He knows the way that I take; when He has tested me, I will come forth as gold. My feet have closely followed his steps; I have kept to his way without turning aside. I have not departed from the commands of his lips; I have treasured the words of his mouth more than my daily bread. But He stands alone and who can oppose him? He does whatever he pleases. He carries out his decree against me, and many other such plans he still has in store. That is why I am terrified before him; when I think of all this, I fear him. God has made my heart faint; the Almighty has terrified me." {Job 23: 10-16}

Interestingly enough Job knew where he was going at least after a certain period of time and my how he came forth as gold. God's refining process therefore proved to be of immense value in the life of this great man. A hard lesson though it was to learn and live through but one in which Job ultimately benefited from and this especially where his faith was concerned. For though Job had faith at the beginning of his trial it was largely based upon what he had known about God from others and we know this because of the confession he made which makes his story all the more remarkable:

"My ears had heard of you but now my eyes have seen you. Therefore I despise myself and repent in dust and ashes." {Job 42:5}

After having gone through what he went through however it became something much more personal and tangible seeing how he came face to face with the power and presence of Almighty God. A matter of which actually occurred and brings us now to the topic of climate change for as we see it was the weather that was affected by this man's life. God actually used the weather to communicate to this man the first of which occurred in a negative sort of way when God allowed that nemesis of His and ours, namely Satan, to use the elements to inflict harm upon Job. Events of which began first by way of a fireball which was probably a meteorite of some kind then to that windstorm that collapsed the home of his eldest son resulting in his death and the death of his brothers and sisters. {Job 1:16-20} Then to having it all culminate in God using the elements Himself when He finally spoke to Job with his own voice out of a tornado. {Job 38:1} This is what this man came to see and experience with Almighty God so is it any wonder then that his faith took on an entirely new perspective and dynamic in not only his life but also in the lives of those within his particular community. A matter which was apparently the intended purpose of this entire story in the first place next to this issue of character that is for what Job ultimately was faced with here was an education into the very things of God and if that isn't easy enough to see given the way in which the story unfolds for us and the amount of questions that are being asked? Two hundred and eighty nine of them to be exact being bantered about by eight different individuals seventy-four of which are recorded as having come from God Himself. There is an enormous amount of education and learning going on here and to find God asking questions Himself is rather astounding if not altogether odd considering the nature of some of them. Like for example these:

"Have you entered the storehouses of the snow or seen the storehouses of the hail, which I reserve for times of trouble, for days of war and battle?"{Job 38:22}

"Does the rain have a father? Who fathers the drops of dew?" {Job38:28}

"From whose womb comes the ice?" "Who gives birth to the frost from the heavens when the waters become hard as stone, when the surface of the deep is frozen?" {Job 38:29 -30}

"Who has the wisdom to count the clouds? Who can tip over the jars of the heavens when the dust becomes hard and the clods of earth stick together? {Job 38: 37-38}

Can you raise your voice to the clouds and cover yourself with a flood of water? {Job 38:34}

It appears Almighty God wasn't about to let that teenager Elihu have all the fun, who, when speaking under the inspiration of God made what is the most clear and succinct an explanation ever on matters of faith and this issue of climate change:

"God's voice thunders in marvelous ways, he does great things beyond our understanding. He says to the snow, 'Fall on the earth, and to the rain shower, be a mighty downpour.' So that all men may know his work, he stops everyman from his labor. The animals take cover; they remain in their dens. The tempest comes out from its chamber, the cold from the driving winds. The breath of God produces ice and the broad waters become frozen. He loads the clouds with moisture he scatters his lightning through them. At his direction they swirl around over the face of the whole earth to do whatever he commands them. *He brings the clouds to punish men or to water his earth and show his love.*" {Job 37:5-13}

God though wasn't satisfied with just this alone and as we see gets into the fray Himself with Job. How astonishing it is to find though that He actually does this by using questions along with the weather which came up in the form of a whirlwind out of which God spoke and communicated with this man. Now is that not something rather astounding if not altogether significant especially in view how these questions are spoken in an almost objective kind of way? For God is not so much telling this man the way it is but rather wants him to discover and answer for himself why things work and exist the way they do. Accordingly if science didn't have its beginnings further back in history than in what occurred with Galileo and the Roman Catholic Church and look if only they had bothered to pay attention to this book and its questions, I'm sure the history of our world and science would have looked much different than what it is. Look there are some serious questions to be pondered and answered here with two of the most interesting if not significant ones surely being these; *"Does the rain have a Father?" "Who fathers the drops of dew?" {Job 38:28}*

Now why would Almighty God the Creator be the one asking questions such as these? Why is He of all individuals placing such an emphasis here on this particular aspect of the weather? Could it be because rain is essentially water and water is the one substance that nothing on this planet can live or survive without and we're talking about literally everything? From the tiniest of insects that roam about in the driest of deserts, to the creatures that live in the clefts of the rocks of the highest mountain ranges, to the creatures that live in the rivers and lakes of the world and to every kind of vegetation that exists in every corner of our world. Literally everything that lives has to drink from this liquid called water to survive. A liquid that by the way to handle and examine is found to be totally transparent, colorless, tasteless and odorless now how odd is that? A liquid that in light of this thirst of ours gives science the reason to believe that water was where life must have originally begun. For as the late scientist Carl Sagan pointed out:

> "The origin of life on Earth seems to have occurred in oceans and shallow tide pools. Life on Earth is made mainly of water, which plays an essential physical and chemical role. Indeed, it's hard for us water-

besotted creatures to imagine life without water."
{Pg. 111 Sagan}

"Life on Earth is intimately connected, for the
most basic chemical reasons, with liquid water. We
humans are ourselves made of some three quarters
water." {ibid. pg. 233}

Now what an incredible and profound if not an altogether
significant observation this is to make! An observation that
is exactly what we find written in the bible:

*"In the beginning God created the heavens and the
earth. Now the earth was formless and empty, darkness was over the surface of the deep, and the Spirit
of God was hovering over the __waters__."* {Genesis
1:1-2}

Now look at this!!! Not only was water the first element
to exist, but was in existence even as God was about to bring
about the creation of life. Now how utterly astonishing and
profound is that? Imagine here we find both science and
religion agreeing together on something water is the stuff
of life surely a not too insignificant a matter and one that
raises a number of interesting questions where the weather
is concerned. For what is the one substance that the weather
goes about providing this planet? Is it not water? Of course
most certainly it is and my how vitally important a work
of nature it is that it should do so. Now consider what can
account for such a remarkable system of hydration as this?
Evolution!? Are we to actually believe that? Surely that
can't be! Not for such a complex and purpose driven system
as this that exists and works because of the interaction of
everything from the suns radiation upon the atmosphere, to
the effects of the moon and its gravitational forces upon our

ocean tide systems and to the way in which the electrical forces of the earth and the air combine together to provide the needed precipitation. Forces that all combine together to work in a most remarkable way to provide just the right kind of an environment so that life can thrive on this terrestrial ball called Earth. A system that by the way revolves over a period of twelve months that are broken up into four seasons of three months each of spring, summer, fall and winter. A system of four seasons that provides this planet with its own particular variety of weather patterns and this as a constant that never really changes from one year to the next. Now if this doesn't bespeak an intelligence of enormous creative power? Certainly that would be the only logical explanation for it and for a system to exist like this could it not in the hands of its very Creator become a perfect kind of communication tool? That is could not He who created it be able to also manipulate it all according to His own whims as He saw fit? Well most certainly He could with the story of Noah being the greatest example of it where the Creator used it to great effect. For what better way for a God to clean out a world than to use wind and water. Water that in the form of rain became the perfect communication tool by which God ultimately destroyed by water the very creation He created from water. It would only make sense wouldn't it and so there we surely have it! An explanation and answer to not only those two questions of God's but even this whole matter of origins. We need to be hydrated it's as simple and as straightforward as that! So astonishing isn't it? Indeed, and yet if something like this isn't or hardly enough to prove to ones conscience the truth of what is written herein well then perhaps a better way of looking at climate change and/or the existence of Almighty God would be to answer that question of His concerning the 'the storehouses of the snow or seen the storehouses of the hail, which I reserve for times of trouble, for days of war and battle?' {Job 38:22}

Now again why would Almighty God be the one asking a question like this? Or rather given the nature of the question does this really happen? Could we in fact actually see this as occurring as the question presumes we actually can during a time of trouble and war? Well, if we were to take a look at what happened in 1998-1999 with that Ice Storm of the Century that occurred over an area that extended from Toronto to New York, Boston, Washington, Chicago and right across the entire Atlantic Provinces and it appears that could very well be the case? Something definitely strange was going on with that particular weather system. A weather system that quite literally brought that entire part of the world to a complete and utter shutdown going so far as to even affect the entire North American continent. A climate change that occurred oddly enough right at the turn of the millennium. Now why if as the above scripture implies Almighty God was directly responsible for it would He do something like this? Could it have been in response to what the Lord knew about those terrorists and their plans to destroy the world trade towers? You want to talk about trouble and war there you have it! The implications and consequences of which would have been that much more serious and grave a matter if as this writer believes the events of 9/11 was supposed to occur with the arrival of the millennium rather than when it did two years later. The correlation between the two events more than makes that a plausible scenario especially in view of that rental truck bombing of the World Trade Towers shortly before. Accordingly those terrorists I think one can assume and can make a good argument for were up to something far more sinister. It only makes sense doesn't it given how this Ice Storm of the Century occurred when it did? Nobody was out committing crimes in those terrible conditions. In fact, where air travel was concerned this ice storm literally disrupted the entire air traffic system in North America grounding as it so many hundreds if not thousands of flights. So God it appears was looking out for the nation though the weather brought for a time a terrible amount of suffering and do you know what really shocks this writer where the events of 9/11 is concerned. While watching an evening television newscast there was this report about a terrible and terrifying thunderstorm that had descended in quite abruptly over the city of Boston. A weather system that apparently had been so severe that it resulted in spectators who while watching some game in the cities stadium caused them to run in fear for their lives. They actually scattered out of the stadium in droves. It was an event that so totally shocked the lady news reporter reporting it that she had this flabbergasted look of disbelief on her face which in turn left me wondering what could God have possibly been up to? Why I thought to myself would He do something like this? The answer to which I began to reflect upon far more seriously given how it was only three days later that the hijacking of those planes and the destruction of the world trade towers occurred! Was there a connection to it I asked myself, the answer to which is most assuredly a yes given what we find written herein. Wow!

The Moslems, the Moslems?!! You know my word it's one thing to have faith in God but to turn around and use that faith as justification for killing others is really something quite incredible if not utterly unbelievable. A matter of which turned this writers thoughts towards communism of all things and why that in particular? Well because was it not the communists like Stalin for example who thought and lived by the philosophy that the best revolutionary was a youth without morals. The best revolutionary I surmised after looking at the smoldering ruins is not a youth without morals but rather someone who thinks that it is their God given duty which they believe God will in turn honor and bless to kill others by using the act of suicide. No youth without morals is going to strap a bomb to his chest for the purposes of killing others along with themselves. They have too much to live and look forward to in this life. So imagine what then would the likes of a Stalin had done if he had been faced with or embarked upon the destruction of the Moslem faith and religion as he did the Christian one? With a murderous brigand like him behind the reigns of power who hated everything religious coupled with Islam's jihadist ways and it would surely have resulted in nuclear oblivion. Wow, never underestimate the power of peoples resolve I shockingly mumbled to myself when it comes to ones faith and religion, a matter of which all but left me thinking and believing that the western world has made a terrible, terrible mistake where the real danger lies in our world. For ultimately the dangers can't be or aren't so much the philosophies of communism or any other political philosophies for that matter but rather what is happening in the Middle East. For the religious tensions that are being exerted now in that part of the world is something frightening to behold and how bizarre if not incredible it is that a people would actually commit to doing such acts of terrorism in the name of God. What do they think that the Creator of all life needs them to exact some kind of vengeance? Most certainly the Almighty, and I stress here <u>Almighty God,</u> does not need anyone to go about exacting any kind of vengeance, and my how dreadful and serious a matter is this. For again do not and will not these kinds of things reflect upon God Himself? Most certainly they will and do, and how long do you think that His Majesty is going to put up with that? Not even a human king or queen like for example the Queen of England or for that matter the King of Saudi Arabia would stand for someone who was never called to be a spokesman running around the world speaking and acting using his/her name and seal as justification for their actions. You want to talk about swift vengeance there you have it. How then a people can presume to think that they can do the same with Almighty God who has more than enough power do to anything He wishes is surely the epitome of ignorance if not outright fear. In fact, look at those earthquakes that struck Sumatra, Indonesia, and isn't it odd that they would occur when they did. That is the main one occurring on Christmas and then the other one at Easter. I think we should find this really quite extra-ordinary. Again what though should we believe about this- just some kind of a coincidence? Given the murdering of all those people with the most shocking and horrifying murders being the beheadings of those three teenage Christian schoolgirls and this as a gift to God for the holy month of Ramadan and this writer doesn't think so. Wow what a frightening thing to do to God's children and then to find another earthquake hitting Indonesia and this on the very eve of the holy month of Ramadan {September 12, 2007} and if it doesn't go to show and prove that God was and is being provoked. My word could there actually be more acts of terrorism and murdering being planned by these jihadists in Indonesia? This can't be just a coincidence folks! This can't be just a coincidence! So again wow, the Moslems, the Moslems?!

You know what do they actually think and believe that it's all really just about heaven and the hereafter where God is going to bless and honor them? Where they along with everyone that they have murdered here on earth will live in an Edenic paradise with God? A paradise that as this writer heard coming out of Lebanon by the Hamas included the belief that the sacrificed in this way are going to be bestowed with 70 virgins in the kingdom of heaven? What heaven is a brothel? It really is quite strange? Imagine here on earth their men are forbidden to even look at women but in heaven with Almighty God they can fill themselves to their heart's content? Wow what ignorance truly lies within people regarding everything called God and religion and that apparently by literally everyone no matter what the religious persuasion. May God have mercy! Truly what do people think? That Almighty God is ultimately powerless to do anything about what is happening in this world of His? That faith is blind? Most certainly it is not! On the contrary it is people who are blind to God. That is the real issue and how the book of Job goes about trying to change that. Imagine whoever would have thought that God would actually use both the display of His glory and power along with questions to say; 'hey you there, tap, tap on the umbrella answer this will you about the how and why of everything. Unbelievable! What a truly amazing book and look no one bothers to pay much attention to it. Literally no one!!? Again what a mistake. What a terrible, terrible mistake! So much so in fact that what will surely become the most alarming thing of all where meteorology is concerned and it would have to be meteorites and why meteorites? Well because as we see in the life of Job he was faced with one that resulted in him losing his entire heard of sheep and even servants. If it isn't one of the most astounding of all events within the book of Job, one in which sadly is what most people sight and zero in on as the reason for their rejection of the entire book. Indeed after having laughed about it, it along with the rest of the bible ends up getting discarded. Guess what though? Have not and are not such events actually happening in our own day and age? They most certainly are and one need only open their newspapers to see it for themselves:

'Terror as huge a meteor hits'
Wellington- "A search began yesterday for the remains of a large a meteor that exploded over New Zealand's North Island with enough force to shake buildings, leaving a plume of blue smoke that covered hundreds of square miles.
Falling debris from the meteor, which eyewitnesses said was as bright as the sun, was blamed for starting a forest fire near Napier, on the East Coast.

The spectacular explosion was seen by people on both sides of the North Island and from as far north as Auckland to Christchurch in the South Island. Witnesses said the fireball had a long, fiery tale. Airline pilots reported sightings and a meteor was picked up on radar by air traffic controllers.

Rodney Austin, information officer for the New Zealand Astronomical Society, said the meteor could have been as large as a railway locomotive. Phone lines to the emergency services were jammed by anxious callers. Jocelyn Nancarrow of Wanganui on the West Coast said: "It was like a huge, dynamite kind of explosion. The house shook, the ground shook. It appeared to be quite close. I was trembling with fear because I thought it was a plane that had exploded."

Another Napier witness, Tony Unsworth, said: "It was an amazing, bright, white ball heading down at about 45° degrees to the earth.

As it got further down, it just seemed to explode and bright blue smoke came after it."

Unsworth said the smoke covered the city of 60,000 people for at least an hour before sunset.

It is feared the remains could be difficult to find in New Zealand's rugged and sparsely populated landscape." {The Province Newspaper Thursday, July 8, 1999}

Now what a frightening event this is, one in which is more than comparable to the one we find in the book of Job. One which is also shockingly similar to the biggest event of them all and that is the Tunguska event of central Siberia, where on the morning of June the 30 of 1908, a large fireball plunged out of the sky with a force strong enough to incinerate some 850 square miles of forest along with an entire herd of reindeer. It is said that the sound of it was so loud and deafening that not only was it heard some 1000 km away but it knocked a man seated some 60 km away from the blast sight flat on his back. It is an event that to this day still shocks and awes all those who study it because of the magnitude of the destruction it left in its wake, and not one human being was killed by that event or it appears by the one that occurred over New Zealand. Surely a not to insignificant a matter given the size of planet earth, it's oceans and its human populations. Again though what should we believe about this? Was this just a natural phenomenon? The world of science certainly seems to think so pointing out as they do that since the universe is full of millions of these kinds of rocks it is only logical that a few of them would make it into our atmosphere and whew we were lucky on that one. *Lucky?!* Well perhaps yes indeed we certainly were given where it landed. For just imagine if you will what the outcome would have been if something like the Tunguska event had landed into the ocean? The fallout would no doubt have destroyed practically every coastline throughout the entire world. So lucky, maybe, although for this particular writer I don't think luck had really anything to do with it. For just ask yourselves what are the actual chances of a meteorite the size of the Tunguska event actually making its way through the universe and then our solar system bypassing every other planet and meteorite in the process and then into our atmosphere and then landing in what is one of the remotest regions of the entire planet? What are the chances of that actually occurring? A million to one? A billion to one? A trillion to one? More like a quadrillion billion to one I would think and that coupled with this 'fire of God' from the book of Job surely places these meteorites as an act of God and that quite literally! Surely that would be the only logical explanation for it. Accordingly Almighty God I think one can assume and can make a good argument for was up to something, the connection to which could have had some-thing to do with the events of the Russian revolution and the destruction of religious faith in that one time Christian nation. The dates again you will find are very close to each other and what's more if it didn't come as quite a shock to this writer to discover that according to the 1966 version of the Guinness Book of World Records and if the Tunguska Event had occurred 4 hours and 47 minutes later it would have obliterated the city of St. Petersburg, the beginning point of the Bolshevik revolution. Now how utterly unbe-lievable if not altogether significant is that? Yes can't forget about the rotation of the earth now can we? WOW! www. answers.com/tunguska%20event

As for this event over New Zealand and Australia and the why of it well that I think is for those particular countries to ponder over and answer. As for this writer I think there is a very good case to be made that the world is ultimately being **_warned_** for just consider this the scriptures make it abundantly clear that the time will come when these events will not happen over land but right into the very ocean as St. John prophesied:

> "The second angel sounded his trumpet, and something like a huge mountain, all ablaze, was thrown into the sea. A third of the sea turned into blood, a third of the living creatures in the sea died, and a third of the ships were destroyed."
>
> The third angel sounded his trumpet, and a great star, blazing like a torch fell from the sky on a third of the rivers and on the springs of water-the name of the star is Wormword. A third of the waters turned bitter, and many people died from the waters that had become bitter." {Revelation 8: 8-11}

Ultimately if the Day of Judgment isn't fast approaching and if it isn't something that we could all very well live to see and experience for ourselves? Looking at the state of affairs of our world and if the wickedness and violence of mankind isn't beginning to reach some truly unimaginable proportions. So much so in fact that when it comes to talk shows like Jerry Springer and Maury Povich and perhaps what they should do when concluding programs such as, 'I had sex with 300 hundred men' or 'Please don't cheat on me with my Mother' or 'Which of 27 men is the father of my child,' is instead open a bible and read passages from Psalms 126:6 or Matthew 23:33. Indeed if that wouldn't be the wise and prudent choice to make? Then again maybe a more knowledgeable choice would be to point everyone in the direction of this important and significant passage spoken by Christ Jesus Himself:

> "I counsel you to buy from me gold refined in the fire, so you can become rich; and white clothes to wear, so you can cover your shameful nakedness; and salve to put on your eyes, so you can see. Those whom I love I rebuke and discipline. So be earnest and repent." {Revelation 3:18-19}

His Majesty certainly wasn't talking just about worldly wealth here that is for certain but rather purity and perfection of character and that in the words of Job and Isaiah no less *gold refined in the fire*. This is the crux of it all where God is concerned and look one should be careful to pay attention to this and submit to God accordingly for you can be sure of this you do not want to end up in the shoes of some people. Like for example that man Armin Miewes from Germany, who after killing his male lover cannibalized him? It is rather astounding and stupefying to find him praying for forgiveness while proceeding to kill and eat his friend. It is really quite strange. What did he think that Almighty God would receive his friend into heaven for such unbelievable and deplorable acts of sin? My word if this isn't something Satanic beyond belief. In fact it's almost like Satan was pulling all of the strings here and why is to ultimately poke fun or rather mock God for His loving and merciful ways. It is actually a satanic version on what St. Paul spoke about concerning what needs to be done with certain individuals:

"hand this man over to Satan, so that the sinful nature may be destroyed and his spirit saved on the day of our Lord." {1Corinthians 5: 5}

When it comes to sin its effects upon us can go much farther than just our souls but rather can so corrupt the human conscience and physical body that there is simply nothing left to do for some but to hand them over to Satan. So imagine this, a believing individual but totally and completely reprobate! If that doesn't bring also to mind a recent news report that came out of the city of Edmonton and the rape of a three year old child by her drunken father? A rape that according to the attending at the hospital came within a fraction of an inch of killing the poor child! You see this is what can and will ultimately happen to a people when they don't care to retain the knowledge of God. {Romans 1:28} The human mind can become so affected and polluted by sin and its desire for wicked pleasures that they end up having no way of recognizing or delineating between what is right or wrong. In the end they will be <u>purified one way or the other</u>! Accordingly <u>*beware the dangers of sin it can and will kill you*</u>. It is not a pollution that you want to take lightly, Job certainly didn't and what a truly fascinating and none to important example we have in him! Truly a diamond will never become a thing of beauty unless it is cut and polished to perfection and if God desires anything it is that we become just like a polished diamond. That is a people who are not arrogant and rebellious but rather a people whose characters shine as brilliantly as a just cut and polished diamond with no inclusions of any kind! This is the crux of what the religion of Almighty God is all about. As for our topic of climate change well as we have clearly seen pollution is not at all about that which comes from industrial sources but rather from that which comes out of the human heart and character of mankind. That invariable poison of the human character that manifests itself by way of a lawlessness involving everything from cursing to lying, stealing, adultery, greed, pride and murder, the seven great pillars of the worst of human conduct and behavior. This the arbiter Elihu summed up totally and completely for us in one simple and straightforward paragraph:

"God's voice thunders in marvelous ways, he does great things beyond our understanding. He says to the snow, 'Fall on the earth, and to the rain shower, be a mighty downpour.' So that all men may know his work, he stops everyman from his labor. The animals take cover; they remain in their dens. The tempest comes out from its chamber, the cold from the driving winds. The breath of God produces ice and the broad waters become frozen. He loads the clouds with moisture he scatters his lightning through them. At his direction they swirl around over the face of the whole earth to do whatever he commands them. _He brings the clouds to punish men or to water his earth and show his love_." {Job 37:5-13}

This is what climate change is really all about and it is called Divine Communication!

CHAPTER THREE

THE HISTORY OF ISRAEL

Having laid the important foundation into understanding climate change and the real reasons behind it and what we need to do next is of course look into the history of the nation of Israel. For when it comes to climate change no other nation in the entire world and its history has been affected by, and continues to be affected by climate change than they have. It is a history utterly fascinating and yet tragic at the same time, but why? Well as we shall see if it hasn't got everything to do first of all with the issue of faith, then this issue of the pollution of sin that exists within the human heart and character and ultimately with Almighty God of course.

Now where climate change and the history of the Jewish people are concerned and what for most people usually come to mind are the lives and stories of Moses and Joseph. Like for example Joseph and his coat of many colors and his being sold into slavery by his own brothers. A matter of which ultimately led to his rise into political leadership in the land of Egypt which quite astonishingly occurred because of climate change. For it was Joseph ultimately who was able to interpret those dreams of Pharaoh about those seven years of famine that would come upon the land of Egypt? Dreams that communicated a fourteen year span of time in which the land of Egypt would first experience a time of unparalleled prosperity only to be followed by seven years of famine that would so ravage their land that they would most likely not have survived. {Genesis 41}

Survive though they did because of Joseph and his admonishment to the king to prepare storage facilities ahead of time so that they could all survive. A hundred thirty five years later though this was largely forgotten under a new Pharaoh who now felt threatened by the Israelites who lived among them and prospered. A matter which moved him to reduce the Israelites to slavery, largely forgetting the God of creation who was their protector. An extremely stupid thing to do and one that under the leadership of Moses led the nation into judgment and destruction which occurred quite astonishingly by climate change! A judgment that was the result not just of their persecution of the Jewish people but ultimately their idolatrous ways:

> "Then the Lord said to Moses, "Get up early in the morning, confront Pharaoh and say to him, 'This is what the Lord, the God of the Hebrews, says: Let my people go, so that they may worship me, or this time I will send the full force of my plagues against you and your officials and your people, so you may know that there is no one like me in all the earth. For by now I could have stretched out my hand and struck you and your people with a plague that would have wiped you off the face of the earth. You still set yourself against my people and will not let them go. Therefore, at this time tomorrow I will send the worst hailstorm that has ever fallen on Egypt, from the day it was founded till now. Give an order now to bring your livestock and everything you have in the field to a place of shelter, because the hail will fall on every man and animal that has not been brought in and is still out in the field, and they will die. When Moses stretched out his staff toward the sky, the Lord sent thunder and hail, and lightning flashed down to the ground. So the Lord rained down hail on the land of Egypt; hail fell and lightning flashed back and forth. It was the worst storm in all the land of Egypt since it had become a nation. Throughout Egypt hail struck everything in the fields-both men and animals; it beat down everything growing in the fields and stripped every tree. The only place it did not hail was the land of Goshen, where the Israelites were." {Exodus 9:13-25}

This is where it all began a history of which is what most people are largely aware of given the emphasis always placed upon these two men and their leadership. Something of which unfortunately is looked at as either just a quaint story that can't really be true or taken seriously or one that largely ended with them alone. This however, is a grave mistake to make for the truth of the matter here is that climate change actually became something that was promised to them by Almighty God. A promise that actually occurred in conjunction with that promise of God's to Abraham many centuries earlier regarding their inheritance of the land of Canaan:

> *"Observe therefore all the commands I am giving you today, so that you may live long in the land that the Lord swore to your forefathers to give them and their descendants, a land flowing with milk and honey. The land you are entering to take over is not like the land of Egypt, from which you have come, where you planted your seed and irrigated it by foot as in a vegetable garden. But the land you are crossing the Jordan to take possession of is a land of mountains and valleys that drinks rain from heaven. It is a land that the Lord your God cares for; the eyes of the Lord your God are continually on it from the beginning of the year to its end.*
>
> *So if you faithfully obey the commands I am giving you today to love the Lord your God and to serve him with all your heart and with all your soul –* then I will send rain on your land in its season, *both autumn and spring rains, so that you may gather in your grain, new wine and oil. I will provide grass in the fields for your cattle, and you will eat and be satisfied.*
>
> *Be careful, or you will be enticed to turn away and worship other gods and bow down to them. Then the*

*Lord's anger will burn against you, <u>and he will shut</u>
<u>the heavens so that it will not rain and the ground</u>
<u>will yield no produce, and you will soon perish from</u>
<u>the good land the Lord is giving you</u>. Fix these words
of mine in your hearts and minds!*" {Deuteronomy
11:8-18}

You see here we find Israel being told that not only were
they to be blessed with a land flowing with milk and honey
but with the promise that if they would live to love and obey
their God, He would in return make sure that their land
would never suffer from the effects of droughts. So imagine
this then, the weather for them wasn't to be just something
of a happenstance or luck for that matter. Rather, it was to
be something that they could fully expect to see happen in
perpetuity if they remained faithful to their God that is. For
if they didn't then what they could fully expect to see happen
was a kind of punishment or discipline as it were by way
of droughts. Any kind of a drought therefore would have or
rather should have served to tell Israel that something was
not right concerning their relationship with God. Now how
utterly astonishing is that! Imagine it wasn't enough for God
to give these people literally everything by the world's stan-
dards, but it was to include even good weather. Now if that
isn't something utterly astounding and did this in fact actually happen? Did Israel actually experience these kinds of
things as it is written? Well they most certainly did and that
in practically every generation beginning shortly after their
arrival into the Promised Land:

"In the days when the judges ruled, there was a
famine in the land, and a man from Bethlehem in
Judah, together with his wife and two sons, went to
live in the land of Moab." {Ruth 1:1}

In just a few short years after their entering into the land that God had promised to them they ended up receiving exactly what God had warned and why? Well with it occurring during the days of the judges and what one can readily see is that it had something if not everything to do with that. For the days of the judges was not a time of faithfulness, righteousness and peace but rather a time of unparalleled trouble seeing how the nation fell directly into sin, and one that they actually picked up and were enticed into from those heathen nations that surrounded them. Nations that they failed to dispossess as God had explicitly commanded them to do. As a result God all but turned a blind eye to them but not entirely interestingly enough for in his great love and mercy He did deliver the people under leaders like Othniel, Ehud, Deborah, Gideon, Jepthah, and Samson. Due to the lack of any kind of real knowledgeable leadership however among these judges sadly resulted in the people largely succumbing to a life of wickedness that was most deplorable in nature. Actually, so great became the wickedness that it led to some rather bizarre and unfortunate practices like for example what happened with that judge and warrior named Jephthah who sacrificed his only child a daughter to God because of a vow that he made {Judges 11:29-39}. A vow that he made apparently in haste and ignorance and one in which he never realized could have been redeemed by a payment in some other way {Lev. 27} for such was the lack of knowledge of God's laws among these people. Imagine what a thing to do to ones own child and how could something like this actually happen? Consider that faith in God for these people should have come as easily as sliced bread, seeing how God provided it for them by way of a climate change that would give them nothing but droughts. For an agricultural society this would have been utterly devastating! So what was going on here then that Israel would not stay faithful to the God of their forefathers? Well the answer to that is not so much in their lack of faith for at that time everyone believed in the existence of God. Rather the problem became one of idolatry wherein the chosen people of God took what was unholy in the practices of the surrounding heathen nations and mixed that with what was holy and righteous to God. They confused the God of creation and His character with created things like snakes, birds, the sun, the moon, fish or whatever they fancied or imagined. A matter of which became a most serious issue given the paralyzing fear that came with believing that ones success in life came by appeasing these idols in some way which often meant activities that were wholly evil in nature. The most extreme of which was the sacrificing of children which became an accepting practice by some cultures like the Canaanites for example. That incredibly despicable race of people that God commanded Israel to utterly destroy and remove from the Promised Land which they unfortunately failed to do and how it came to haunt them in later years. Indeed is that not why Jepthah could so easily end up sacrificing his daughter? What he learned, he learned by observing what he saw happening in the surrounding nations. Accordingly as we see then for Israel it was this kind of idolatry that became a never-ending source of trouble for her. A constant stumbling block to all of their endeavors and one that infuriated the one true God to no end and look how God dealt with them. He used the weather of all things to both govern and communicate His peculiar ways and purposes and character. Weather was the key to everything and Israel lived more or less oblivious to this and this apparently even after God used the weather as a kind of military weapon against her enemies. Like for example in this one particular battle with the Philistines:

"While Samuel was sacrificing the burnt offering, the Philistines drew near to engage Israel in battle. But that day the Lord thundered with loud thunder against the Philistines and threw them into such a panic that they were routed before the Israelites." {1Samuel 7:10}

Israel along with her enemies was to learn just who God was exactly and what a fearful thing to be faced with. To go up against a nation that has as its protector, a God, who can manipulate the weather like this is not a nation you want to mess with and the Philistines learned this quickly enough. Indeed after this war Israel was a nation that was more or less left to live in peace with the surrounding nations largely leaving them alone {1Samuel 7: 11-17}. God made sure of that especially under the leadership of Samuel who turned out to be one of Israel's greatest leaders. A prophet and judge who knew God intimately and lived always being careful to obey Gods words and laws and made sure that Israel would as well.

When Samuel grew old however, and could no longer fulfill his duties as priest, prophet, and judge before the people and seeing that his sons did not walk in the ways of the Lord either, Israel was faced with a dilemma. For who now was going to lead them and guess what? Taking again their cue from the surrounding nations around them they desired that it was time now for a human king to lead and rule over them. To replace the Eternal Creator though with a human King was not a wise choice by any stretch of the imagination to make for it would ultimately bring about the beginnings of man made politics and taxes over the affairs and laws of God. To ask for a king was to reduce the populace to servant-hood and even slavery and that as the Creator illustrated through Samuel would not lead to happy endings {8: 9-18}. Endings of which as Samuel alluded to would result in them being shut out from God when that day came when they would cry out to Him for relief from their King and all of the taxes {1 Samuel 8:18}.

Now what were they thinking? Was not God a capable leader before them? Did He not provide for them in their time of need? Did He not save them from their enemies the Philistines with that thunder that was used against them, an event that surely should not have been forgotten that easily? Was not He playing the part of a Father and a true one at that? Indeed He was, but by the time of Samuel's gray hair this was largely forgotten by a younger generation that desired now to make the jump from a theocracy to a monarchy. The asking of which pained Samuel terribly for he felt that they were rejecting him and that it was his own leadership that was at fault. As it turned out though it was not Samuel that they were rejecting but God:

"And the Lord told him: '*Listen to all that the people are saying to you; it is not you they have rejected, but they have rejected me as their king. As they have done from the day I brought them out of Egypt until this day, forsaking me and serving other gods, so they are doing to you. Now listen to them; but warn them solemnly and let them know what the king who will reign over them do.*'" {1Samuel 8:7-9}

God however knew different, for their actions revealed just how unfaithful a people they had become to Him. Actions that caused God now to confront the people with both a review of their past and to the display of His glory and power that came with what? Well with thunder and rain of course and this during of all things harvest season:

"Now then, stand still and see this great thing the Lord is about to do before your eyes! Is it not wheat harvest now? I will call upon the Lord to send thunder and rain. And you will realize what an evil

thing you did in the eyes of the Lord when you asked
for a King.

Then Samuel called upon the Lord, and that same
day the Lord sent thunder and rain. So all the people
stood in awe of the Lord and Samuel." {1 Samuel
12:16-18}

The weather again was to be used by God to communicate,
here I am Israel. A Divine Communication that quite literally
redisplayed before them that promise of Deuteronomy 11:8-
18 in such a way that it should have never again brought into
question just who God was and what He wanted. A display
of God's power that should have sealed once and for all this
nation's relationship to their God in holiness and righteousness and Israel did what in the face of it? They drew back
in fear crying out for Samuel to pray for them so that they
would not end up perishing at the hands of God. Something
which was not going to happen for all God was trying to do
here was open the eyes of this nation to the fact that they
already had a king in God Himself.

"Do not be afraid," Samuel replied. "You have done
all this evil; yet do not turn away from the Lord, but
serve the Lord with all your heart. Do not turn away
after useless idols. They can do you no good, nor can
they rescue you, because they are useless." "For the
sake of His great name the Lord will not reject His
people, because the Lord was pleased to make you
his own. As for me, far be it from that I should sin
against the Lord by failing to pray for you. And I
will teach you the way that is good and right. But be
sure to fear the Lord and serve Him faithfully with all
your heart; consider what great things He has done
for you. Yet if you persist in doing evil, both you

and your king will be swept away." {1Samuel
12:19-25}

So, as a result then Israel accordingly got what they
desired a monarchy and guess what? True to God's words
a monarchy did just as God foretold. They largely reduced
the people to servitude to serve their own needs and ends.
Strange how a people would not understand this and to think
that a people any people, for that matter, would want to
replace the Eternal Creator as governor with a human king
instead, has got to be one of the most foolish of things to do.
For unlike God, a human king is subject to the same kinds
of passions and vices as everyone else is, with their selfish
lustful thoughts, pride, and actions. Human behavior which
of course will always lead to sins and sufferings of all kinds.
To think of mixing that then with the power of a political
nature can be and often is a dangerous mix. Just take as an
example King David and the abuse of his power with the
young damsel Bathsheba and the treacherous murder of her
husband Uriah. You see his lust got the better of him and
to cover up his sins he had her husband quietly murdered
and that under the guise of warfare no less. David paid the
price though before God with the loss of his firstborn child
and then to living the rest of his days without peace having
a sword against him even within his own home {2 Samuel
12}. Then if that wasn't enough, along comes David's son
Solomon who couldn't live up to the ideal either with his fall
from grace actually shattering the kingdom of Israel altogether. In fact after his fall the kingdom was divided into
two between Judah and Israel with the final collapse of Israel
occurring altogether under those most despicable of all kings
Manasseh and Ahab. Two kings who had filled the nation
of Israel with so much evil that it included everything from
the building of altars to worship idols, to the practicing of
sorcery and divination, to prostitution and this in the temple

of God and to the shedding of a great amount of innocent blood. To the degree that it filled the entire city of Jerusalem, King Manasseh having gone so far as to sacrifice even his own son in a fire to the worship of man made idols:

"And you took your sons and daughters whom you bore to me and sacrificed them as food to the idols. Was your prostitution not enough? You slaughtered my children and sacrificed them to the idols." {Ezekiel 16:20-21}

Wow, look what was warned against many generations earlier now came into full bloom with idolatry and its accompanying child sacrifice being adopted by the Israelites? Having learned nothing a new generation had now succumbed to a paganism that did not even exist in the surrounding nations for quite some time and how interesting looking back on all of this history now are the words of the historian Josephus:

"Some nations place the sovereignty of their land in the hands of a single ruler {monarchy], some in the hands of a number of rulers {oligarchy}, and some in the hands of the people {democracy]. Moses our Teacher taught us to place our faith in none of these forms of government. He taught us to obey the rule of God, for to God alone did he accord kingship and power. He commanded the people always to raise their eyes to God, for He is the source of all good for mankind in general and for each person in particular and in Him will people find help when they pray to Him in their time of suffering, for no act is hidden from His understanding and no hidden thought of man's heart is hidden from Him." {Josephus Flavius, Contra Apion, Volume One}

If anyone had an interesting take on things historically it would certainly have been him and so as we see then this asking and receiving of a king did nothing to prevent their society from being attacked and plundered by foreign nations. Actually it had the direct opposite effect with her kings becoming fueled with a lust and greed for power that it drowned that entire region of the world into violence. A violence and bloodshed that became such that it so shocked God into proclaiming that none of it would ever be forgotten by Him:

> *"The Lord has sworn by the Pride of Jacob:" "I will never forget anything they have done."* {Amos 8:7}

Jacob, Jacob how utterly devastated he would have been, indeed to the point of tearing apart his own chest and that quite literally! Horrified beyond belief he would have been for what was going on in the land of their forefathers in the 6th Century B.C. Activities that ultimately moved God now to punish that nation in the gravest of ways:

> "The Lord said through his servants the prophets: *Manasseh king of Judah has committed these detestable sins. He has done more evil than the Amorites who preceded him and has led Judah into sin with his idols. Therefore this is what the Lord, the God of Israel, says: I am going to bring such disaster on Jerusalem and Judah that the ears of everyone who hears of it will tingle. I will stretch out over Jerusalem the measuring line used against Samaria and the plumb line used against the house of Ahab. I will wipe out Jerusalem as one wipes a dish, wiping it and turning it upside down."* {2 Kings 21:10-13}

Gravest of ways that did not just come by way of Israel's exile from their land to the land of Persia by the invading and conquering Babylonian armies but by way of severe climate change. A climate change that was so severe in fact, that it more or less reduced the land of promise to a barren landscape and totally obliterated the city of Jerusalem. The prophet Ezekiel summing it up quite succinctly with these words:

> "Rain will come in torrents, and I will send hailstones hurtling down and violent winds will burst forth... In my wrath I will unleash a violent wind, and in my anger hailstones and torrents of rain will fall with destructive fury." {Ezekiel 13: 8-13}

And the prophet Jeremiah:

> "When He thunders, the waters in the heavens roar; He makes clouds rise from the ends of the earth. He sends lightning with the rain and brings out the wind from His storehouses." {Jeremiah 51:16}

And the prophet Isaiah:

> "The Lord will cause men to hear His majestic voice and will make them see His arm coming down with raging anger and consuming fire, with cloudburst, thunderstorm and hail." {Isaiah 30:30}

> "I will make justice the measuring line and righteousness the plumb line, hail will sweep away your refuge, the lie, and water will over flow your hiding place." {Isaiah 28:17}

"See the Lord has one who is powerful and strong. Like a hailstorm and a destructive wind, like a flooding downpour He will throw it forcefully to the ground." {Isaiah 28:2}

And the prophet Haggai:

"I struck all the work of your hands with blight, mildew, and hail yet you did not return to me declares the Lord." {Haggai 2:17}

My word what happened to this nation? To go from bad to worse is hard to understand the why of. What a huge and terrible price she had to pay for her wicked and sinful and unfaithful ways. Get this though, God was not one to utterly forsake these people and though this was the way it was at that time anyway He only used such predicaments as a stepping-stone towards something better. One that came in a number of different ways with reformation and revival occurring under leaders like Ezra, Nehemiah and Daniel, who were used mightily by God to bring a people back from the brink. Speak comforting words to Israel God declared in Isaiah 40:1 and comforting words they certainly were especially with a declaration like this that harked back to that promise that started it all in Deuteronomy 11: 8-18.

"The poor and needy search for water, but there is none; their tongues are parched with thirst. But I the Lord will answer them; I the God of Israel, will not forsake them. I will make rivers flow on barren heights, and springs within the valleys. I will turn the desert into pools of water, and the parched ground into springs. I will put in the desert the cedar and the acacia, the myrtle and the olive. I will set pines in the wasteland, the fir and the cypress together, so

that the people may see and know, may consider and
understand, that the hand of the Lord has done this,
that the Holy One of Israel has created it." {Isaiah
41: 17-20}

Water in the form of rain is again the key to literally everything, and for Israel this occurred when? Well it occurred
during the time of her reformation and revival under Ezra
and Nehemiah. Two great leaders who during and after the
exiles return from Babylon caused Israel to realize the extent
of their unfaithfulness to God and led them into a time of
repentance and confession for their sins before God and the
making of restitution. Israel was again to learn the hard way
that intermingling with the foreign nations around her was a
bad idea and both Ezra and Nehemiah made sure that they
understood this going so far as to even cause Israel to send
back to those nations the men and women that they took
from there as husbands and wives. Nehemiah going so far
as to even beat and shout in such extreme anger at the house
of Israel giving them as an illustration the life of their king
Solomon whose ultimate destruction along with the nation
came because of his and their numerous marriages and adulterous affairs with these kinds of woman.

"I rebuked them and called curses down on them. I
beat some of the men and pulled out their hair. I made
them take an oath in God's name and said: "You are
not to give you're daughters in marriage to their
sons, nor are you to take their daughters in marriage
for your sons or for yourselves. Was it not because
of marriages like these that Solomon king of Israel
sinned? Among the many nations there was no king
like him. He was loved by his God, and God made
him king over all Israel, but even he was led into sin
by foreign women. Must we hear now that you too

are doing all this terrible wickedness and are being unfaithful to our God by marrying foreign woman?" {Nehemiah 13:25-27}

"Within three days, all the men of Judah and Benjamin had gathered in Jerusalem. And on the twentieth day of the ninth month, all the people were sitting in the square before God, greatly distressed by the occasion and because of the rain. Then Ezra the priest stood up and said to them, "You have been unfaithful; you have married foreign women, adding to Israel's guilt. Now make confession to the Lord, the God of your forefathers, and do his will. Separate yourselves from the peoples around you and from your foreign wives." {Ezra 10: 9-11}

These two great leaders understood the importance of keeping a people from the influences of what was happening in the surrounding nations. They understood the importance of righteousness and holiness and look how a monsoon rain accompanied all of this. Yet again God was to use the weather to communicate that He was there. Yet again another generation was to learn the truth of what they should have already been well aware of. Did they though? Did they in fact understand the truth of what was happening here with the rain accompanying this time of reformation and revival? Well we really have no idea whether they did or not except to say that surely they must have realized something was up with the weather; for shortly after their return from exile they ran into, yet another drought and this apparently was because Israel had become too preoccupied with their own lives to bother with the rebuilding of God's Temple. They seem to have thought that the rebuilding of the wall of Jerusalem was enough. God however made it quite clear to them that this was a mistake:

"This is what the Lord Almighty says: *Give careful thought to your ways. Go up into the mountains and bring down timber and build the house, so that I may take pleasure in it and be honored, says the Lord. You expected much, but see, it turned out to be little. What you brought home I blew away. Why? Declares the Lord Almighty. Because of my house, which remains a ruin, while each of you is busy with his own house. Therefore, because of you the heavens have with-held their dew and the earth its crops. I called for a drought on the fields and on the mountains, on the grain, the new wine, the oil and whatever the ground produces, on men and cattle, and on the labor of your hands.*" {Haggai 1: 5-11}

Rather astonishing isn't it? Yet again another drought came to afflict that land but not so extreme as to render that land uninhabitable. Yet again God was to use the weather as a means of communicating that for Israel there existed between them a special kind of relationship with their God. What a nation and what a history! Truly they were a people who had it all. They had it all and yet because of this one despicable practice of idolatry they ended up becoming a race of people who never really understood or experienced all that God had in store for them. Rather they simply went from bad to worse and this largely because they could never get a grip on stopping this despicable practice of taking what was unholy and wicked from the nations that surrounded her and mixing that with what was holy and righteous to God. Having misunder-stood everything about God they continually went the way of the yo-yo, although after what happened with the exile and God's punishment of her this matter of idolatry would largely never again be dabbled in. At least not to the extent of what it was originally. It was just too emotionally devas-tating what happened to them during that time. Certainly that was the case where her kingdom was concerned for no king would ever again lead her politically. Rather she would only end up coming under the auspices of other nation's kings who would come and conquer them and their land like the Greeks for example and then the Romans. A conquering of which by the way now took the most terrible toll of all upon them with their capital city of Jerusalem being destroyed by Rome in 70A.D. with the final destruction occurring altogether under Roman governor Tinneas {Turlus} Rufus in 135A.D. who had the Temple Mount plowed under for the last time. An event that interestingly enough should be paid special attention to here, weather wise, that is; for after these events God would never again be seen to concern Himself with anything having to do with this city. Rather as history teaches God would end up ignoring the city of Jerusalem altogether including that Temple of His which He would never allow to be rebuilt in anyway again. In fact as the history of it reveals God apparently was against its rebuilding altogether and we can know this because of the rather unusual circumstances that surrounded the Jewish people's attempts to do exactly that. Like for example what occurred on May 20th in 363 A.D. and that earthquake that struck the city. To find that it should have occurred on this particular date is not without great significance given how it was on this date that the Jews of Jerusalem were about to begin the rebuilding efforts of the Temple:

"The stones were piled high and ready. Costly wood had been purchased. The necessary metal was at hand. The Jews of Jerusalem were rejoicing. Tomorrow - May 20, 363 A.D.-the rebuilding of the Temple would begin!... Suddenly, and without warning, at the third hour of the night...the streets of Jerusalem trembled and buckled, crushing two hundred years of hope in a pile of dust. No longer would there be

any possibility of rebuilding the Temple." {pg. 31
Thomas Ice & Randall Price}

My word! What happened to this nation now that God
would go to such extremes? Well of course with it happening
during the Roman occupation and it would surely have to
point to only one thing, and that is the crucifixion and resurrection of Christ. That one all-important and central event
that changed history for all time and sadly led Israel to its
final downfall, something of which this very Christ foretold
would happen and my how He cried because of it...

*"If you, even you, had only known on this day what
would bring you peace-but now it is hidden from
your eyes. The days will come upon you when your
enemies will build an embankment against you and
encircle you in on every side. They will dash you to
the ground, you and the children within your walls.
They will not leave one stone on another, because
you did not recognize the time of God's coming to
you."* {Luke 19:42-44}

*"O Jerusalem, Jerusalem you who kill the prophets
and stone those sent to you, how often I have longed
to gather your children together, as a hen gathers
her chicks under her wings, but you were not willing.
Look, your house is left to you desolate. For I tell
you, you will not see me again until you say, Blessed
is he who comes in the name of the Lord."* {Matthew
23:37-39}

The Christ and true King of Israel had finally arrived but
sadly for the house of Israel they were all but oblivious to
His coming. Again they had misunderstood everything about
God and looking back over the last 2000 years of history

and what Christ said about their house being left desolate has certainly been fulfilled in its entirety. Indeed, looking at the history of it all where will one find anything having to do with anything where God is concerned? All we find ourselves looking at is nothing but war and bloodshed by numerous nations who have come and gone and raped this land of virtually everything leaving just a desert in their wake. Jerusalem moreover being taken over by the Moslem's who to spite the Crusaders along with the Jews, their half brothers, built for themselves a temple of their own on the very spot where the previous temple of God had stood. The building of which by the way did nothing to cause God to send plentiful rain showers upon that dry and thirsty land as He once did under the revivals of Haggai, Daniel, Ezra and Nehemiah. Surely a not too insignificant matter given Israel's past with climate change and the promises made to her and looking at what is happening today in that land makes one wonder where is this all going to go? Indeed with all of the talk now about the rebuilding of the temple according to the Old Testament pattern and what Israel is hoping for is some kind of a miracle that will again place the Temple Mount into their hands. A hope that some were expecting would have been fulfilled by a wayward rocket that Saddam Hussein had fired into that nation during the Gulf War. That was not be of course and with the way in which things are continuing to progress in that land are causing many people to realize that nothing short of divine intervention will ever bring about the rebuilding of that Temple. A divine intervention that given what happened during the Roman occupation seems to be a fore gone conclusion now that the Christ of God has come. For He was the fulfillment of everything regarding the Old Testament Law with its sacrifices and procedures having replaced it all with his own sacrifice.

He was the atonement for sin!

Of course Israel doesn't believe this though and for the Christ to say to the Jews of that time, "*I have come in my fathers name, and you do not accept me; but if someone else comes in his own name, you will accept him*" {John 5: 43} can surely mean only one thing. That another like unto the Christ of God will arrive to take his place and give to the Jewish people what they want. That is peace with her enemies and a restored temple to worship at, and for anyone to give to the Jews their Temple Mount under the conditions that exist there today would surely be received by that nation as ultimately god. Given what the prophet Daniel has to say however {11: 31-44} and what we find is that if this were to actually happen then this king will not be the true king of Israel but only an impostor. One who will end up bringing about what the bible refers to as the 'Abomination of Desolation' the final act in a long history that will see a mere mortal of a man, Satan's avatar, proclaiming himself to be god and demanding the world worship him as that. A matter which we are told interestingly enough by St. John the Revelator will result in something utterly astonishing happening. For guess what ends up occurring during this period? Well climate change of course. God will again have to intervene to teach truth but this time it ends up happening in a very unusual manner. For what St. John illustrates for us is that this will occur not primarily from heaven as it were but rather by way of two witnesses who we find will arrive in the city of Jerusalem to prophesy and speak on behalf of the one true God. Two witnesses who will have been given by Almighty God the kind of power to render the skies cloudless and to inflict on mankind all sorts of plagues:

> "And I will give power to my two witnesses, and they will prophesy for 1260 days clothed in sackcloth. These are the two olive trees and the two lamp stands that stand before the Lord of the earth. If anyone

tries to harm them, fire comes from their mouths and devours their enemies. This is how anyone who wants to harm them must die. These men have the power to shut up the sky so that it will not rain during the time they are prophesying; and they have power to turn the waters into blood and to strike the earth with every kind of plague as often as they want."

"Now when they have finished their testimony, the beast that comes up from the Abyss will attack them, and kill them. Their bodies will lie in the street of the great city, which is figuratively called Sodom and Egypt, where also their Lord was crucified. For three and a half days men from every people, tribe, language and nation will gaze on their bodies and refuse them burial. The inhabitants of the earth will gloat over them and will celebrate by sending each other gifts, because these two prophets had tormented those who live on the earth."

"But after three and a half days a breath of life from God entered them, and they stood on their feet, and terror struck those who saw them. Then they heard a loud voice saying to them, Come up here. And they went up to heaven in a cloud, while their enemies looked on. *At that very hour there was a severe earthquake and a tenth of the city collapsed. Seven thousand people were killed in the earthquake, and the survivors were terrified and gave glory to the God of heaven.*" {Revelation 11:1-13}

So imagine here we go yet again with the weather and look what further happens here. Another earthquake will end up striking this city which given what occurred under the Temple Mount in the year 363 AD is surely not to an insignificant a matter. Actually if it doesn't go to show and prove that the May 20 earthquake was not just some kind of a coincidence! Rather Almighty God was the one directly responsible for it and if that wasn't enough look yet another earthquake is going to strike except this one will end up becoming global in scope and impact. Moreover hailstones are going pummel whatever is left of man upon the earth! Apparently this is where God will finally have had enough:

> "The seventh angel poured out his bowl into the air, and out of the temple came a loud voice from the throne, saying, 'IT IS DONE!' Then there came flashes of lightning, rumblings, peals of thunder and *a severe earthquake. No earthquake like it has ever occurred since man has been on earth, so tremendous was the quake.* The great city split into three parts, and the cities of the nations collapsed. God remembered Babylon the Great and gave her the cup filled with the wine of the fury of His wrath. Every island fled away and the mountains could not be found. From the sky huge hailstones of about a hundred pounds each fell upon men. And they cursed God on account of the plague of hail, because the plague was so terrible." {Revelation 16:17-21}

What an unimaginable judgment and look for the most part the Jewish people and nation are completely and totally oblivious to this thinking that a rebuilt Temple is going to usher in for them and the world a kind of utopia. Their hope is for a rebuilt Temple! What a mistake! Accordingly any attempts to rebuild that Temple therefore in the future should be looked upon with the greatest of trepidation especially in view of how it will lead to this Abomination of Desolation. The final act in a long history wherein a mere mortal of a man will raise himself to godhood and demand under death no less that the entire world worship him as that. A matter of which actually occurs with this incredible matter called the

666. For this to ultimately happen a temple has to exist and what better way for that to happen than for some individual who through cunning and deceitful behavior uses the hope of a people to do exactly that. It's certainly something to think about isn't it especially in view of what the bible further has to say on the subject like for example in these words from both the prophet Daniel and St. Paul:

> "He will confirm a covenant with many for one seven. In the middle of the seven he will put an end to sacrifice and offering. And on a wing of the temple, he will set up an abomination that causes desolation, until the end that is decreed is poured out upon him." {Daniel 9:27}

> "Don't let anyone deceive you in any way, for that day will not come until the rebellion occurs and the man of lawlessness is revealed, the man doomed to destruction. He will oppose and will exalt himself over everything that is called God or is worshiped, so that he sets himself up in God's temple, proclaiming himself to be God." {2 Thessalonians 2:3-4}

Here we have it, the very explanation of everything and that from both the Old and New Testaments. Events of which we find ultimately will conclude with Armageddon and for those who are interested in the Old Testament interpretation of the finality of this will find its conclusion in the words of the prophet Zechariah:

> "A day of the Lord is coming when your plunder will be divided among you. I will gather all the nations to Jerusalem to fight against it; the city will be captured, the houses ransacked, and the women

raped. Half of the city will go into exile, but the rest of the people will not be taken from the city.

Then the Lord will go out and fight against those nations, as he fights in the day of battle. On that day his feet will stand on the Mount of Olives, east of Jerusalem, and the Mount of Olives will be split in two from east to west, forming a great valley, with half of the mountain moving north and half moving south. You will flee by my mountain valley, for it will extend to Azel. You will flee as you fled from the earthquake in the days of Uzziah king of Judah. Then the Lord my God will come, with all the holy ones with him. On that day there will be no light, no cold or frost. It will be a unique day, with out daytime or nighttime a day known to the Lord. When evening comes, there will be light.

On that day living waters will flow out from Jerusalem, half to the eastern sea, and half to the western sea, in summer and in winter.

The Lord will be king over the whole earth. On that day there will be one Lord, and his name the only name." {Zechariah 14: 1- 9}

The coming of Armageddon will result in the true King of Israel that is the one who holds the scars of Calvary finally returning to fulfill all that was spoken of Him through the prophets. An event which will find Israel finally coming to that place of salvation that she so desperately needs but could never find. A salvation that will surely be a severely emotional one if not altogether an excruciating painful one seeing how her eyes will finally be opened to the truth of what all her prophets have been prophesying about since the time of antiquity:

"And I will pour out on the house of David and the inhabitants of Jerusalem a spirit of supplication. They will look on me, the one they have pierced, and they will mourn for him as one mourns for an only child, and grieve for him as one grieves for a first-born son. On that day the weeping in Jerusalem will be great, like the weeping of Hadad Rimmon in the plain of Megiddo.

On that day a fountain will be opened to the house of David and the inhabitants of Jerusalem, to cleanse from sin and impurity.

On that day I will banish the names of the idols from the land, and they will be remembered no more, declares the Lord Almighty. I will remove both the prophets and the spirit of impurity from the land. And if anyone still prophesies, his father and mother, to whom he was born, will say to him, You must die, because you have told lies in the Lord's name. When he prophesies, his own parents will stab him.

On that day every prophet will be ashamed of his prophetic vision. He will not put on a prophets garment of hair in order to deceive. He will say, I am not a prophet. I am a farmer; the land has been my livelihood since my youth. If someone asks him, What are these wounds on your body? He will answer, The wounds I was given at the house of my friends."
{Zechariah 12:10-11 to 13:1-6}

The return of Christ will be a special day for Israel and the world. One in which will result in both the remnants of Israel along with the rest of mankind who will have come out of the great tribulation living to see a day and age like no other. An age that the scriptures refer to as the millennial age where Christ will reign over the entire planet for a 1000 year period of sublime peace, harmony and righteousness. It will be the beginnings finally of Israel's true golden age where Israel along with the rest of the world will come to experience a world like no other. Everything will change under the leadership of Christ except for one incredible and important factor, and that is how climate change will remain a fixture over the earth. A climate change that like unto what was written many thousands of years previously will again result in droughts and famines. Unlike what happened at that time though the reason for it occurring now will be because of the lack of attendance to a certain feast called the Feast of Tabernacles:

> "Then the survivors from all the nations that have attacked Jerusalem will go up year after year to worship the King, the Lord Almighty, and to cele-brate the Feast of Tabernacles. If any of the peoples of the earth do not go up to Jerusalem to worship the King, the Lord Almighty, they will have no RAIN. If the Egyptian people do not go up and take part, they will have no RAIN." {Zechariah 14:16-18}

A feast that God will apparently require that literally everyone, Jew and Gentile, keep otherwise no rain will fall, and why is this? Well, because of thanksgiving of course! For this feast interestingly enough was a harvest feast falling as it did during the week of 15th to the 22nd of the month of Tishri that is October. Harvest is dependant upon rain and the rain was dependent upon the people loving and obeying God. So it comes back to this issue of faithfulness and thanksgiving of course which was to be celebrated with great joy during this particular feast. It was to be a celebration of thanks-giving for everything that God did from Israel's salvation from bondage under Egyptian rule, to the salvation of our sins by the cross of Christ and ultimately to the continued blessings of Almighty God. This is what it is all about.

Accordingly is it any wonder then that God would make it a requirement that such a feast be celebrated throughout the millennial period. It speaks of His salvation ultimately and doesn't that astonish that He would connect it to the weather of all things!

So imagine this then-yet again the weather is to become the means by which a people will learn that being unfaithful to God their Creator is a most foolish if not grave mistake to make. One in which by all appearances will never be made by anyone living in the principle area of Israel ever again. This return of Christ will once and for all change that forever! As for those living in the furthest regions of the world however, whether they come under droughts or not we have been given no details of in scripture other than to find that after these 1000 years are over something quite terrible is going to happen. For according to what both the prophet Ezekiel and St. John have to say in their visions an enormous group of nations that God refers too as Gog and Magog will be completely destroyed:

> "*I will summon a sword against Gog on all my mountains, declares the Sovereign Lord. Everyman's sword will be against his brother. I will execute judgment upon him with plague and bloodshed; I will pour down torrents of rain, hailstones and burning sulfur on him and on his troops and on the many nations with him and on his troops and on the many nations with him. And so I will show my greatness and my holiness, and I will make myself known in the sight of many nations. Then they will know that I am the Lord.*" {Ezekiel 38: 21-23}

"When the thousand years are over, Satan will be released from his prison and will go out to deceive the nations in the four corners of the earth-Gog and

Magog-to gather them for battle. In number they are like the seashore. They marched across the breadth of the earth and surrounded the camp of God's people, the city He loves. But fire came down from heaven and devoured them. And the devil, who deceived them, was thrown into the lake of burning sulfur, where the beast and the false prophet had been thrown. They will be tormented day and night for ever and ever." {Rev. 20: 7-10}

Destroyed because they will all collectively decide together to go to war against the land of Israel for the purposes of plunder and conquest. A war which they could in no way possibly win going up as it were against the land and city of Christ, that is the Son of Almighty God who will actually be residing within the walls of that city and my how strange a thing is this to find occurring. Now why would Almighty God commit to doing such a terrible thing? Well given what we have seen so far in the scriptures specifically from the book of Job and if the answer to that isn't as simple as the word test with perhaps the prophet Jeremiah summing it up the best for us here with these words:

"I the Lord search the heart and examine the mind, to reward a man according to his conduct, according to what his deeds deserve." {Jeremiah 17:10}

At that future time man's character and faith will apparently have to be tested yet again and to find a people who will have lived without any kind of evil influence in their lives and this under the rulership of Christ, no less, succumbing to an evil and that by this Satan, will ultimately prove to be to much for Almighty God. Accordingly His Majesty will be forced to act in the most severe of ways by judging and destroying these people along with Satan himself:

"This is what the Sovereign Lord says: On that day thoughts will come into your mind and you will devise an evil scheme. You will say, I will invade a land of unwalled villages; I will attack a peaceful and unsuspecting people all of them living without walls and without gates and bars. I will plunder and loot and turn my hand against the resettled ruins and the peoples gathered from the nations, rich in livestock and goods, living at the center of the land." {Ezekiel 38:10-12}

"On the mountains of Israel you will fall, you and all your troops and the nations with you. I will give you as food to all kinds of carrion birds and to wild animals. You will fall in the open field, for I have spoken, declares the Sovereign Lord. I will send fire on Magog and on those who live in safety in the coastlands, and they will know that I am the Lord." {Ezekiel 39: 4-6}

"And the devil, who deceived them, was thrown into the lake of burning sulfur, where the beast and the false prophet had been thrown. They will be tormented day and night for ever and ever." {Rev. 20: 10}

God will destroy them and again how odd it is to find that this should happen this way to them. For consider these people will not be a people like us born as it were without the knowledge of God. Rather these people will be born into a world where the knowledge of God and His Christ will be everywhere. God will be a living reality right before their very eyes. Faith therefore will not be so much a struggle but a living reality one in which they will experience day in and day out. Surely *that promise of rain and the Feast*

of Tabernacles proves that out well enough. More significantly though is how this issue of ones sinfulness will be
manifested for what it is disobedience to God. For no longer
will there be the kind of blindness that exists now and this
because of this Satan who blinds the consciences of men in
order to deceive them:

> "And I saw an angel coming down from heaven,
> having the keys to the Abyss and holding in his hand
> a great chain. He seized the dragon, that ancient
> serpent, who is the devil, or Satan, and bound him
> for a thousand years. He threw him into the Abyss,
> and locked it over him, to keep him from deceiving
> the nations anymore until the thousand years were
> ended. *After that he must be set free for a short time.*"
> {Rev. 20:1-3}

Sinfulness will therefore be dealt with, and that in a manner
where it will all but been removed from the consciences of
mankind during this millennial period. At least to the extent
of where willful disobedience and wickedness to God's laws
are concerned. By the time of this 11th generation though it
appears that this matter of sinfulness will have all but been
forgotten or rather just cast aside as it were and we can know
this because too easy will be their seduction and fall to the
influences of Satan and how incredible is that? For how
can it be that such a pathetic and despicable creature as this
Satan could so easily deceive a people like this? Or more
to the point is how could these people allow themselves to
end up being deceived by this individual especially in view
of how this is already written? To open the bible to Ezekiel
chapter 38 and Revelation, chapter 20 and read of the future
should more than cause one to be educated and prepared *in
what not to do.* These people it appears though will apparently be more or less ignorant of this and why should that

be so strange and unusual given the state of affairs in our own world and generation? For if a people today hardly find time or give any credence to the bible why should any other generation be any different? Accordingly what then can we assume is really going on here? Well I think one can assume that it as usual comes back to this matter of what is in the heart of mankind with Christ Jesus of course giving us the best example of it with these words:

"This is the verdict: Light has come into the world,
but men loved darkness instead of the light because
their deeds were evil." {John 3:19}

As usual mankind will find sin delightful and to find that this should happen in a generation such as theirs will be the ultimate of grave mistakes to make. You see the picture here is not that they will attack the nation of Israel per-se as the reason for their destruction *but rather that they will literally have committed the ultimate of all treasonous acts against Almighty God. It will be rebellion of the most serious and dreadful kind against His Majesty.* Look why else would we find His Majesty using these words; *"Then they will know that I am the Lord."* {Ezekiel 38:23, 39:6}

So this ultimately is the real reason why they will be destroyed and imagine it will take those living in the land of Israel some seven months to bury the dead and some seven years to clean the land of their weapons of war {Ezekiel 39: 9-16}. That is a great deal of death! So imagine then what a terrible and dreadful end this is going to be to a long and peaceful life under the ruler-ship of Christ and do you know that according to the book of the Revelation of Christ, this end will be the end to literally everything including the look of planet earth. For shortly after these events will come the great white throne judgment wherein the books will be opened, including the book of life wherein everyone will be judged according to what they have or haven't done to determine which of them will inherit the lake of fire or eternal life. Then will come the beginnings of a new earth and a new heaven with a new city called the New Jerusalem descending from out of heaven wherein God will make all things new and will wipe away all tears {Revelation 20:11-15 to 21:1-27}.

This is the picture of how the scriptures say things will ultimately come to an end and my how interesting it is to find and see that what Ezekiel prophesied as ending Israel's long exile the apostle John brings to a conclusion with his vision of God's glory in a new heaven and earth where her capital city will be utterly glorious. A Jerusalem that will radiate God's magnificent glory forever and ever! Now if that isn't something incredibly fascinating, in fact to the degree of whoever would have thought that studying climate change of all things would take us right into the future history of our world? With the God of the bible though that is the way it is; that He made abundantly clear for all to see and read:

"I am God, and there is no other; I am God, and there is none like me. I make known from the beginning, from ancient times, what is still to come. I say: My purpose will stand, and I will do all that I please." {Isaiah 46: 9-10}

A matter which was also reiterated by his Son Christ Jesus who likewise revealed the same abilities:

"I have told you now before it happens, so that when it does happen you will believe." {John 14:29}

Wow, and so Israel then we find is in for an interesting future if not an extremely difficult and suffering one. A future history that given what the words of God have to say could have been prevented if only they had but paid attention to everything that God had ever said to them. Especially where this matter of climate change is concerned, for as we have seen looking back through their history it winds its way through practically every generation. Even today not much has changed with rain water being a scarce commodity. So scarce in fact that it has actually led to wars being fought over what little remains and if that isn't something utterly unbelievable? For how can it be that in a land where practically everyone believes in God and nobody it seems can make the connection that this is a direct result of God? Have things really gone so far that even today in the holy land people and were not talking just about the Jews but about Moslem's and Christians as well have been suckered into believing what science has to say regarding the weather. That it is just some kind of a natural process that exists and works because of the interaction of air temperature, air pressure and humidity the three factors that science says makes up the weather. Apparently so, except that is for one rather interesting individual who this writer heard on a television news cast had been yelling to the people in the streets of the city of Baghdad something to the effect of, 'hey look what God is doing to the American forces!' {Paraphrase mine} A matter of which immediately caused this writer to stop what he was doing and quickly run out to get a copy of a newspaper to try and find out what exactly this individual was referring to and guess what I came across. This incredible report written by Matthew Fisher of the Canwest News Service concerning Bravo Company:

CENTRAL IRAQ - "Neither hail, sandstorm, pestilence nor rugged terrain can halt the slow, inexorable advance of U.S. forces toward Baghdad.

A tempest of biblical proportions swept across the Mesopotamian plain Tuesday, cutting visibility first to 40 to 50 metres, then to as little as one or two meters.

The storm sprang out of nowhere after a pleasant start to the day.

At the height of the tempest, the wind was so strong no one could go outside our light armored vehicle {LAV}. It was also so dark, the sun could not be seen. Everything was bathed in an odd orange glow.

Inside our vehicle, we felt almost as if we were in a small boat, as the heavy gusts of wind shook the 14 tonne LAV.

Six of us were crammed inside, along with extra ammunition, personal belongings, military equipment, radios and communications gear.

After several hours, the wind subsided, then the sandstorm became a hailstorm, with thunder and lightning, which turned the desert floor into a silky mud almost bogging down the eight-wheel drive vehicles.

A small pool of water, a little lake almost, quickly formed behind our vehicle. We had to move to avoid getting swamped."{The Vancouver Sun, Wednesday, March 26, 2003 pg. A4}

Now look at this! Everything that we have been discussing in this chapter is displayed right before us in our daily headlines and it took a citizen of the city of Baghdad and a Moslem no less to recognize it for what it was. *__An act of Almighty God!!!!__*

He of all people could see what others could not and this was no doubt due more to his acclimatization to that particular environment than anything revolving around his education of the bible or rather the Koran if there is anything in that book regarding the weather that is. For in the desert no one ever lives to see such weather phenomena as a hailstorm and this in such an abrupt manner and this especially directly over an army. A matter of which given this study coupled with this scripture from the book of Isaiah will no doubt engender a great many questions and concerns about what is happening not only in the land of Iraq but throughout the entire world:

> "The Lord will cause men to hear his majestic voice and will make them see his arm coming down with raging anger and consuming fire, with cloudburst, thunderstorm and hail." {Isaiah 30:30}

Alarming isn't it? Indeed! Accordingly, the next time one hears or sees or experiences climate change, maybe what one should do is take a good hard long look at the sinful reasons for it. For more likely than not there will be a connection to it with some wickedness that mankind is or has been committing. That has certainly been the way it has been for this particular writer with some meteorological events having come as quite a shock and surprise like the one above of course. More interestingly though would have to be that severe tornado with accompanying hailstones that landed in Israel of all places on April 4, 2006. Again another inexplicable weather phenomenon for an area of the world that never sees such things because of the dryness of the region and one that fortunately occurred not directly over one of her cities but rather out in some desert region. Now again what should we make of this just an odd and inexplicable work of nature? Doubtful given what we have just learned and to look further into the news of the day from that region of the world and guess what further happened just a few days later? A suicide bombing that took the life of more innocent civilians. Again was there a connection?

My word you know isn't faith supposed to result in something called the fear of God? That is a fear that tells them that if you commit sin and wickedness you will be punished for it accordingly. Where has that disappeared? Do people really think that it applies only to the life hereafter? That it has more to do with a hell and a heaven? If so then that is a very grave mistake to make and with that I'll leave you my reader with one last thing to mull over. When Mel Gibson made that movie called The Passion of the Christ there occurred a most astounding and incredible meteorological event, a lightning strike of all things hit the set during the filming of one particular scene. Now was that just some kind of a coincidence, or do you think that maybe someone was trying to communicate something of great importance? Wow! Accordingly think well I think one should on the events of Luke chapter 23:44 with particular emphasis upon chapter 24: 25-27 while surely keeping a finger on this passage from the book of Zechariah:

"Rejoice greatly, O daughter of Zion! Shout, Daughter of Jerusalem! See your king comes to you, righteousness and having salvation, gentle and riding on a donkey, on a colt, the foal of a donkey. I will take away the chariots from Ephraim and the war-horses from Jerusalem, and the battlebow will be broken. He will proclaim peace to the nations. His rule will extend from sea to sea and from the River to the ends of the earth." {Zechariah 9:9-10}

CHAPTER FOUR

ARCHAEOLOGY - ITS FASCINATING DISCOVERIES

Of all of the arguments ever given by science regarding faith and religion that it is really nothing more than conjecture and it would be that God can't be observed to exist. Looking at the topic of climate change however and what we are presented with is something altogether different. For according to the bible it makes no bones about the fact that when it comes to the weather God is the One ultimately responsible for it all. This we have clearly seen a matter which surely no one will be able to gainsay or reject given the enormous historicity of it all. If however there are or would be those who would question this and this because what it's just the biblical record and accordingly are in need of something more current or scientific well then perhaps this chapter will be of some significance. For what you are about see in this chapter is how everything that is written in the bible is exactly what our scientists are themselves beginning to observe now from their own investigations. It is something really quite fascinating if not utterly mind-boggling in fact that it has created in the heart of this writer a kind of eureka moment. Indeed whoever would have thought to find a subject like global warming which is on the minds of practically everyone today being a topic of such paramount importance in the bible as well? Let me tell you it sure makes for an interesting study as we shall see in this utterly fascinating chapter.

Recently a landmark study entitled What Drives Societal Collapse was published in the journal Science. In it anthropologists Dr. Harvey Weiss of Yale University and his colleague Dr. Raymond S. Bradley from the University of Massachusetts in Amherst published the remarkable news that climate change is not something unique to just our own day and age. Rather, climate change it has been observed now has been an on going event in one way or another throughout mankind's entire history. So much so in fact that many societies along with some entire civilizations have actually collapsed under the weight of it all. A rather star-tlingly discovery that has so stirred the halls of academia with many questions and concerns for it was always believed that the collapse of such societies in the past was the result of social, political, and or economic factors. That however is no longer the case as these scientists clearly point out...

"That perspective is now changing with the accumulation of high-resolution paleoclimatologic data that provide an independent measure of the timing, amplitude, and duration of past climatic events. These climatic events were abrupt, involved new conditions that were unfamiliar to the inhabitants of the time, and persisted for decades to centuries. They were therefore highly disruptive, leading to societal collapse-an adaptive response to otherwise insurmountable stresses." {pg. 609 Science}

"Climate during the past 11,000 years was long believed to have been uneventful, but paleoclimatic records increasingly demonstrate climatic instability. Mulitdecadel-to multicentury-length droughts started abruptly, were unprecedented in the experience of the existing societies, and were highly disruptive to their agricultural foundations because social and techno-logical innovations were not available to counter the rapidity, amplitude, and duration of changing climatic conditions." {ibid pg. 610}

Now if this isn't something utterly astounding if not altogether significant?! What profound statements to make regarding something that is at the very heart of what the bible has been saying and that for the past 11,000 years as well. What an enigma this has been proving though to be for those within the scientific community. Indeed to the degree that they are at a complete and total loss to explain what could have possibly been responsible for these past climate changes especially where droughts and famines are concerned. For what exactly could have possibly been responsible for droughts lasting entire centuries? Certainly not mankind, for they of course did not have the kind of industrialization that we have today. They did not pour millions of tons of industrialized pollutants into the atmosphere every hour of everyday. Nor did they poison their rivers, lakes and oceans with chemicals of every sort and description under the sun. Neither did they electrify their world with hydro poles and telecommunication lines spanning the entire globe. The air they breathed was relatively pure in comparison to our own. What then did they have that would cause weather patterns to change so drastically? Our scientists have no answers whatsoever other than to be of the opinion now that the weather is not as stable as originally thought. A matter of which on a side note here has actually led politicians and even oil company executives to quickly jump on and use in their pursuit to somehow discredit the whole idea that industrial pollution is the cause of our troubles and why? Well because of economics and money of course, for to accept the argument that industrialization is the guilty party would mean the complete changing of energy policy and that would be detrimental to the bottom line. So profits as usual takes center stage which is really something given how the world has already spent in the neighborhood of some 40 billion dollars and counting studying climate change. What an absurd amount of money for something that can be easily explained by simply opening the bible, and to look at some of these scientists examples of past climate changes and if they don't mirror the very words and history of the bible. Like for example this utterly astounding illustration:

"In the Middle East, a ~200 year drought forced the abandonment of agricultural settlements in the Levant and northern Mesopotamia. The subsequent return to moister conditions in Mesopotamia promoted settlement of the Tigris-Euphrates alluvial plain and delta, where breachable river levees and seasonal basins may have encouraged early Mesopotamia irrigation agriculture. By 3500 B.C. urban Late Urak society flourished in southern Mesopotamia, sustained by a system of high yield cereal irrigation agriculture with efficient canal transport. Late Urak "colony" settlements were founded across the dry-farming portions of the Near East. But these colonies and the expansion of Late Urak society collapsed suddenly at about 3200 to 3500 B.C. Archaeologists have puzzled over this collapse for the past 30 years. Now there are hints in the paleoclimatic record that it may be related to a short {less than 200 year} but severe drought." {pg. 610 Science}

Or to this rather phenomenal and significant find regarding other Middle Eastern civilizations:

"Following the return to wetter conditions politically centralized and class-based urban societies emerged and expanded across the riverine and dry- farming landscapes of the Mediterranean, Egypt, and West Africa. The Akkadian empire of Mesopotamia, the pyramid constructing Old Kingdom civilization of Egypt, the Harrapan C3 civilization of the Indus valley, and the Early Bronze III civilization of Palestine, Greece, and Crete all reached their economic peak at about 2300 B.C. This period was abruptly terminated before 2200 B.C. by catastrophic drought and cooling that generated regional abandonment, collapse, and habitat-tracking. Paleo-climatic data from numerous sites document changes in the Mediterranean westerlies and monsoon rain-fall during this event, with precipitation reductions of up to 30% that diminished agricultural production from the Aegean to the Indus." {ibid}

Wow, what a fascinating resemblance if not outright corroboration and substantiation this is to what happened to such nations as the Hittites, Amorites, Edomites, Assyrians, Philistines, Israelites, and Egyptian kingdoms? The biblical accounts of the weather related demise of these nations is quite graphic. Again that we clearly saw in our last chapter and if perchance one needs to be reminded or needs more from the bible just consider again these words in relation to the house of Israel from the 6th Century B.C. through their prophet Amos:

> *"I also withheld rain from you when the harvest was still three months away. I sent rain on one town, but withheld it from another. One field had rain; another had none and dried up. People staggered from town to town for water but did not get enough to drink, yet you have not returned to me, declares the Lord.*
> *Many times I struck your gardens and vine-yards, I struck them with blight and mildew. Locusts devoured your fig and olive trees, yet you have not returned to me, declares the Lord.*
> *I sent plagues among you as I did to Egypt. I killed your young men with the sword, along with your captured horses. I filled his nostrils with the stench of your camps, yet you have not returned to me, declares the Lord.*

I overthrew some of you as I overthrew Sodom and Gomorrah. You were like a burning stick snatched from the fire, yet you have not returned to me, declares the Lord. {Amos 4: 7-11}

And or the prophet Ezekiel:

"*When I shoot at you with my deadly and destructive arrows of famine, I will shoot to destroy you. I will bring more and more famine upon you and cut off your supply of food. I will send famine and wild beasts against you, and they will leave you childless. Plague and bloodshed will sweep through you, and I will bring the sword against you. I the Lord have spoken.*" {Ezekiel 5:16}

"The word of the Lord came to me, *Son of man, if a country sins against me by being unfaithful and I stretch out my hand against it to cut off its food supply and send famine upon it and kill its men and their animals, even if these three men Noah, Daniel and Job were in it, they could save only themselves by their righteousness, declares the Sovereign Lord.*" {Ezekiel 14: 12-14}

Here we find the explanation of what our scientists do not understand themselves climate change is the work of Almighty God and look as we saw in an earlier chapter if there isn't one truth about life that prevails on this planet and it is that we need to be hydrated? Again water is the name of the game isn't it where life is concerned and that for literally everything whether human, plant or animal life, a matter which surely no scientist worth his salt would ever argue against or reject? Its existence therefore can't be just some kind of an evolutionary process or creation! As much as rain water is vital to life though the more important and serious matter here would of course be the issue of sin, that invariable poison of the human character that manifests itself by way of lawlessness involving everything from cursing to lying, stealing, adultery, greed, pride and murder. The seven great pillars of the worst of human conduct and behavior that has for countless generations been responsible for an immeasurable amount of pain and suffering, again this the Christ of God made clear enough:

> *"Are you so dull? Don't you see that nothing that enters a man from the outside can make him unclean? For it doesn't go into his heart but into his stomach, and then out of his body. What comes out of a man is what makes him unclean. For from within, out of men's hearts, come evil thoughts, sexual immorality, theft, murder, adultery, greed, malice, deceit, lewdness, envy, slander, arrogance, and folly. All these evils come from inside a make a man unclean,"*
> {Jesus from Mark 7:18-23}

Look it is the only pollution that exists and that we have in common with previous generations and if only the experts had paid attention to this then they would of course not be going around so perplexed and confounded by these previous climate changes. As usual though everything ends with the story of the great flood of Noah doesn't it? People just can't get past the idea that a flood could occur to the degree that it could cover the entire planet let alone a man building a boat big enough to handle a bunch of animals. If anything is going to prove the mistake of that though and it is surely going to be this issue of climate change now. Certainly no one can argue that of all of the evidences that point towards the truth of the great flood and it is going to be this matter of climate change both past and present. Guess what though, we do not have to base our faith on just this one area alone but rather we can look now to another form of evidence for the great flood? An evidence if not outright a corroboration that comes to us now by way of another branch of science and that is Geology and their startling discovery that Nova Scotia was once a part of Africa. Part of some kind of an African-American, European supercontinent this land mass apparently broke apart and drifted until eventually becoming present day Canada, United States, Britain, France, Spain, Mexico etc, etc. This they determined by using new rock and fossil data that clearly reveals each coastline as having been fused together at one time in the ancient past. Now wow if that isn't something utterly phenomenal if not altogether significant and what do they attribute this breaking apart to? Well they mention only that as water filled the basin of the Rheic Ocean which was the precursor to the present day Atlantic Ocean these continents were pushed apart due to weak seams caused as a result from collisions with other land masses. All of which supposedly occurred some 480 million years ago. {pg. 325-328 Geology} Wow, imagine that? No mentioning of cataclysms, no earthquakes, no volcanoes, no nothing?! Just a gradual drifting apart of land masses that apparently took millions of years to do? Of course millions of years for how else from their perspectives could an ocean fill to the capacity of the Atlantic and still be able to push and/or float entire continents as large as the British Isles. So look again were back to this issue of water and what does the bible have to say on the subject?

"In the six hundredth year of Noah's life, on the 17th day of the second month- on that day all the springs of the great deep burst forth, and the floodgates of the heavens were opened. And rain fell on the earth 40 days and 40 nights." {Genesis 7:11-12}

Yes, I think one can make a good case that the breaking apart of the '*great deep*' was the result of a massive global wide earthquake that split apart the land masses to a terrible degree. Everything imploded in on itself and then exploded outward with such force that the entire planet probably shook from the very vibrations of it all. Similar probably to what occurred with that earthquake that struck Sumatra, Indonesia a few years ago and imagine this: the waters of Noah are still with us today made up of the Atlantic and Pacific Oceans and if not all of the frozen ice at both poles as well. It only makes sense doesn't it and why our geologists don't point this out is just another continuing saga in the fight for religious faith. Will it never end?

So look if we aren't back to this issue of sin! Again it is the only pollution that exists and that we have in common with previous generations and wow to look at what another branch of archaeology has discovered of late and if this next illustration doesn't reveal the truth of that in a most shocking and startling way!

In yet another landmark discovery that was published this time in the National Geographic a team of archaeologists working at an altitude of 22,110 feet {6,706 meters} found on the summit of Mount Llullaillaco the mummified remains of three children. It was quite the extra-ordinary find because to the surprise and excitement of the archaeologists the three mummies were found to be in a perfect state of preservation having decomposed little because of the high altitude of the site. Upon exhuming the three bodies however and the excitement turned to sadness with the discovery that the three children, two girls and a boy, were found bundled in the fetal position with cords tied around their legs. Victims apparently of an Inca religious sacrifice the children had died from being buried alive. Now how could a people subject their children to such a horrible fate? Well apparently for the Inca they believed that such human sacrifices were important in the appeasing of their gods and the children themselves had all but become willing participants. Participants because it was believed that they were purer than adults, accordingly their sacrificial offering would somehow result in the child's deification thereby enabling them to become direct representatives of their people living with their idols. Imagine a moral factor of all things comes into play here with the use of children!? It was not just children who paid the price though for this mountain along with others is apparently full of many corpses who had come to violent deaths:

"People living near Llullaillaco must have believed the mountains controlled the weather as well as the fertility of animals and abundance of crops in the region-which is why people still worship the mountains today. The Inca authorities in Cuzco-the seat of the empire-knew that making offerings on sacred mountains was a way to incorporate those deities into the state religion, giving themselves greater control over the outlying people they subjugated...Inca sacrifices reportedly died by being buried alive, by strangulation, or by a blow to the head -which is how the Ice Maiden died. The Lulluaillaco children, however, have benign expressions and bear no obvious physical scars, suggesting that they died while unconscious or semiconscious, probably stupefied by a combination of ritual alcoholic drinks and altitude." {pg. 47 National Geographic November 1999}

Hard to believe isn't it and this occurring in a pre-modern day society as early as 500 years ago? Did not such sacrifices end with the biblical history of the Old Testament wherein God said:

"And you took your sons and daughters whom you bore to me and sacrificed them as food to the idols. Was your prostitution not enough? You slaughtered my children and sacrificed them to the idols." {Ezekiel 16:20-21}

And how did the Creator deal with Inca society? Well of course if it wasn't in the same manner as He did previous generations and that is with climate change, and if we can't see and know this here by way a most shocking discovery? For to the utter dismay of the archaeologists, one of the young girls it was discovered had been severely burned on her ear, shoulder and chest by a lightning strike that had apparently penetrated some five feet into the top of the mountain. The smell of burnt flesh was actually still fresh as though it happened that very day and overpowered those who had exhumed the body. Now what an odd event for a lightning strike to occur at such a high altitude {22,000 feet} and in exact proximity to the corpses of the children. What though should we believe about this? Was this just a coincidence or do you think that maybe someone was fuming at the ears for such a terrible crime? Again the book of Job:

"See how He scatters His lightning about Him, bathing the depths of the sea. This is the way He governs the nations and provides food in abundance. He fills His hands with lightning and commands it to strike its mark. His thunder announces the coming storm; even the cattle make known its approach." {Job 36:31-33}

Now if this doesn't illustrate with pinpoint accuracy what our archaeologists discovered high in the mountains of Argentina. So look it's not just about droughts and famines but rather anything and everything that God has in His arsenal. A matter which for the Inca surely must have proved utterly disastrous after this kind of wickedness for the Father of life surely wasn't about to allow the murderers of His children to go free. Neither them nor their entire civilization for that matter and is there any evidence to the truth of this? Well to look back at what Dr. Weiss and Dr. Bradley have to say and it sure points that way:

"High-resolution archaeological records from the New World also point to abrupt climatic change as the proximal cause of repeated social collapse. In northern coastal Peru: the Moche civilization suffered a 30 year drought in the late 6th century A.D., accompanied by severe flooding. The capital city was destroyed, fields and irrigation systems were swept away, and widespread famine ensued. The capital city was subsequently moved northward, and new adaptive agricultural and architectural technologies were implemented. Four hundred years later, the agricultural base on the Tiwanaku civilization of the central Andes collapsed as a result of a prolonged drought documented in ice and in lake sediment cores. In Mesoamerica, lake sediment cores show that the Classic Maya collapse of the 9th century A.D., coincided with the most severe and prolonged drought of that millennium. In North America, the Anasazi agriculture could not sustain three decades of exceptional drought and reduced temperatures in the 13th century A.D., resulting in forced regional abandonment." {pg. 610 Science}

This may not speak directly to the Inca but it's surely close enough. So look yet again the bible is proven correct and isn't it fascinating how different branches of archaeology are all coming together with the same observations.

Archaeology, geology the more they continue to dig into the past the more conclusive and concrete the history and teachings of the bible will and is becoming apparent. If it isn't something utterly fascinating and exciting to watch if not altogether shocking especially given what was further discovered except this time on the other side of the world. That is in the Himalayan Mountains.

Dated from the 9th Century a discovery was made near the glacial Roopkund Lake region of the remote Himalayan Gahrwal region back in 1942. It was a discovery that like the Inca find resulted in the unearthing of bodies, hundreds of them in fact being in a perfect state of preservation having decomposed little because of the altitude of the region {5030 meters, 16,500 feet}. What they were doing there though and who they were exactly has for many decades perplexed the experts. What is more astonishing however is how these people had died for upon exhuming the corpses the only noticeable damage to them was to the tops of their skulls? That is their skulls had deep cracks and even holes in them:

"The most startling discovery was that many of those who died suffered fractured skulls.' We retrieved a number of skulls which showed short, deep cracks,' said Subhash Walimbe, a physical anthropologist at the college. These were caused not by a landslide or an avalanche but by blunt, round objects about the size of cricket balls." {pg. A8 by David Orr as reported in The Vancouver Sun, Monday November 8, 2004}

"The only plausible explanation for so many people sustaining such similar injuries and at the same time is something that fell from the sky,' said Walimbe.' The injuries were all to the top of the skull and not to other bones in the body, so they must have come from above. Our view is that death was caused by extremely large hailstones." {ibid}

Now what could have possibly been going on here? Well as it turns out if the answer to that doesn't come by way of some interesting data that reveals that these people were on some sort of a religious pilgrimage. Recent discoveries have the experts concluding that these people belonged to the high caste Brahmin sect of India and were apparently seeking to offer worship to God in the mountains. Accordingly if that then doesn't reveal something very telling about these people with perhaps the most insightful issue here being a song sung to this day by members of this particular community which speaks about the very judgment of Almighty God!

"Wolfgang Sax, an anthropologist at Heidelberg University in Germany, cited a traditional song among Himalayans that describes a goddess so enraged at outsiders who defiled her mountain sanctuary she rained death upon them by flinging hailstones 'hard as iron." {ibid}

So isn't that interesting? Teaches us doesn't it or rather takes us back to the bible and its teaching about idolatry? More seriously though would have to be this matter of trying to pay homage to the divine being in the feminine. Wow, what an extremely dangerous if not an absurd thing to do! No one should ever, ever dare try approach Almighty God in anyway whatsoever without first going through His Son Christ Jesus. Again the pollution of sin has to be dealt with in the heart at the cross before any of that can ever occur. So thank you archaeology for again proving the truth of what the bible has to say:

"See, the Lord has one who is powerful and strong. Like a hailstorm and a destructive wind, like a driving rain and a flooding downpour, He will throw it force-fully to the ground." {Isaiah 28:2}

More significantly though would surely have to be these rather fascinating words from the prophet Jeremiah:

*"See the storm of the Lord will burst out in wrath, a whirlwind swirling down on the heads of the wicked. The anger of the Lord will not turn back until He fully accomplishes the purposes of his heart. **In days to come you will fully understand this**."* {Jeremiah 23:19-20}

Imagine we are certainly "seeing it" today aren't we? Indeed we are and if these examples don't prove the truth that pollution is again not at all about that which comes from industrial sources. On the contrary it has got everything to do with the pollution of sin which is lawlessness that is at the heart of what is really going on? Certainly no one can argue that climate change is not just a phenomenon for our own day and age. It's been going on since the beginning of time or least from the days of Noah. Again it is something that has really shocked and perplexed the experts and looking towards the future the seriousness of it all is leading to some pretty profound and scary conclusions. For if this was the way it was with our weather thousands of years ago then what pray tell does this mean for us today and/or our future generations? For to add mankind's industrial pollution to the mix leaves many scientists with some very grave predictions and conclusions. Again just take as an example the words of Dr. Weiss and Dr. Bradley on this:

"These past climate changes were unrelated to human activities. In contrast, future climatic change will involve both natural and anthropogenic forces and will be increasingly dominated by the later; current estimates show that we can expect them to be large and rapid. Global temperature will rise and atmospheric circulation will change, leading to a redistribution of rainfall that is difficult to predict. It is likely, however, that the rainfall patterns that societies have come to expect will change, and the magnitude of expected temperatures gives a sense of prospective disruption. These changes will affect a world population expected to increase from about 6 billion people today to about 9 to 10 billion by 2050."
{pg 610 Weiss & Bradley Science}

What is more mind-blowing though or rather wacky is what came out of the Pentagon of all places concerning climate change. In an apparently secret report that was leaked to the press the Pentagon is claiming that climate change could well become more of a threat to our way of life than even terrorism. They go so far as to say that climate change should be immediately elevated from just a scientific debate to a U.S. National security concern and why? Well as we have clearly seen if parts of our world begin to experience and suffer from 200 hundred year droughts the consequences of that will be utterly staggering if not truly disastrous. Millions upon millions of people will literally be on the move to find new sources of food and water supplies and what do you think that will lead to? War and conflict of course as country after country try to secure their own dwindling food and water supplies. It will quite literally be an unimaginable catastrophe:

"Britain will have winters similar to those in current-day Siberia as European temperatures drop off radically by 2020.

By 2007 violent storms will make large parts of the Netherlands uninhabitable and lead to a breach in the aqueduct system in California that supplies all water to densely populated southern California.

Europe and the U.S. will become 'virtual fortresses' trying to keep out millions of migrants whose homelands have been wiped out by rising sea levels or made unfarmable by drought.

'Catastrophic' shortages of potable water and energy will lead to widespread war by 2020. {Agence France Presse, The Province- Monday, February 23, 2004}

Wow, can you imagine? What scary conclusions and so accordingly then with emphasis such as these from both the world of science and the military now and it surely doesn't take much to understand the truth of those words from Almighty God;

'in days to come you will fully understand this.'
[Jeremiah 23:20}

Looking for solutions and answers mankind will eventually be forced to look back to the stories of the bible and why that hasn't happened already is really quite odd. For surely one would think that something would register in the minds of the experts with so much data now coming from so many branches of knowledge. Or then again maybe it is time now to hook up those huge radio telescopes to some extra juice of power in the hopes that those aliens who apparently according to some supposedly created this world could somehow save us from ourselves? ***Please, please*** let's get our sensibilities back in order and return to the bible for our answers. Answers which are as simple as returning to the Lord as our Lord and Savior made quite clear in those statements from a few pages back:

> *"I also withheld rain from you when the harvest was still three months away. I sent rain on one town, but withheld it from another. One field had rain; another had none and dried up. People staggered from town to town for water but did not get enough to drink, <u>yet you have not returned to me, declares the Lord.</u>*
>
> *Many times I struck your gardens and vineyards, I struck them with blight and mildew. Locusts devoured your fig and olive trees, <u>yet you have not returned to me, declares the Lord.</u>*
>
> *I sent plagues among you as I did to Egypt. I killed your young men with the sword, along with your captured horses. I filled his nostrils with the stench of your camps, <u>yet you have not returned to me, declares the Lord.</u>*
>
> *I overthrew some of you as I overthrew Sodom and Gomorrah. You were like a burning stick snatched from the fire, <u>yet you have not returned to me, declares the Lord.</u>* {Amos 4: 7-11}

King Solomon interestingly enough points this out as well:

> "When the heavens are shut up and there is no rain because your people have sinned against you, and when they pray toward this place and confess your name and turn from their sin, because you have afflicted them, then hear from heaven and forgive the sin of your servants, your people Israel. Teach them

the right way to live, and send rain on the land you gave your people for an inheritance.

When famine or plague comes to the land, or blight or mildew, locusts or grasshoppers, or when an enemy besieges them in any of their cities, whatever disaster or disease may come, and when a prayer or plea is made by any of your people Israel -each one aware of the afflictions of his own heart, and spreading out his hands toward this temple- then hear from heaven, your dwelling place. Forgive and act; deal with each man according to all the he does, since you know his heart {for you alone know the hearts of all men}, so that they will fear you all the time they live in the land you gave our fathers. {1 Kings 8: 35-40}

More significantly though would have to be the words spoken by the only true King, Jesus of Nazareth, concerning climate change:

"Therefore everyone who hears these words of mine and puts them into practice is like a wise man who built his house on the rock. The rain came down, the streams rose, and the winds blew and beat against that house; yet it did not fall, because it had its foundation on the rock. But everyone who hears these words of mine and does not put them into practice is like a foolish man who built his house on sand. The rain came down, the streams rose, and the winds blew and beat against that house, and it fell with a great crash." {Matthew 7:24-27}

If this isn't a great illustration of what happened to Noah and his generation? Noah listened and accordingly built his house on a rock and when the rains came it wasn't destroyed.

It's also a great illustration of Joseph and his interpretation of the dreams of Pharaoh about those fourteen years of climate change that could have resulted in the destruction of Egypt. For it was Joseph who admonished the king to build storage facilities to see them through the seven years of drought that came upon their land. So you see what Christ Jesus spoke here goes to the very heart of the matter; we all need to be prepared for the weather will in one way or another always speak to mankind's behavior. This is the crux of everything—make no mistake about this! Make no mistake either about the fact that a theocracy is in operation over this world of ours. Accordingly people had better wake up! Had better wake up entire nations before they find themselves faced with the truth of that scripture from the New Testament in a far, far more serious way; for *"It is a dreadful thing to fall into the hands of the living God."* {Hebrews 10:31} Accordingly whatever fear mongering therefore that is going on should be directed towards our not obeying Almighty God and not as those in the Pentagon or science have been seeking to do. In fact, if it shouldn't be mentioned here that where that article from the Pentagon is concerned and if they shouldn't be looking at their own actions as the threat to National Security. One need only look at the Vietnam War as a prime example of that and why that conflict in particular? Well because as this writer learned while watching a documentary on that conflict the U.S. Air Force was engaged in weather control. They actually tried to change the weather over the skies of Vietnam because it would never stop raining. It rained so much apparently that when the soldiers woke up in the morning it was raining. When they went out on patrol it was raining and when they returned to their camps it was raining. It rained went they went to sleep. It rained when they went to get a shower. It rained when they went to the latrine. It rained so much that even Hollywood got into the act of complaining about it by inserting it into the movie Forrest Gump and his reminiscing about it raining so much that it seemed as though it came up from below ricocheting as it was off the rivers. Watching and hearing this I was totally and completely flabbergasted and shocked that what our ignorance of everything called God and religion has us now turning our attack on God Himself!? Brought well it did to my mind General MacArthur and his belief that the next war would be fought against evil beings from outer space. {See chapter 6}Unbelievable! What was God possibly thinking when faced with aircraft pouring whatever it was into His clouds to try and clear the skies from pouring His tears into what was happening? Again unbelievable and then to come across a documentary on weather and learn about those 148 tornadoes that struck the heartland of America over a period of a day {April 3-4, 1974} left this writer in quite a state of shock, horror and disbelief. In fact trembling I thought to myself wow could this have been in response to what was happening over in Vietnam as well as in America herself? Was there a connection between the two? Most certainly I surmised given the teachings of the bible regarding this whole matter of climate change. Again the bible:

> "Rain will come in torrents, and I will send hailstones hurtling down and violent winds will burst forth...In my wrath I will unleash a violent wind, and in my anger hailstones and torrents of rain will fall with destructive fury." {Ezekiel 13: 8-13}

So alarming isn't it? Indeed! Accordingly climate change a threat to national security? No! Rather its our ignorance of everything called God and religion that is the real threat and do you want to know what is the most incredible if not alarming thing of all where the military and the weather is concerned? Well if it wasn't the monsoon conditions that accompanied the development of the nuclear bomb in the New Mexico desert on July 16, 1945. In studying the events of that day this writer discovered and that to his utter amazement that the creation of the atomic bomb was hammered constantly by monsoon like conditions. It rained and rained so much that it could be said that never in the whole history of mankind did a desert see so much rain in such a short period of time. It rained so hard and so much in fact that it actually grounded test flights of the B-29 bombers and even hindered the actual development of the bomb itself leading no less to the changing of the dates of detonation. The article in the Seattle times even mentioned that on the final day of the detonation which was to occur at 0400 hours there was a pre-dawn lightning storm which delayed detonation to 0529:45 hours.

{http://seattletimes.nwsource.com/trinity/articles/part1. html}

The lightning storm even woke up Joe McKibben who had slept near ground zero to prevent anyone from tampering with the bomb as well as laying out mattresses underneath it to prevent it from going off by mistake if it broke free from its moorings so heavy it was. Now how does that saying go again?

"If the radiance of a thousand suns/Were to burst into the sky/That would be like/ The splendor of the Might One.../I am become death, the shatterer of worlds." {Pg, 209-210 Roger H. Stewuer}

Wow! So climate change a threat to national security? No! Although with Almighty God a flood the size of Noah's would not be a very hard thing for Him to do yet again. As He promised though no flood of that size would ever again be used to destroy all life:

123

"And God said, *"This is the sign of the covenant I am making between me and you and every living creature with you, a covenant for all generations to come: I have set my rainbow in the clouds, and it will be the sign of the covenant between me and the earth. Whenever I bring clouds over the earth and the rainbow appears in the clouds, I will remember my covenant between me and you and all living creatures of every kind. Never will the waters become a flood to destroy all life."* {Genesis 9:12-15}

CROP CIRCLES!?

You know truly if the pursuit of scientific knowledge and investigation is leading mankind anywhere it is to the enthronement of men upon their own thrones. Look what we have become capable of, it is almost godlike now and isn't this where the absurdity of Darwin's evolutionism comes into play. For if we really did just evolve from some kind of a big bang then that leaves mankind in a very precarious position in that we have no one to look to but ourselves if something catastrophic were to occur. Really, what are we to actually do place our trust in men who don't know the end from the beginning where scientific knowledge and investigation is concerned? Like for example these very scientists who when developing the nuclear bomb were totally and completely oblivious to what the effects of the detonation would actually be and they went ahead and did it anyway? Just look at how the events at Bikini Atoll prove that out:

"In San Diego, I talked with Captain Eddy. He had been with the expedition in the Marshall Islands on November 1, 1952, when America exploded her first hydrogen bomb. In a sober voice, Captain Eddy said, 'No one could visualize the awfulness of that sight unless he were there in person.' Two hundred miles above the Pacific, the mighty hydrogen bomb was detonated. The blast lighted up thousands of miles of Pacific sky. At Auckland, New Zealand, 3,800 miles away from the scene of the blast, New Zealanders said the ocean showed a reflection that was blood red. 'The scientists present at the scene were dreadfully shaken,' said Eddy. 'They thought they had set the heavens aflame with a chain reaction of exploding atoms that would surely go around the world.' On returning from his mission, Captain Eddy asked to be transferred to another department of service, and was given a position in the field of seismology, studying earthquakes back in the South Pacific." {pg. 91-92 Cantelon}

Frightening isn't it? Indeed and how people and governments can gamble with everyone's lives including their own children the way they do is something utterly unbelievable. Brings well to mind those words from Albert Einstein:

"Two things are infinite: the universe and human stupidity; and I'm not sure about the universe." {www.brainyquote.com/quotes/a/alberteins148795. html}

Words that were spoken by him shortly after this explosion at Bikini Atoll and it don't end there either:

"That there is a connection between atom bombs and earthquakes might sound humorous to some, but the facts allow little room for humor or ridicule.
On an island called Amchitka, southwest of Anchorage, Alaska, man sank a 53-inch shaft deep into the heart of the ground. On September 6, 1971, man created the largest man-made earthquake in

history. The bomb he detonated in the island of Amchitka was 250 times more powerful than the one that had been dropped on Hiroshima. The explosion rocked not only the island of Amchitka; it caused the earth to tremor on the other side of the globe.

Professor Marcus Baath in Uppsala, Sweden, declared that the underground blast from Alaska caused his Richter scale to show a 7.4 earth tremor— -in Sweden!" {pg. 92 Cantelon}

Unbelievable and then if this wasn't enough along came the communists who detonated their own devices, one which {October 23, 1961} was so large that the shock wave was reported to have encircled the earth three times! Now what did the scientists do with this one? Wiping the sweat off their brow did they just exclaim to each other we were lucky on that one? That and/or perhaps exclaiming something to the effect of lets hope that the earth can somehow magically heal itself? Incredible! Its truly too bad that Charles Darwin wasn't around today, I'm sure that he would be the first to take his theory of evolution, natural selection and the survival of the fittest and make quick use of a paper shredder by throwing it all in the garbage can. My word and look what an interesting song we have here composed interestingly enough by the artist Edwin McCain...

"Seven million years of progress handed down on silver wings
Of gossamer and protein still we haven't learned a thing
Are we caught up in our anger, locked up in our rage
In the opera of selection on this our earthly stage
And Charlie's laughing, laughing in his grave
Laughing at the prophecy the prophecy he gave
Can we spread our wings like angels, can we break out of the grind

Are we destined to be Darwin's children this time
The ribbons of our cigarettes vanish in the air
In the glow of our great teacher we sit and blankly stare
And the sky could open up and what would we have to
say
Something cute about burning out, better than fading
away
On the wings of invention now we hurtle towards our
fate
As sure as the sunset burns
Collective resignation, evolutionary fate

When will we ever learn?" {Edwin McCain from the album Misguided Roses}

When will we ever learn is certainly the correct and proper question to ask or rather end with isn't it? Wow if this song isn't something utterly and truly amazing if not altogether prophetic. Congratulations Edwin McCain! Congratulations on being inspired surely by Almighty God.

So again climate change a threat to National Security? No!! Rather it is our own behavior that is the real threat. Sin which is lawlessness is the real danger and if perchance one need's something more to understand the truth of this well just look at the horrendous behaviors and wickedness of individuals like Jeffery Dahmer, Carla Holmolka, and Paul Bernardo. The wickedness of their actions is something utterly unbelievable to behold and do you know what shocks this writer the most where Paul Bernardo and Carla Holmolka are concerned specifically? Well if it wasn't the reporting in the newspapers of an extremely violent thunderstorm that descended quite abruptly in over the city of Toronto. It's reporting in the newspaper was quite unusual given how Toronto is used to extreme weather conditions. Not this particular weather event though it apparently got everyone's attention! Accordingly if the question isn't one of did this have anything to do with or was in response to what was occurring in the cities court house? I think we should find it rather curious how the reporting of this thunderstorm coincided with the reporting in the newspapers as well of the proceedings of the horrendous murders of Kristen French and Leslie Mahaffy. What was coming out during the deliberations no judge or lawyer was prepared for. Not there or for that matter the shocking proceedings of the Jeffery Dahmer case. So again, the words of Almighty God:

"The Lord will cause men to hear His majestic voice and will make them see His arm coming down with raging anger and consuming fire, with cloudburst, thunderstorm and hail." {Isaiah 30:30}

The bible, the bible, what a truly glorious and fascinating collection of books we have here. Truly it really does provide everything; literally everything that mankind could possibly want or need and with that we bring this chapter to a close. Before we move on though, just one last thing to mention or rather ask; and that is what pray tell is going on in the nation of Australia? To find a plague of a hundred million mice running around farmers fields gorging themselves on every available piece of food was something utterly shocking to behold. What is there an Egyptian Pharaoh running around loose somewhere? http://www.youtube.com/watch?v=2LMxhc8WwGU

My word whoever would have thought to find and see the very acts of Almighty God and that from the book of Exodus no less being re-created in the modern day nation of Australia! This is in no way just a natural act of an animal species procreating in large numbers. That's absurd! Moreover to find this nation suffering from what is apparently the worst drought in its entire history causes this writer to shudder with fear. Remember those words from a few pages back:

> "*The word of the Lord came to me, Son of man, if a country sins against me by being unfaithful and I stretch out my hand against it to cut off its food supply and send famine upon it and kill its men and their animals, even if these three men Noah, Daniel and Job were in it, they could save only themselves by their righteousness, declares the Sovereign Lord.*"
> {Ezekiel 14: 12-14}

So again what is possibly going on in that nation that the Creator would be provoked in such a dreadful way? Looking for answers this writer has certainly poured over numerous articles in print and T.V. and some of the things I have come across is quite disturbing like for example something called the puppetry of a certain male anatomy. You have got to be kidding! Do people no longer have any shame? Are parents of children no longer disciplining and that with the strap no less their sons and daughters evil and wicked behaviors? May God have mercy! May God have mercy!

Please, please let's get our sensibilities back in order and return to our Heavenly Father for look if eternity doesn't await?

CHAPTER FIVE

'EL NINO'

One Easter while I was engaged with activities with my family, I happened to mention to my mother who was doing some cooking my how it was raining outside. To that my mother replied back to me while affirming to herself that it always rains at Easter time. What I said! It was a statement that caught me off guard and actually made me smile because of my understanding of the bible. What an astonishing thing to say I said too myself causing me to reflect upon our ancestry. Viva Slovenia and Croatia I shouted to myself! Viva Slovenia and Croatia! Of far more significance though it was some time later while doing research for this book that I was quite intrigued to learn that the term used to explain certain types of climate change it was El Nino and why? Well because El Nino means "the Christ child" a term that was actually coined by fisherman in South America who noticed that it always rains at Christmastime. What I said?! Here we go again more proof that climate change is the work of Almighty God and what proof it is. In fact as we shall see in this chapter and the following ones revolves around the work and person of Christ in an astounding and glorious and no less exciting way. Just take as an example what occurred over the city of Singapore back in the early 1980's as described by Dr. Cho in his book More Than Numbers:

> "Last year, the business leaders of Singapore got a vision from the Holy Spirit. They were to sponsor a national crusade to reach all of Singapore. They rented the local soccer stadium, which seats 70,000 people. One business leader alone, Mr. Wy Wy Wong, paid for the total advertising in every newspaper in the country. The committee was composed of pastors, professional people and businessmen. These men and women had one thing in common. They had a burning desire for revival in Singapore, which had a small Christian population. *Night after night, for five*

straight nights, the rain came in torrents. But by six o'clock every evening, the sky would clear and we were able to have large crowds gather to hear the gospel. The total count of people that came forward to accept Christ amazed me. I repeated nightly. 'Please only those who want to accept Christ as their personal Savior for the first time in your life, only you come forward.' Yet, we counted more than 50,000 people making decisions for Christ." {pg. 130 Cho}

Of all of the events ever to happen in the history of mankind no event was more important than what occurred in the city of Jerusalem 2000 years ago. The death and resurrection of God's own Son Christ Jesus was the single most important factor in the life of the entire human race. For what Jesus did for us all on that day quite literally paid for our forgiveness before our Heavenly Father this the bible makes abundantly clear:

"The Lord your God will raise up for you a prophet like unto me from among your own brothers. You must listen to him." {Det. 18:15}

"Therefore the Lord Himself will give you a sign: The virgin will be with child and will give birth to a son, and will call him Immanuel." {Isaiah 7:14}

"Surely he took up our infirmities and carried our sorrows, yet we considered him stricken by God, smitten by him and afflicted. But he was pierced for our transgressions, he was crushed for our iniquities; the punishment that brought us peace was upon him, and by his wounds we are healed." {Isaiah 53:4-5}

"For God so loved the world that He gave His one and only Son, that whoever believes in him shall not perish but have eternal life." {John 3:16}

It was a phenomenal life that Jesus lived and yet an extremely sorrow filled one in that he was born really for only one purpose and that was to die a horrible death and why exactly? Well as the scriptures make abundantly clear it is ultimately because with Almighty God there really is no forgiveness of sins without the shedding of blood:

"In fact, the law requires that nearly everything be cleansed with blood; and without the shedding of blood there is no forgiveness." {Hebrews 9:22}

Under the Old Testament Law this is why animals were sacrificed. When a person sinned against the law it was required that they pay for that sin by way of some animal sacrifice. So imagine this then you having committed some transgression and for that transgression to be forgiven before God you had to bring before the priest an offering of some kind perhaps a bird or some other creature. You then had to take its life in payment for the sin you had committed as well as any financial restitution to your brother. This is the way it was and given the severity of some sins that payment or sacrifice rather led to some very expensive and serious payments like for example the offering of a bull, goat and or lambs. So imagine the effects then this must have had on people? For ones sin some innocent animal had to pay the ultimate price so talk about feeling guilty and remorseful which is what God was after ultimately. All of these kinds of things though were supposed to change with the coming of the Christ of God for under Him there was to be a different kind of administration, one that took away all manner of animal sacrifices by replacing them all with His own death and blood. For as the scriptures again make abundantly clear:

"Sacrifices and offerings you did not desire, but a body you prepared for me; with burnt offerings and sin offerings you were not pleased. Then I said, Here I am-it is written in the scroll-I have come to do your will, O God." {Hebrews 10:6-7}

Accordingly what Almighty God was and is after then is perfection and that ultimately began and ends with the coming of Christ Jesus, the Alpha and the Omega. He ultimately was the payment for sin and it takes nothing more than for us to acknowledge His sacrifice by way of confession and belief. Again the scriptures:

"That if you confess with your mouth, Jesus is Lord, and believe in your heart that God raised him from the dead, you will be saved. For it is with your heart that you believe and are justified, and it is with your mouth that you confess and are saved." {Romans 10:9-10}

Everything changed with this life that was given to us so much so in fact that it also resulted in our being given by Him the gift of the Holy Spirit. A counselor and comforter of sorts whom Jesus said would come to us so that we could learn to and live the life of righteousness in an altogether new way:

"Now I am going to him who sent me, yet none of you asks me, where are you going? Because I have said these things, you are filled with grief. I tell you the truth: It is for your good that I am going away. Unless I go away, the Counselor will not come to you;

but if I go, I will send him to you. When he comes, he will convict the world of guilt in regard to sin and righteousness and judgment: in regard to sin, because men do not believe in me; in regard to righteousness, because I am going to the Father, where you can see me no longer, and in regard to judgment, because the prince of this world now stands condemned.

I have much more to say to you, more than you can now bear. But when he, the Spirit of truth, comes, h*e* will guide you into all truth. He will not speak on his own; he will speak only what he hears, and he will tell you what is yet to come. He will bring glory to me by taking from what is mine and making it known to you. All that belongs to the Father is mine. That is why I said the Spirit will take from what is mine and make it known to you. In a little while you will see me no more, and then after a little while you will see me." {John 16: 5-16}

"Do not leave Jerusalem, but wait for the gift my Father promised, which you have heard me speak about. For John baptized with water, but in a few days you will be baptized with the Holy Spirit." {Acts 1:4-5}

It was to be a new kind of baptism as it were into the things of God for as things stood God knew that with mankind nothing would ever change unless possessed by this Spirit of His:

"And I will put my Spirit in you and move you to follow my decrees and be careful to keep my laws." {Ezekiel 36: 26-27}

"The fortress will be abandoned, the noisy city deserted; citadel and watchtower will become a wasteland forever, the delight of donkeys, a pasture for flocks, *till the Spirit is poured upon us from on high*, and the desert becomes a fertile field, and the fertile field seems like a forest." {Isaiah 32: 14–15}

"And afterward, I will pour out my Spirit on all people. Your sons and your daughters will prophesy, and your old men will dream dreams, your young men will see visions. Even on my servants, both men and women, I will pour out my Spirit in those days." {Joel 2: 28}

Accordingly if it wasn't shortly after Jesus' return to the Father then that those who were gathered together in that little room overlooking the city of Jerusalem were overcome with the wind of this irrepressible Spirit:

"When the day of Pentecost came, they were all together in one place. *Suddenly a sound like the blowing of a violent wind* came from heaven and filled the whole house where they were sitting. They saw what seemed to be tongues of fire that separated and came to rest on each of them. All of them were filled with the Holy Spirit and began to speak in other tongues as the Spirit enabled them. {Acts 2:1-4}

An event that quickly saw the Spirit of God setting about the empowering of the people gathered together with the ability to speak in other languages and why that in particular? Well if it wasn't because Jerusalem was and is not a one language city but rather was filled with so many different languages that for many of its citizens it must have been a confusing mess. That and of course its location sitting as it is in a thoroughfare between the Mediterranean and the Near East which meant that it was a city constantly filled with travelers and tourists of all kinds everyone of them in pursuit of getting a glimpse of or partaking somehow in the events of the great Temple of God which stood in its midst. Accordingly from God's perspective therefore the best way to set about this new work of His Spirit was to have these Galileans speak to these peoples and cultures in their own languages. To everyone standing around it would have been a most astounding kind of thing proving to them that what was being said was truly an act of Almighty God. Can you imagine you an Englishmen speaking under the power of God lets say Chinese and then being confronted by English speaking Chinese communicating back to you what you just said in Chinese? This is what was going on here as evidenced by the writer:

> "Now, there were staying in Jerusalem God-fearing Jews from every nation under heaven. When they heard this sound, a crowd came together in bewilderment, because each one heard them speaking in his own language. Utterly amazed, they asked: 'Are not all these men who are speaking Galilean's?' 'Then how is it that each of us hears them in his own native language?' Parthians, Medes, Elamites; residents of Mesopotamia, Judea and Cappadocia, Pontus and Asia, Phrygia and Pamphlia, Egypt and the parts of Libya near Cyrene; visitors from Rome [both Jews and converts to Judaism}; Cretans and Arabs-we hear them all declaring the wonders of God in our own tongues?' Amazed and perplexed, they asked one another; 'What does this mean?'" {Acts 2:5-12}

So you see God's intelligence at work here? If this was any other city like for example a London or a Moscow

Almighty God would never have gone about trying to communicate in this way. Rather he would have employed some other means or methods to get across His words and communicate. For many are God's gifts as St. Paul said to the Corinthian Church:

> "There are different kinds of gifts, but the same Spirit. There are different kinds of service, but the same Lord. They're different kinds of working, but the same God works all of them in all men.
>
> Now to each one the manifestation of the Spirit is given for the common good. To one there is given through the Spirit the message of wisdom, to another the message of knowledge by means of the same Spirit, to another faith by the same Spirit, to another gifts of healing by that one Spirit, to another miraculous powers, to another prophecy, to another distinguishing between spirits, to another speaking in different kinds of tongues, and to still another the interpretation of tongues. All these are the work of one and the same Spirit, and he gives them to each one, just as he determines." {1 Corinthians 12: 4-11}

Now what though has any of this possibly got to do with the topic of the weather and/or climate change? Well what do you think that Almighty God likes to go around constantly punishing the human race for its wickedness by using the weather to do exactly that? That Almighty God is content at always being angry at a world that has gone insane with living in wickedness. No! Rather Almighty God wants change! He wants the same kind of things for the human race that the human race wants itself and that is love, joy, peace, happiness, and all of the other things that go with it. An interesting way of looking at it would be that just as we need to be **hydrated physically {the rain} so to do we need**

to be hydrated spiritually. This interestingly enough is no doubt why John the Baptist was commanded to baptize with water. You see it began the process of regeneration and one of the best illustrations that this writer has ever come across that would best explain the spiritual part of this would have to be what was witnessed in a church service one morning. Our guest speaker Dan Bilinski, bless his memory, had set up a table with a large clear plastic empty salad bowl on it. He then took another clear glass container and poured water into it then proceeded to add barbecue sauce to it so that the water became extremely dirty and did it ever look dirty and disgusting. He then placed this glass container into the large clear salad bowl on the table without spilling any of it into it. He then proceeded to explain to us that this glass container with the barbecue sauce in it was an illustration of us with all of our sins. He then took another container and again filled it with water which he left clean and pure. This we were told was an illustration of God's Holy Spirit and with that he proceeded to pour this clean pure water into the glass container that was full of the dirty water. When this pure water fell into the glass of dirty water it naturally began to overflow into the larger bowl. As it did so the contents of the glass of dirty water naturally began to be replaced by the clean and pure water that was flowing into it. This we were told was how God works and acts within us to clean and purify us from all of our sins. It was an incredibly stunning demonstration which caused me to exclaim and that quite loudly yep that is exactly the way it is with us and our Heavenly Father causing Dan in turn to smile. Christ Jesus referred to it as being 'born again' and the analogy here shouldn't be lost on anyone. It certainly wasn't for Arthur Wallis who wrote in that immortal book of his Revival the Rain from Heaven.

"Rain is a continual picture throughout Scripture of the outpouring of the Holy Spirit. Before the Israelites had entered their inheritance, Moses describes to them the land of Canaan,

'The land which you are going over to possess is a land of hills and valleys, which drinks water by the rain from heaven...And if you will obey My commandments...to love the Lord your God, and to serve Him with all of your heart and with all of your soul, He will give the rain for your land in its season, the early rain and the later rain, that you may gather in your grain and your wine and your oil.'" {Deut.11: 11, 13-14}

The similarity between this rainy season and the age of the Spirit is striking. We see in the ministries of John the Baptist, and Jesus, when multitudes heard the message of the Kingdom, the first showers that heralded the time of rain. These told all those 'looking for the consolation of Israel' that the long dry season was over, and that the time of rain had come. Those heavy showers of the former rain commenced to fall at Pentecost, when God poured out His Spirit in fulfillment of Joel's prophecy. Through the ensuing centuries the showers continued here and there now and again, though the heavier down pouring were few and far between. Since the Reformation these have been more distinct and frequent. Jesus Himself told us, 'The harvest is the close of the age' that is, the time of the latter rain, when the fruit of the earth is being prepared for the final harvest. In striking confirmation of this is the exhortation of James: "Be patient, therefore, brethren, until the coming of the Lord. Behold, the farmer waits for the precious fruit of the earth, being patient over it until it receives the

early and late rain. You also be patient. Establish
your hearts, for the coming of the Lord is at hand."
{James: 7-8} {pgs. 29-31 Wallis}

Nor was it lost on what is for this writer one of the most
lost opportunities ever of being a part in terms of music
something utterly and truly glorious:

"On May 24, 2000 the historic Ryman Auditorium
was booked to offer Nashvillians an evening of
sublime beauty. Label executives and soundtrack
producers so loved the music of O Brother, Where Art
Thou? that they brought it to life as a benefit concert
for the Country Music Hall of Fame. Filmmakers
Joel and Ethan Coen loved it so much that they hired
famed documentary filmmaker D.A. Pennebaker to
record the show for posterity.
The concert that unfolded that night was one of
the greatest musical moments in the annals of Music
City. Holly Hunter was there, and T. Bone Burnett
and Jim Blake Nelson. But the stars who shone
brightest were the unassuming acoustic performers
who made audio magic the old fashioned way on that
hallowed stage.
The Fairfield Four earned an ovation for their
stark, a cappella gospel treatments of "Po Lazarus"
and "Lonesome Valley." John Hartford fiddled, sang
and served as the evenings emcee. Dan Tyminski
offered "Blue and Lonesome Too," as well as his
soundtrack contributions. The Cox Family brought
down the house with "Will There Be Any Stars in
My Crown." Gillian Welch and David Rawlins had
the crowd grinning from ear to ear with their old-
timey "I Want to Sing That Old Time Rock and Roll."
The Whites augmented their set with the toe tapping

"Sandy Land." The Peasall Sisters were adorable beyond measure.

One by one, Chris Thomas King, Allison Krauss, & Union Station, The Nashville Bluegrass Band, Emmylou Harris and the other soundtrack participants took the stage. And one by one, they took us back to a time when music sprang from the heart and not the corporate boardroom. In their simplicity and eloquence, these performers were by far more emotionally moving than anything that can be manufactured in our modern studio electronic wonderlands. By the time the entire cast assembled around Ralph Stanley for "Angel Band." eyes were moist throughout the hall.

It was a night of healing, a night to restore the spirit, a night of blessing, and wonder. *Rain cascaded on the city streets as we made our way home, which was a fitting metaphor for the cleansing that the music had given us.*

The ghosts in country's most revered venue rested easy that night. We all did." {Robert K. Oermann Nashville, Tennessee August 2000}

So fascinating isn't it? Unfortunately though what has been looked upon as just a metaphor is not a metaphor at all. That we clearly see by way of what happened in the city of Singapore and of all of the scriptures within the bible that perhaps explains it the best for us it would be these from the prophet Hosea:

"Let us acknowledge the Lord; let us press on to acknowledge him, As surely as the sun rises, He will appear; He will come to us like the winter rains, like the spring rains that water the earth. {Hosea 6:3}

"Sow for yourselves righteousness, reap the fruit of unfailing love, and break up your unplowed ground; for it is time to seek the Lord, until He comes and showers righteousness on you." {Hosea 10:12}

Again this is not just a metaphor for some inexplicable work of Almighty God as some have apparently been led to believe and think. Rather with God the weather becomes a rather interesting and important way of communicating His peculiar ways with mankind. The prophet Isaiah also makes this abundantly clear when he wrote:

"For I will pour water on the thirsty land, and streams on the dry ground; I will pour out my Spirit on your offspring, and my blessing on your descendants." {Isaiah 44:3}

You see they go hand and hand with each other. So interesting isn't it? Again Christ Jesus referred to it as being 'born again' and isn't interesting to that He particularly would use the words '***born of water***' here and why?

"Jesus answered, *'I tell you the truth, no one can enter the kingdom of God unless he is **born of water and the Spirit**. Flesh gives birth to flesh, but the Spirit gives birth to spirit. You should not be surprised at my saying, You must be born again. The wind blows wherever it pleases. You hear its sound, but you cannot tell where it comes from or where it is going. So it is with everyone born of the Spirit."* {John 3:5-8}

Well because as we saw in an earlier chapter water is where everything originally began. Remember those words of Carl Sagan's:

"The origin of life on Earth seems to have occurred in oceans and shallow tide pools. Life on Earth is made mainly of water, which plays an essential physical and chemical role. Indeed, it's hard for us water-besotted creatures to imagine life without water." {Sagan pg. 111}

"Life on Earth is intimately connected, for the most basic chemical reasons, with liquid water. We humans are ourselves made of some three quarters water." {ibid. pg. 233}

Statements that not even the bible would disagree with given what we find written in Genesis chapter one verse two:

"In the beginning God created the heavens and the earth. Now the earth was formless and empty, darkness was over the surface of the deep, and *the Spirit of God was hovering over the waters.*"

Water it is again the key to everything isn't it? Look though and understand something else here, for doesn't Jesus also add an analogy here to the *wind?* Most certainly He does and why would He do that and/or why would that be of any importance? Well if it isn't because no other element best describes the power of Almighty God than the wind. I mean you can't see it, you can't touch it, you don't know from where it comes from or where it's going. You can sure feel it though can't you? Most certainly and at times one can even see it but only as it rustles the leaves and what not. Furthermore and perhaps most significant of all its invisible isn't it which is what Almighty God is Himself? So what a perfect analogy then the wind is to the work of Almighty

God and look isn't that exactly what we find happening on the day of promise:

"When the day of Pentecost came, they were all together in one place. *Suddenly a sound like the blowing of a violent wind* came from heaven and filled the whole house where they were sitting. {Acts2:1}

Most certainly it is! So again phenomenal isn't it? Accordingly when it comes to the weather then it's simply God's method of taking what He created originally to communicate and bless His people. Climate change as we see then is not all about an angry and vengeful God but it's about love, mercy, righteousness and peace. Imagine what was applicable to the Jewish people and nation was and is just as applicable to the Gentiles. If it isn't something utterly and truly glorious and if not more so when one looks at what happened to a little church in a place called Swan Quarter, North Carolina back in the year 1876:

"There are only two possible explanations for what you are about to read. It was either the most phenomenal coincidence that ever occurred-or it was an act of God.
Literally!
And remember, as you learn what happened on that rainy Thursday afternoon a hundred summers ago, that a stack of sworn statements and legal documents say that it was so.
There was just one problem with Swan Quarter, North Carolina. It was lowland, so naturally the choicest real estate was on the highest ground. In the event of a heavy rain, the closer you were to sea level, the harder you were hit.

A little more than a hundred years ago the Methodists of Swan Quarter, North Carolina had no church, and the only lot available on which to build one was a plot of low-lying property on Oyster Creek Road.

It was far from an ideal location, but they acquired the land and construction began.

The church was to be white frame, small but sturdy, propped up on brick pilings. In 1876 the building was completed and on Sunday, September 16, a joyous dedication ceremony was celebrated.

That was Sunday, September 16.

Three days later, on Wednesday, a terrible storm lashed Swan Quarter. All day the wind howled and the rain came down in a gray wall of water.

By nightfall, devastation.

Much of the town was flooded; many roofs were ripped from homes by the cyclonic turbulence. The storm raged on all through the night and into the bleak morning.

By Thursday afternoon the wind subsided, the rain all but stopped. For the first time in more than a day, there was an almost eerie calm. One by one the citizens of Swan Quarter threw back the shutters and peered from what was left of their homes.

Most saw only a desolate waterscape, a community ravaged by nature. But those within sight of Oyster Creek Road beheld the most incredible sight they had ever seen.

The church-the Swan Quarter Methodist Church-the whole building, intact-was floating down the street! The floodwaters had gently lifted the entire structure from the brick pilings on which it had rested and had sent it off, slowly, silently, down Oyster Creek Road.

147

Within minutes, several concerned townsfolk were sloshing about in the street, waist-deep, fighting the rushing current, trying desperately to reach the still moving church so that they could moor it with lengths of rope.

The ropes were fastened, but the effort was in vain. There was no stable structure secure enough to restrain the floating chapel.

And as the building passed by, more attention was attracted, more aid was enlisted. To no avail. The church moved on.

By now the building had made it to the center of town, still on Oyster Creek Road. Then as dozens, amazed, helpless, watched, the Swan Quarter Methodist Church, still floating, made a sharp inexplicable right turn and continued down that road, as though the chapel were alive-as though it had a mind of its own.

For two more blocks the townspeople fought the ropes to hold it back, unsuccessfully. And then, in the same decisive manner with which it had moved, the church veered off the road, headed for the center of a vacant lot...and there...stopped.

While the floodwater receded, the church remained-and is there to this day.

Over a hundred Septembers have passed since the little white-framed church removed itself to the most desirable property in Swan Quarter.

In the process of making up your own mind as to how and why what happened happened, you ought to know this one thing more, THE REST OF THE STORY.

The choice highland lot where the chapel settled was the first choice of the town Methodists for the site of their church. And the shrewd, prosperous landowner whose property it was originally turned them down.

But the next morning after the flood-after discovering the church in the middle of his lot-that same landowner went to the Methodist minister and, with trembling hands, presented him with the deed." {pg. 190-192 Paul Aurandt}

Now talk about Divine Communication or what? Of all of the meteorological events ever to happen in the history of pre-modern day mankind this one surely stands out as one of the most astounding comparable in fact to the very story of Noah. Why though a Methodist Church? Well if that hasn't got something if not everything to do with its founder and leader John Wesley who along with the Moravians under one Count Nicolas Ludwig von Zinzendorf had similar experiences to that of the city of Singapore. The history of it is really quite amazing if not utterly astounding with their biographers going so far as to say that nothing their equal had ever been seen on the European Continent. Apparently they had their own book of Acts chapter two experience. It occurred on August 13, 1727 while that little band of brothers and sisters were in prayer. The record given to us is by a Dr. Greenfield:

"...and verily the 13th of August was a day of the outpouring of the Holy Spirit. We saw the hand of God and His wonders, and we were all under the cloud of our fathers baptized with their Spirit. The Holy Ghost came upon us and in those days great signs and wonders took place in our midst. From that time, scarcely a day passed but what we beheld His Almighty workings among us. A great hunger after the Word of God took possession of us so that we had to have three services every day, viz., 5:00 and 7:30

A.M. and 9 P.M. Everyone desired above everything else that the Holy Spirit might have full control. Self-love and self-will as well as all disobedience disappeared and an overwhelming flood of grace swept us all out into the great ocean of Divine Love." {pg. 10 Greenfield}

"Exactly what happened at Wednesday forenoon, August 13th, 1727 in the specially called Communion service at Berthelsdorf, none of the participants could fully describe. They left the house of God that noon 'hardly knowing whether they belonged to earth or had already gone to heaven.'" {ibid}

"Zinzendorf, who gives us the deepest and most vivid account of this wonderful occurrence, says it was a sense of the nearness of Christ bestowed in a single moment, upon all the members that were present; and it was so unanimous that two members, at work 20 miles away, unaware that the meeting was being held, became at the same time deeply conscious of the same blessing." {ibid pg 11-12}

"In this divine presence of their bleeding dying Lord they were overwhelmed with their own sinfulness and his more abounding grace. Hushed were their controversies and quarrels; crucified were their passions and pride as they gazed upon the agonies of their 'expiring God.' With the apostle they learned to die daily unto the world, the flesh and the devil, and to live for Him who died for them. Hence forth their one passion was to gaze upon the King in His beauty and to proclaim the 'slaughtered Lamb' as the 'chief among ten thousand and the one altogether lovely." {ibid pg. 44}

"The great Moravian Pentecost was not a shower of blessing out of a cloudless sky. It did come suddenly, as suddenly as the blessing of its greater predecessor in Jerusalem, when the Christian Church was born. *Yet, for long, there had been signs of an abundance of rain, though many recognized them not.* In short, the blessing of the thirteenth of August 1727 was diligently and earnestly prayed for. We know of no annals of Church history which evidence greater desire for an outpouring of the Holy Spirit and more patient and persistent effort in that direction than those of our own church between the years 1725 and 1727. Two distinct lines of preparation and spiritual effort for the blessing are evident. One was prayer; the other was individual work with individuals. We are told that men and woman met for prayer and praise at one another's homes and the Church of Berthelsdorf was crowded out. Then the entire company experienced the blessing at one and the same time." {ibid pg. 86}

Now what a glorious thing this is! Look what we saw with the city of Singapore event was in full evidence over a community of believers in the country or region rather of Moravia. As for John Wesley well it apparently wasn't until some 12 years after the fact, when after becoming intimately acquainted with these Moravians that he along with a number of others of his group became immersed in this great experience of Pentecost as well. It occurred back in London in the year 1739:

"About three in the morning, as we were continuing instant in prayer, the power of God came mightily upon us, insomuch that many cried for exceeding joy, and many fell to the ground. As soon as we were recovered a little from that awe and amazement at the presence of His Majesty, we broke out with one voice, We Praise Thee, O God, we acknowledge Thee to be the Lord." {ibid pg. 34-35}

So what was essentially the Moravians own unique experience under Almighty God now came to be the experience of the Methodists as well. It was something that changed them into an entirely new breed of men and ultimately led them to become some of the world's greatest evangelists and missionaries. Actually for John Wesley who up until this time suffered greatly regarding his faith and theology this epiphany was so life transforming that for the rest of his life he dedicated everything he had to the service of his Lord. It is why he went on to become one of England's greatest sons ultimately becoming known or crowned rather as being the Father of the entire Evangelical Movement. Not only that but perhaps most significant of all is how historians look to him as being one of the chief reasons for having prevented England from plunging into the horrors of the French Revolution.

"What a truly noble soul John Wesley was!"
"No wonder he preached in demonstration of the Spirit and of power and caused more than 130,000 persons to rally around him during his lifetime. Eighty years after Wesley's death Methodism could boast of twelve million adherents; today of nearly thirty millions. Dean Farrar has well said: 'The Evangelical movement, the Oxford movement, even the recent enthusiasm of the Salvation Army are traceable to Wesley's example, and to the convictions which he inspired.' Bishop Lightfoot also testified that 'The Salvationists, taught by John Wesley, have learned and taught the Church again, the lost secret of the

compulsion of human souls to the Savior.'" {ibid pg. 38-39}

What a testimony to our blessed Lord and Savior Christ Jesus! The significance of all this then can't be emphasized enough but what is more important or rather pertinent for us here however is of course the weather. The weather was affected by these people and this quite astoundingly especially so where John Wesley was concerned. For when one studies his life and his writings in particular and what one quickly learns and sees is how very preoccupied he is with what the weather does at times. Like for example this pulled from his diary:

"Monday, 17 As we were walking toward Wapping, the rain poured down with such violence that we were obliged to take shelter till it abated. We then held on to Gravel Lane, in many parts of which the waters were like a river. However, we got on pretty well till the rain put out the candle in our lantern. We then were obliged to wade through all, till we came to the chapel yard. Just as we entered, a little streak of lightning appeared in the southwest. There was likewise a small clap of thunder and a vehement burst of rain, which rushed so plentifully through our shattered tiles that the vestry was all in a float. Soon after I began reading prayers, the lightning flamed all around it, and the thunder rolled over our heads. When it grew louder and louder, perceiving many of the strangers to be much affrighted, I broke off the prayers after the collect, 'Lighten our darkness, we beseech thee, O Lord,' and began applying, 'The Lord sitteth above the water flood; the Lord remaineth a king forever' {Ps. 29:10} Presently the lightning, thunder, and rain ceased, and we had a remarkably calm evening. It was observed that exactly at this hour they were acting Mac Beth in Drury Lane, and just as the mock thunder began, the Lord began to thunder out of heaven. For a while it put them to a stand; but they soon took courage and went on. Otherwise it might have been suspected that the fear of God had crept into the very theater!" {pg. 8-9 Wesley}

It appears John Wesley was well aware of God's work with the weather accordingly an event like the Singapore event and/or the Swan Quarter Methodist Church event would not have come as a surprise or shock to him. Wow, what a truly faithful Creator God is; John Wesley would have been astounded. That and perhaps jumping up and down for joy this would have only fired his zeal for the things of Christ Jesus that much more. Doesn't it astonish how His Majesty works? To think that God's Son who you would think would surely have other far more important things on His mind than to consider some small and insignificant little church building is something utterly unique in the history of the Christian Church if not the whole world! It just goes to show and prove what a truly glorious God we serve and if all of this doesn't bring to mind and clarity those words of His from the Old Testament:

"Call to me and I will answer you and tell you great and unsearchable things you do not know." {Jeremiah 33:3}

Whoever said that faith was blind or that the existence of God is just conjecture is really quite unbelievable if not altogether scandalous. Talk about barking up the wrong tree! In fact ludicrous ultimately for what do people really think and/or believe? That Almighty God the 'Creator' is really just some sort of an absentee landlord. That He who created this magnificent world just decided one day to up and leave? Most certainly not! Rather He who created this magnificent planet cares enormously about what happens to it and/or more significantly us! He loves us and loves us with such a deep and everlasting love that cares enormously about what happens to you! The problem however, is again this love for wickedness that exists within the heart of mankind which of course is what separates us from God. ___Again it is why Christ Jesus had to die the way He did___.

His sacrifice bought our forgiveness and it takes nothing more for us to believe in His death and resurrection for us to be saved. {Romans 10:9} Something in the course of history though went horribly, horribly wrong. For to bring to the forefront such an argument that faith and religion is just a matter of conjecture proves to this writers mind that something within either the leadership of the church and/or our universities went horribly wrong and look if climate change doesn't ultimately prove out what that is!? In fact just consider that where the Swan Quarter event is concerned {1876} we are not even a decade removed from the work of Charles Darwin here. {1809-1882}The church with one simple illustration coupled with the book of Job and its questions and that of a scientific nature and we could have obliterated this mans ridiculous postulations and look how we still fight. Accordingly what does this tell us then? Well it tells us doesn't it that Hosea was right about what he wrote?

"My people are destroyed from a lack of knowledge." {Hosea 4:6}

Is this not the truth? Imagine what was and continues to be applicable to the Jewish people from the 6th Century B.C. was and is just as applicable to the entire Christian Church of today. If it isn't something utterly astounding if not altogether perplexing and especially so where this particular writer is concerned? For in looking to try and find teachings regarding this matter of climate change and/or to here from our leaders the religious perspective on climate change and we find and here nothing! Literally nothing and that even by the Methodists which given what happened in Swan Quarter and you would think that there would be entire volumes dedicated to the explanation of what happened there but there exists little to nothing? Literally nothing!? It is something really quite odd? Look if anyone was qualified to speak on matters of climate change it should have been the Methodists and /or the Moravians specifically. Looking to find teachings regarding it though and one will look in vain for any kind of writing concerning anything in relation to climate change, Divine Communication or the book of Job for that matter. Not even from those who were a part of what happened in the city of Singapore do we find or hear anything being taught or explained? Even Oxford along with Cambridge of all places is apparently oblivious to the teachings of the bible regarding climate change? Now if that isn't something altogether perplexing. I guess it just goes to show you just how blind and/or deceived everyone really is to what the bible has to teach and people are of the opinion and argument that it is faith that is blind. That the existence of Almighty God is just a matter of conjecture! What was the church really that deeply affected and/or ashamed by the whole Galileo affair that they ended up throwing the baby out with the bath water so to speak where some of the teachings of the bible are concerned? If so, then wow do we ever need to be more careful and/or watchful regarding what we believe! That is just one part of the equation though, for as St. Paul said to the Corinthians:

"My message and my preaching were not with wise and persuasive words, *but with a demonstration of the Spirits power, so that your faith might not rest on men's wisdom, but on God's power."* {1 Corinthians 2: 1-5}

This issue of faith for St. Paul was never to be a matter of just words or preaching the good news of the gospel of Christ or just some belief about God. Rather for him it was all about being possessed by God's Holy Spirit as well as the display of God's power and throughout his life that was certainly true. Even for us it is supposed to be the same way for as St. Paul taught the gifts of the Spirit of God are many and are freely available for all. {1 Corinthians 12:1-11}Why we don't see more of this though in our own lives and churches is something that surely needs to be emphasized here or rather questioned. Why don't these kinds of miraculous gifts occur in many if not all of our churches? Well there are probably thousands of reasons for it some of which we will discuss in following chapters but for the most part this writer believes it comes down to one basic thing-*no desire for it.* I mean consider:

"Dr. George W. Gale had failed to receive that divine anointing of the Holy Ghost that would make him a power in the pulpit and in society for the conversion of souls. He had fallen short of receiving the baptism of the Holy Ghost, which is indispensable to ministerial success. When Christ commissioned his apostles to go and preach He told them to abide at Jerusalem till they were endued with power from on high. This power was the baptism of the Holy Ghost poured out upon them on the day of Pentecost. This is an indispensable qualification for success in the ministry and I have often been surprised and pained that to this day so little stress is laid upon this qualification for preaching Christ to a sinful world." {pg. 18 Greenfield}

"I believe there is one thing for which God is very angry with our land, and for which his Holy Spirit is so little among us, viz., the neglect of united prayer, the appointed means of bringing down the Holy Spirit. I say it, because I believe it, that the Scotch with all their morality so called, and their outward decency, respectability, and love of preaching, are not a praying people. Sirs, is not this the truth? The neglect of prayer proves to my mind, that there is a large amount of practical infidelity. If the people believed that there was a real, existing, personal God, they would ask Him for they wanted, and they would get what they asked. But they do not ask, because they do not believe or expect to receive. Why do I say this? Because I want to get Christians to remember that though preaching is one of the great means appointed by God for the conversion of sinners, yet, unless God give the increase, Paul may plant and Apollos may water in vain; and God says He will be inquired of. O ministers, excuse me,-you gave me this chance of speaking- urge upon your people to come to the prayer meeting. O Christians, go more to the prayer-meetings than you do. And when you go to the prayer-meeting, try and realize more that there is use in prayer." {Evangelist Brownlow North to the Presbyterian General Assembly of Scotland ibid pg. 66}

Sadly somewhere something went terribly wrong with a people believing that this possession of His Spirit was no longer necessary. Somewhere a people became selective in what they wanted to believe about Almighty God and that sadly is no doubt why the church in her long history has seen so much confusion and pain. The struggles have been tremendously difficult and the divisions sinful beyond belief:

"Our church {United Methodist} goes limping along in anemia because both in the pulpit and in the pew, we have people today who are not converted. We have the same situation in our churches today that John Wesley faced in the Church of England."

{Dr. George Morris, Professor of Evangelism at Emory University, a United Methodist scholar, speaking to the Southeastern Jurisdictional Laity Conference at Lake Junaluska, North Carolina in August, 1987 pg. 110 Relfe}

"The state of the Church in America today is without a sense of the reverence and holiness of Almighty God and is absolutely filled with lost church members.

I am deeply convinced out of 14.5 million Southern Baptists on our church rolls, a full 50% might not be born into the kingdom of God...and where others are saved, many are walking in carnal Christianity."

{Dr. Glen Shepherd, home Mission Board Executive, November, 1987 in Jackson, Mississippi ibid}

As strange as it is a people have all but forgotten those admonishments of God's from His prophets:

"Ask the Lord for rain in the springtime; it is the Lord who makes the storm clouds. He gives showers of rain to men, and plants of the field to everyone."
{Zechariah 10:1}

"For I will pour water on the thirsty land, and streams on the dry ground; I will pour out my Spirit on your

offspring, and my blessing on your descendants."
{Isaiah 44:3}

Unfortunately what was ignored by the Jewish people so to it has been ignored by those under God's son Christ Jesus as well? It is a sad and unfortunate mess but as we see by way of what happened in the city of Singapore things are and will surely change. In fact they have to change for heavens sakes given the enormous and unbelievable amount of sin and wickedness that is occurring. We need another revival of religion surely and with that we will bring this to a close. Before we go though, just one last thing to mention and that is when Jesus had succumbed to death upon the cross a soldier pierced His side and what poured forth from Him? Well we are told it was blood mixed with water. Blood mixed with water and why would that be of any importance? Well because of these words of Christ:

"He said to me, 'It is done. I am the Alpha and the Omega, the Beginning and the End. To him who is *thirsty I will give to drink without cost from the spring of the water of life.*" {Revelation 20:16}

And:

"The Spirit and the bride say, Come! And let him who hears say, Come! *Whoever is thirsty, let him come; and whoever wishes, let them take the free gift of the water of life.*" {Revelation 22:17}

It appears that the fountain of youth from Greek Mythology does indeed exist!!! Water, people, water! It's as simple and straightforward as that! So consider this then...

JESUS! A TWO THOUSAND YEAR OLD THIRTY THREE YEAR OLD!

WOW!!! Although of course He no doubt is a great deal older given his deity, ageless in fact being of the same substance with the Eternal Father. So those fishermen were right about climate change...

"EL NINO" — —THE CHRIST CHILD — — YES!!!!!!!!!

CHAPTER SIX

LUCIFER

Early one morning while attending a Sunday School lesson I happened to over hear something to the effect that what was happening in relation to our weather was because of Satan and the reason the minister gave for this was because of what happened with Job. It was a statement that came as quite a shock and surprise to me for this is not what the bible teaches. Rather as we see it is Almighty God who is in control of the weather. Satan only ended up doing what he did with the weather because God just happened to allow it. So this minister I thought then was making a rather grave mistake and that left me with a number of concerns and questions regarding his particular knowledge of the bible. Of far more concern at the time though was how it caused me to realize that when it comes to this 'Satan' too many people go through life totally and completely ignorant and /or oblivious of what and who it is. Accordingly if it isn't a subject then that we should have a look at and study before we move on with the subject of climate change. It's important to understand who and what this creature is for as the scriptures note he is the god of this present world. With a statement like that and one would think that we should all be very well educated and aware of what this creature is and what role it plays in all of our lives.

Now to begin with what the bible teaches us about this particular individual is that it was at one time some sort of a guardian angel who held an enormous amount of power and responsibility in heaven. His original name was actually Lucifer which translated from the Latin means a messenger of light. This however was changed by God to the name Satan which translated means more or less a liar, thief and usurper of everything that is holy and righteous and just. An excellent description of him can be found in these words of the prophet Ezekiel:

"You were the model of perfection, full of wisdom and perfect in beauty. You were in Eden, the garden of God; every precious stone adorned you: ruby, topaz and emerald, chrysolite, onyx and jasper, sapphire, turquoise and beryl. Your settings and mountings were of gold; on the day you were created they were prepared. You were anointed as a guardian cherub, for so I ordained you. You were on the holy mount of God; you walked among the fiery stones. You were blameless in your ways from the day you were created till wickedness was found in you. Through your widespread trade you were filled with violence, and you sinned. So I drove you in disgrace from the mount of God, and I expelled you O guardian cherub from among the fiery stones. Your heart became proud on account of your beauty, and you corrupted your wisdom because of your splendor. So I threw you to the earth; I made a spectacle of you before kings." {Ezekiel 28:12-17}

And from the prophet Isaiah:

"How you have fallen from heaven, O morning star, son of the dawn!

You have been cast down to the earth, you who once laid low the nations! You said in your heart, I will ascend to heaven; I will raise my throne above the stars of God.

I will sit enthroned on the mount of assembly, on the utmost heights of the sacred mountain.

I will ascend above the tops of the clouds; I will make myself like the Most High.

But you are brought down to the grave, to the depths of the pit." {Isaiah 14:12-15}

So as we see this life form apparently was at one time quite a beautiful and powerful being equal probably only to God Himself. His actions though with God and then with Adam and Eve led to his banishment from both Eden and ultimately from out of heaven. A banishment that actually took a third of the host of heaven with him and where exactly were they all banished to? Well, to a realm of the spiritual that exists between heaven and earth that the human eye cannot see and perhaps the best way of understanding this would be to look at what St. Paul had to say regarding the resurrection body:

"But someone may ask, how are the dead raised? With what kind of body will they come? How foolish! What you sow does not come to life unless it dies. When you sow, you do not plant the body that will be, but just the seed, perhaps of wheat or of something else. But God gives it a body as he has determined, and to each kind of seed he gives its own body. All flesh is not the same: Man has one kind of flesh, animals have another, birds another and fish another. There are also heavenly bodies and their earthly bodies; but the splendor of the heavenly bodies is one kind, and the splendor of the earthly bodies is another. The sun has one kind of splendor, the moon another and the stars another; and star differs from star in splendor.

So it will be with the resurrection of the dead. The body that is sown is perishable, it is raised imperishable; it is sown in dishonor, it is raised in glory; it is sown in weakness, it is raised in power; it is sown a natural body, it is raised a spiritual body. If there is a natural body, there is also a spiritual body." {2 Corinthians 15:35-44}

This explains that not only does mankind have a soul but there does exist life forms of a spiritual kind accordingly this idea then of there being a fourth dimension to life could very well be true. Just witness the fact that since there exists the three environments of air, water and space and why could not there exist yet another plane of existence or environment as it were made up of the spiritual? Seems only logical, A matter of which brings to mind a most interesting and fascinating creature of the deep blue sea that surely reveals an interesting quality of the spiritual if not the divine and that would be what exactly? Well that would be a certain species of squid that have bodies that are not only almost transparent but they actually luminesce and that with different colors no less. It is an act of nature so utterly amazing and mind-boggling in fact that the scientists who study them are dumbfounded at the process of it and are to this day still in the dark as to how they do it. The chemical processes are apparently a secret known only to the squid and of course to Almighty God. What a wonder they are to behold though as they maneuver about in the depths of our oceans and that I think makes for an interesting illustration of what these life forms of the spirit are themselves kind of made up of; and please don't make the mistake of thinking that they look like squid. All I'm trying to do here is present an explanation of the spiritual by using what we see from our own environments. Remember creation is really only a reflection of the divine, God having created everything and if this doesn't suffice for you then perhaps something like this would be more to your liking:

"The U.S. Government is being taken over by the space people!"

"This rumor spread throughout the country in 1967, an updated version of the old devil theory. Actually it got its start in 1949 when James V.

Forrestal, the brilliant secretary of defense in the Truman cabinet, went bananas and raced through the corridors of the Pentagon screaming, "We're being invaded and we can't stop them!" He was convinced that his phones were being tapped and some enormous conspiracy was underway. Soon after he was placed in a hospital he leaped out a window to his death. While the press blamed his paranoia on the tensions of the cold war, the UFO enthusiasts knew better. Air force Intelligence had compiled a Top Secret Estimate of the Situation following their UFO investigations in 1947-48. Their conclusion, according to the late Capt. Edward Ruppelt, was that flying saucers were extraterrestrial. Forrestal, so the story went, was one of the few to read that report before Air Force Chief of Staff Hoyt Vandenburg ordered all copies destroyed and it blew his mind.

Two other top military men, Gen. George C. Marshall and Gen. Douglas MacArthur were obsessed with the flying saucer phenomenon. MacArthur made several public statements declaring the next war would be fought against 'evil beings from outer space.' A fabled "think thank," the Rand Corporation, was assigned to feed UFO data into a computer and fight an imaginary war with those evil beings. Since we wouldn't know where they are from, what there technology was, or how to attack their bases, the computer advised us to surrender." {pg. 216-217 Keel}

Now wow if this isn't something utterly bizarre! It appears that the realm of the supernatural is not so unnotice-able after all and why or how could this be? Well if it hasn't got something if not everything to do with mankind's technological advancements that allow us now to penetrate the oceans and outer space to a remarkable degree. In fact where the military is concerned especially so for in trying to protect and defend a country from threats they have inadvertently been forced to look at why certain strange events occur now and then. Like for example UFO's which has quite literally caused alarms to sound and the scrambling of military jet aircraft to pursue, thinking that perhaps they were some sort of secret weapons launched against us from other countries. In addition to this we also have the strange events of missing planes and boats in the Devils Triangle? This is no doubt why there exist special branches of the military that have entire agencies devoted to the documentation and study of this kind of phenomena with what is surely becoming the most fascinating if not distressing matter of all now is this whole matter of crop circles. There are some very strange things beginning to take place throughout the entire world and my how the imagination of mankind is running wild with all kinds of stories of the most unimaginable kind. Like for example one the greatest stories of them all revolving around Roswell, New Mexico and the apparent crash landing and explosion of an alien spacecraft in some farmer's field. It's really quite astounding and even science is beginning to give this idea of aliens some serious consideration and why? Well because this planet, they are finally beginning to realize, is just too complex and intelligent a design to think of it as just a matter of happenstance! Instead of giving credit to whom credit is due though, the God of the Bible they want to postulate that it had something to do with aliens from some other galaxy. They even have a name for it, 'Directed Panspermia' which is the idea that after having traveled millions of light years from some distant galaxy these extra terrestrials just happened to find our solar system which they found to be perfectly suited for life. This then caused them to begin the process of Genesis by sprinkling into the atmosphere the amino acids of life which after falling like rain into the earth started the process of life which eventually came to be known as Darwinian Evolution. This is what is being put forth as an explanation now of our world's existence and people are actually beginning to take this quite seriously which is only logical given the way things are progressing now with the numerous paranormal and supernatural experiences and encounters. Certainly that is the case with these UFO enthusiasts who believe that there is far more going on than meets the eye. Our governments they believe know far more than they are letting on. It's all rather mind-boggling and where and how does religion fit into all of this? Well, no where of course, which is quite odd given how these extra-terrestrials apparently are not out for the good of humankind but rather are turning out to be quite evil in their activities with mankind. Surely a not to insignificant a matter given what the bible has to say about the existence of evil. A matter which should more than bring to mind what Christ Jesus had to say about being able to recognize the profane from the holy by their character or fruit as He puts it:

"Watch out for false prophets. They come to you in sheep's clothing, but inwardly they are ferocious wolves. By their fruit you will recognize them. Do people pick grapes from thorn bushes or figs from thistles? Likewise every good tree bears good fruit, but a bad tree bears bad fruit. A good tree cannot bear bad fruit, and a bad tree cannot bear good fruit. Every tree that does not bear good fruit is cut down and thrown into the fire. Thus, by their fruit you will recognize them." {Matthew 7:15-20}

Accordingly understanding what these creatures are should therefore be relatively easy! Of course though with the way in which religion is treated by most people and what unfortunately happens is they choose to completely tune themselves out to this which is an incredibly foolish if not terrible, terrible mistake. Surely it shouldn't take much to see and understand that especially in view of what happened to this James V. Forrestal, who apparently committed suicide because of his exposure to and knowledge of the paranormal. This should never and would not have happened if he had but paid attention to what Christ Jesus had to say on the subject:

"He replied, I saw Satan fall like lightning from heaven. I have given you authority to trample on snakes and scorpions and to overcome all the power of the enemy; nothing will harm you. However, do not rejoice that the spirits submit to you, but rejoice that your names are written in heaven." {Luke 10: 18 – 20}

In this passage of scripture Jesus reveals the truth about this 'alien' and his numerous minions whom He refers to as snakes and scorpions. Snakes and scorpions who at the mere mention of His name recoil in fear and why? Well because they know that their existence will not be a long one for the time will come when they will be thrown into the lake of fire. That is why when we see encounters between them and Jesus they pleaded desperately for their very lives like for example what happened with one particular man who was possessed with a whole bunch of them:

"When he saw Jesus, he cried out and fell at his feet, shouting at the top of his voice, what do you want with me, Jesus, Son of the Most High God? I beg you, don't torture me! For Jesus had commanded the evil spirit to come out of the man. Many times it had seized him, and though he was chained hand and foot and kept under guard, he had broken his

chains and had been driven by the demon into solitary places."

"Jesus asked him, 'what is your name?' 'Legion,'
he replied, because many demons had gone into him.
And they begged him repeatedly not to order them to
go into the Abyss."

"A large herd of pigs was feeding there on the
hillside and the demons begged Jesus to let them go
into them, and he gave them permission. When the
demons came out of the man, they went into the pigs,
and herd rushed down the steep bank into the lake
and was drowned." {Luke 8: 28 -33}

So imagine these life forms actually care terribly and
immensely about their fate and welfare even though they go
about committing any and all types of evil behavior. Unlike
human being who just ignore and/or mock the blessed Christ
of God these creatures know where the real power lies.
The kind of evil behaviors that can even result in the actual
possession of the human soul of mankind and how and why
could that be possible? Well because of sin of course which
these life forms relish to be a part of and look for in the
human heart of mankind. For what they could not find in
heaven with God they more than found in us. The human
heart with its desire for sinful pleasures is what ultimately
drives these creatures. Accordingly when men and women
pursue and engage themselves in sinful desires what they
inadvertently are ending up doing is opening up their souls
for possession. It is just that serious so please pay attention!

Now as for this Satan though, well he is not one to go
about being full of such fear but rather takes it upon himself
to actually challenge the Creator on all counts. Something
of which we can clearly see quite astonishingly with his
behavior with God's own Son, Christ Jesus in the days
before His earthly ministry. A life form that actually tried

to get the Son of Almighty God to bow to him and actually worship him:

> "The devil led him up to a high place and showed him in an instant all the kingdoms of the world. And he said to him, 'I will give you all their authority and splendor, for it has been given to me, and I can give it to anyone I want to. So if you worship me, it will all be yours."{Luke 4:5-7}

It is a rather astounding kind of thing and yet understandable given its desire to become like the Most High God. It is in fact what he is essentially after, something of which literally became within his grasp when Adam and Eve disobeyed God in the Garden of Eden. For when mankind sinned it ultimately led to this creature being given an authority over this world that he should never have had. By sinning mankind actually became enslaved as it were to this creature and for thousands of years it is he who held the power of judgment over the human race. It is he who by using what was forbidden to us by God that is this knowledge of good and evil that has fueled this creatures rage and lust for power in wanting to become like god. The Eternal Creator however made it quite clear back in the Garden of Eden that this authority of his would not last long for as God said:

> "And I will put enmity between you and the woman, and between your offspring and hers; he will crush your head, and you will strike his heel." {Genesis 3:15}

This was spoken in reference to the incarnation of His beloved Son Christ Jesus who came to deliver us from the grasp of this evil creature. God provided for mankind a way out by that one sacrifice that changed history for all time, the crucifixion of His dear Son Christ Jesus. A death that not only paid for our forgiveness where sin is concerned through repentance, confession and faith but essentially took away from Satan the authority that he had over us all. This is why we find Peter interestingly enough ultimately being spared from the same kind of experience that happened to Job centuries earlier as we saw in our first chapter:

"Simon, Simon, Satan has asked to sift you as wheat. But I have prayed for you Simon, that your faith may not fail. And when you have turned back, strengthen your brothers." {Luke 22:31-32}

With Jesus things changed considerably and dramatically to the extent that at his death Satan lost the ability to judge us before God. That was turned over to Jesus who stands before us and our Heavenly Father:

"Now is the time of judgment on this world; now the prince of this world will be driven out. But I, when I am lifted up from the earth, will draw all men to myself." {John 12:31-32}

That is also why at his death particularly the prisons that had held for centuries the holy people of God were broken and set free. It is why with His resurrection from the dead the graves were opened:

"At that moment the curtain of the temple was torn in two from top to bottom. The earth shook and the rocks split. The tombs broke open and the bodies of many holy people who had died were raised to life. They came out of the tombs, after Jesus resurrection they went into the holy city and appeared too many people." {Matthew 27:51-53}

Satan accordingly is but a beaten foe and it takes nothing more than for us to resist him for him to flee from us as St. James so rightly explains:

"Submit yourselves, then to God. Resist the devil, and he will flee from you. Come near to God and he will come near to you." {James 4:7-8}

Having said this however, it should not be forgotten that we nevertheless are in a war with this creature. A war that is fought not on a General Douglas MacArthur theme but rather one of morality as so many of the writers of the bible has pointed out:

"For though we live in the world, we do not wage war as the world does. The weapons we fight with are not the weapons of the world. On the contrary, they have divine power to demolish strongholds. We demolish arguments and every pretension that sets itself up against the knowledge of God and we take captive every thought to make it obedient to Christ." {2 Corinthians 10:4-5}

"Dear friends, do not believe every spirit, but test the spirits to see whether they are from God, because many false prophets of God have gone out into the world. This is how you can recognize the Spirit of God: Every spirit that acknowledges that Jesus Christ has come in the flesh is from God, but every spirit that does not acknowledge Jesus is not from God. This is the spirit of the antichrist, which you have heard is coming and even now is already in the world." {1John 4:1-6}

"For such men are false apostles, deceitful workman, masquerading as apostles of Christ. And no wonder, for Satan himself masquerades as an angel of light. It is not surprising, then, if his servants masquerade as servants of righteousness. Their end will be what their actions deserve." {2 Corinthians 11:13 -15}

"The god of this age has blinded the minds of unbelievers, so that they cannot see the light of the gospel of the glory of Christ, who is the image of God." {2 Corinthians 4: 4}

You see this is where the real battle lines are drawn and it is a battle that at times can become quite explosive like for example when dealing with the demon possessed as the disciples of Christ learned painfully enough:

"Once when we were going to the place of prayer, we were met by a slave girl who had a spirit by which she predicted the future. She earned a great deal of money for her owners by fortune telling. And this girl followed Paul and the rest of us, shouting, "These men are servants of the Most High God, who are telling you the way to be saved." She kept this up for many days. Finally, Paul became so troubled that he turned around and said to the spirit, "In the name of Jesus Christ I command you to come out of her!" At that moment the spirit left her.

When the owners of the slave girl realized that their hope of making money was gone, they seized Paul and Silas and dragged them into the marketplace to face the authorities. They brought them before the magistrates and said, "These men are Jews, and are throwing our city into an uproar by advocating customs unlawful for us Romans to accept or practice."

The crowd joined in the attack against Paul and Silas, and the magistrates ordered them to be stripped and beaten. After they had been severely flogged, they were thrown into prison, and the jailer was commanded to guard them carefully." {Acts 16: 16 – 24}

These demons aren't stupid. They know how to play with the desires of the human heart knowing full well what it takes to attract and garner our interests. That is why they are so dangerous. So those then who are involved in such things as the occult, séances, divination, spiritism, fortune-telling and a whole host of other such deplorable and dangerous activities had better think twice about what they are doing. For these creatures ultimately do not have your best interests at heart! Rather they will play you for fools until you have been thoroughly and completely beaten and terrorized and that to their enjoyment. Make no mistake about this and don't ever think that you can exact some kind of revenge by going into the exorcising of them at will; that is without Christ's participation with you against these demons. For these creatures aren't ones to be commanded about by mere powerless human beings, something of which we see the Sons of Sceva also learned painfully enough:

"Some Jews who went around driving out evil spirits tried to invoke the name of the Lord Jesus over those who were demon-possessed. They would say, 'In the name of Jesus, whom Paul preaches, I command you to come out." Seven sons of Sceva, a Jewish chief priest, were doing this. One day the evil spirit answered them, Jesus I know, and I know about Paul, but who are you?" Then the man who had the evil spirit jumped on them and overpowered them all. He gave them such a beating that they ran out of the house naked and bleeding."

When this became known to the Jews and Greeks living in Ephesus, they were all seized with fear, and the name of the Lord Jesus was held in high honor. Many of those who believed now came and openly confessed their evil deeds. A number of them who had practiced sorcery brought their scrolls together and burned them publicly." {Acts 19:13- 19}

Again these spirits are not stupid. They know what they are doing and act accordingly and if you perchance are sitting there reading this and thinking to yourself that this is all well and good but hardly applicable for our own day and age think again. For this writer is not speaking about things that he has just read or heard about from others but has actually lived to experience the reality of it himself and that in a rather phenomenal way.

I was barely 19 years old at the time and just a new believer in Christ when I was pushed into the wall by one of these life forms. I had just finished walking up the stairs toward my bedroom when all of a sudden I was shoved into the wall by some invisible force. Apparently it had been waiting for me and as I came around the corner of the hallway and was about to enter into my bedroom it just shoved me right into the wall. I was, as you could well imagine quite startled by this and immediately went into prayer to seek God's help and protection. I prayed for a considerable amount of time as well as singing a number of hymns, and after a few hours of this I then went about my daily activities thinking as I went what a fascinating testimony this was going to be the following Sunday evening in church. Little did I know though at the time just how fascinating this was actually going to be for guess what happened the very next day? Exactly the same thing except this time when it shoved me I actually felt its hand landing right on my upper arm when it did it and I landed right on the door jam because of it. My left foot caught the bottom of the jam causing my baby toe to become quite bruised. With that I again immediately went into prayer this time seeking God for answers to this. I prayed long and hard asking God for protection and for the sanctification of my home as well as trying to understand why this was happening? I asked for forgiveness thinking that perchance I had done something wrong and continued in this state of prayer for a significant amount of time. That is until I became enveloped with such an unbelievable feeling of peace that it quite literally flowed through my entire being. It was as though, like Daniel before, I had got through to God and He answered me by rendering me in total peace. I rejoiced over the experience and after singing a number of praises to God, I then went about my daily activities hardly waiting for Sunday to arrive so that I could share with everyone this experience.

When Sunday arrived however, I was late for church which I was quite upset about. I had slept in, which was a first for me; for I had always liked to arrive early so that I could take my favorite seat which was in the third row near the front and in the middle section. That morning however I was late and after finding the only vacant seat in the house which quite interestingly was in the back row and on the inside corner I settled in to hear the message and WOW was I in for a surprise and a treat. For to my utter astonishment the message that morning was on the subject of Satan, demonology, and spiritual warfare by a guest speaker named Dr. Jefferies, a theologian from LIFE Bible College in California which is affiliated with the Foursquare Church. I was quite intrigued by this given what I had just been through and after listening for a few moments could hardly keep myself from getting up and telling everyone about what I had just experienced with these creatures. I however remained seated and as I continued to listen to this preacher a hand all of a sudden touched me on top of my right shoulder penetrating right through the material of my leather jacket and into my very flesh. I remember the sensation as being quite warm in nature and it actually squeezed its hand into me as though it was trying to comfort me. I immediately whipped my head around me to see who was doing this only to be faced with the back wall. I then glanced at the person next to me but he was embroiled in the pages of the bible. I was stunned and amazed realizing that behind me was standing an angel of the Lord! I became quite excited by this of course and no less agitated wanting to jump up and do or say something but was reserved in my actions given what people would have thought of me if I did such a thing. You know how it is look at that fanatic and so forth! So I remained seated and it was almost like God was just telling me to pay attention to the message for it was an important one which is what I did of course and Dr. Jefferies text from Ephesians 6:10-18 is one scripture I will never forget:

"Finally be strong in the Lord and in His mighty power. Put on the whole armor of God so that you can take your stand against the devil's schemes. For our struggle is not against flesh and blood, but against the rulers, against the authorities, against the powers of this dark world and against spiritual forces of evil in the heavenly realms. Therefore put on the whole armor of God, so that when the day of evil comes, you may be able to stand your ground, and after you have done everything to stand. Stand firm then, with the belt of truth buckled around your waist, with the breastplate of righteousness in place, and with your feet fitted with the readiness that comes from the gospel of peace. In addition to all this, take up the shield of faith, with which you can extinguish all the flaming arrows of the evil one. Take the helmet of salvation and the sword of the Spirit, which is the word of God. And pray in the Spirit on all occasions with all kinds of prayers and requests." {Ephesians 6:10-18}

Now when church was over I wanted to go and tell everybody about what I had just experienced especially this minister Dr. Jefferies who no doubt would have taken quite an interest in my encounters. However, with the way in which everyone was milling about and fellowshipping I left church that morning looking forward to the evening message which Dr. Jefferies would again be giving. I thought that the evening service would be a better place for such a testimony; for it is not as formal as the morning one and as I left Church that morning I thought to myself WOW I never thought Church could be like this and I was just itching to get back to experience more of it.

Now in the evening service I again found myself faced with an interesting situation for Dr. Jefferies message that evening was on the subject of praying for a door of utterance to be opened so that we go out and proclaim the good news of the gospel of Christ. A door of utterance I thought? Well guess what I had just received, exactly that, and my how I became excited at the prospects of it. Indeed my heart was just brimming to the full with the very news of what Christ had just done in my life and all I wanted to do was just jump up and tell everyone the news of what had happened to me. It was really quite an incredible experience sitting there for it was like this Dr. Jefferies was being guided by a hand to reveal and explain to me exactly what God wanted me to do and let me tell you I was listening. I was also quite amazed because the speaker was being used by God in way that he was totally and completely oblivious of. He quite literally had no idea what was happening and though I was going to tell him and everybody else in the place I left that evening with such a desire that for the following three nights all I did was pray for that door to open to me and was there an answer? Well upon returning to church the following Tuesday which was Dr. Jefferies last night with us, which was spent more or less reflecting over the week's message with him summing up a few more things in relation to the work of Satan there occurred a prophetic word from God which came through two individuals. The first by way of the gift of tongues which a man named Larry gave and then through Pastor Ross Fox who spoke these words and I quote:

> "I have opened to you a door of utterance, but are you going to make it through that door. I have many great and wonderful things in store for you, but there are many adversaries in the way. But if you will make it through that door I have many great and wonderful things in store for you."

I was stunned and in awe for to be hearing this after what I had just been through and praying that God would indeed open that door for me was the culmination of everything. I had heard from God that evening and my how it fired my zeal for the things of God. Whoever said Church was boring and insignificant doesn't know anything about Church that is for sure I said to myself. What a struggle it has been though. True to His word there are far, far too many enemies and adversaries. In fact never would I have thought that now after what some twenty-five years there would be so many struggles and so much adversity and evil to deal with. Truly the Christian life is a life of conflict for we fight too many battles on far too many fronts. Satan is a most clever and deceitful liar knowing just where to hurt us the most in our desire to live for God. Certainly this writer has had his fair share of it all and do you know it wasn't even a year after these events with Dr. Jefferies that I encountered another experience with these life forms by way of a young woman who was apparently possessed. I had met her through work and at the time nothing appeared to be wrong and she actually wanted to go to church with me. We talked some especially about that Mazda car of hers and its rotary engine. I was elated about the prospects of taking her to church with me the following week. After returning to work though following a day off I learned she had been let go or rather fired for some inexplicable reason which saddened me. She had a sister though that worked next door so I hoped that it could still be possible for her to attend church. Later that same night however, I became quite stunned by the news that this girl was causing quite a raucous down at the local bar and fuming something about coming to the restaurant to inflict harm upon the owner who fired her. It was something that saddened me and looking into the faces of those who were reporting this to us at the restaurant there was an odd feeling of fear in the air. Something was wrong with this girl for people were afraid of her. How strange I thought to myself for nothing seemed out of the ordinary to me that is until about midnight when she showed up at the front door which immediately sent me into prayer. It was quite a strange experience because I felt as though I needed to get into prayer and that quite quickly. Looking for some solitary place I moved into the staff bathroom and was immediately thrown into a struggle as it were crying out to God and fighting as it were a spiritual battle that I had no idea was about or for. All I knew and felt was to pray and after a considerable amount of time of fighting in prayer like this I again became overwhelmed with that wonderful feeling of peace. I rejoiced over the experience and then after walking out into the general area to resume my work activities I came face to face with one of the waitresses who was in complete and total shock. Horrified actually, for she came into the kitchen to hide from what was happening in the dining room. I remember her saying and that with some serious emotions something to the effect that she had never in her entire life witnessed anything like what just happened. This girl went into a kind of frenzy when she showed up at the restaurant screaming and uttering such threats and language that it was actually quite hideous in nature. All of which was directed towards the owner and it apparently took quite a number of men to keep her away from her. It was really quite a shocking display the waitress said and then for some inexplicable reason this girl just stopped dead in her tracks, glared towards the kitchen and then yelled out as loudly as she could a one word expletive and then abruptly left. The waitress said it was really quite weird; for it was almost like something had grabbed a hold of her and that was that. It left everyone stunned and shocked beyond belief. I thought to myself wow if only she really knew, if only she really knew! Imagine here I said to myself we find ourselves faced with the same kind of phenomena that the original Disciples of Christ were faced with thousands of years ago. I was stunned as well and later became quite upset because after coming across this girl's sister I learned no real deliverance had ever taken place with this young woman. She went on to become quite a handful including having had a number of abortions. It saddened me and reflecting over that experience I often wonder what would have happened if I had walked out into the dining room and faced this girl head on. It actually makes me shudder to think of what the implications would have been me just a mere babe in Christ so to speak facing all alone a demon possessed girl! How I wish now as I look back for a Dr. Walter Martin to have been there. He would have known what to do seeing how he was involved in hundreds of such types of things throughout his life and ministry. He understood it all. He would have understood the need for an exorcism over this girl and so that is my story then and so as you see when it comes to this topic of Satan and demonology I am not just talking off the top of my head. My knowledge of him is not based just upon what the bible has to say or upon what others have to say and so forth. Rather, it is something that I have fully experienced and because of it I am often left astounded by the explanations given by mankind concerning these life forms as being extra-terrestrials. Extra-terrestrials who are coming to visit us from some other galaxy to perhaps see what became of the world they supposedly created? Encounters of which have actually led people like Gen. Douglas McArthur and others to believe a war with these extra-terrestrials is forth-coming? What unbelievable nonsense! That is just so wrong if not totally ludicrous, for what are we supposed to do in the mean time live in fear with the view of finding ways of protecting us from the eventual by perhaps building nuclear arsenals in outer space to try and defend ourselves from these beings? Beings of which present day science believes were actually responsible for this planets creation in the first place? Wow do you think people are in need of a religious education or what? <u>Again by their fruit you will know them!</u> Ah but as some would probably argue how could religion possibly explain the actual eye witness accounts of spacecrafts being seen with there oblong shapes and rolling lights and what not? Well as any military leader worth his salt will tell you there is something called espionage and propaganda wherein an enemy will use practically anything in its arsenal to win a war. Just take as example the Battle of the Bulge during World War Two and the havoc wrought by Germany's use of uniformed English speaking military police personal disguised as Americans. They did a considerable amount of harm and if that is the way it is with us human beings how much more so do you think these life forms of the spirit will go in their attempts to keep you from the truth? Especially with creatures like them who have a great deal at stake given the human ability now to actually observe these creatures. For no longer are they totally hidden to us as they once were to previous generations. Our technological advancements are changing the way in which these creatures have to interact with us. Accordingly is it any wonder then that they would go about disguising themselves as flying saucers and what not. *They're only using our own inventions and imaginations against us and this is where the real war is!* Having said that, though, it appears that there is more going on here than meets the eye and one need only look at the events surrounding the collapse of the Silver Bridge across the Ohio River on December 15, 1967. Events that for a whole year previously actually caused people of that particular region to experience everything from strange lights hovering in the skies, to the appearance of apparitions of men dressed in black and to some kind of a winged humanoid creature referred to as a Mothman who was flying around terrifying people. A creature that from actual eye-witness accounts was quite large, gray in color without feathers and eyes that glowed red. It was and is to this day something that people are totally fascinated with including of course Hollywood which has made movies out of it. Movies that actually poke fun into it all like "Men in Black." "Men in Black," though, is no joke, not for those of us in religion who recognize them as being the messengers of death coming to receive the souls of the dead, the dying and the damned! This is what the bible teaches and how unusual to find that this occurred the way it did in West Virginia. For this creature referred to as the Mothman apparently went about trying to communicate with certain individuals as well as marking those whom it knew beforehand were going to succumb to the bridges collapse and death. A rather unprecedented move for a life form that desires to remain anonymous and unknown among the children of men! Can you imagine that, and what are we to make of something like this or rather what if anything does the bible have to teach us about this? Well given a statement like the one below from the book of Job and what we can readily see is this demons use or rather robbing and stealing from Almighty God what is God's own peculiar work with mankind {Divine Communication} and turned it into something utterly diabolical. It perverted this whole issue of dreams and visions and even suffering to fit its own evil agenda:

"For God does speak-now one way, now another-though man may not perceive it. In a dream, in a vision of the night, when deep sleep falls on man as they slumber in their beds, he may speak in their ears and terrify them with warnings, to turn man from wrongdoing and keep him from pride, to preserve his soul from the pit, his life from perishing by the sword. Or a man may be chastened on a bed of pain with constant distress in his bones, so that his very being finds food repulsive and his soul loathes the choicest meal. His flesh wastes away to nothing, and his bones, once hidden, now stick out. His soul draws near to the pit, and his life to the messengers of death. Yet if there is an angel on his side as a mediator, one out of a thousand, to tell a man what is right for him, to be gracious to him and say, Spare him from going down into the pit; I have found a ransom for him- then his flesh is renewed like a child's; it is restored as in the days of his youth. He prays to God and finds favor with Him, he sees God's face and shouts for joy; he is restored by God to His righteous state. Then he comes to men and says, I sinned, and perverted what was right, but I did not get what I deserved. He redeemed my soul from the pit, and I will live to enjoy the light." {Job33:14-28}

Satan as usual simply went about counterfeiting God's work. Satan played god with the lives of people in West Virginia; it's as simple and straightforward as that! Unbelievable and to think that the U.S. Air Force put together a top secret dossier on this under the heading X-Files and thinks that this has something to do with extra-terrestrials from outer-space is something utterly unbelievable if not totally ludicrous. Wow! My word again do you think that a people need a religious education or what? Do you think that maybe a people need to get past this idea that faith and religion is just a matter of conjecture? Most certainly for look proof and evidence there is a plenty and if this issue of dreams and visions doesn't bring to mind a most interesting testimony that apparently afflicts many millions of people. A dream that you will find numerous people describing causes them to wake up in a fright and sweat because of how they find themselves feeling as though they're falling into some great abyss of some kind. Something is going on here and though many would and unfortunately are passing this off as just some kind of a coincidence the answer for those of us in the know points in the direction of what is spoken of here in the book of Job. A communication from God to you that you are in danger of falling into the pit of death that is hell! Accordingly it is a dream that one should pay special attention to otherwise what will surely come next in your life is as the arbiter Elihu further pointed out will be your own kind of suffering and affliction. A suffering and affliction that will most likely be the result of your own foolish ways and lack of obedience to God's Law's and Commandments rather than by any intervention into your life like unto what happened to Job although that of course is not this writer's place to say so. Rather God can do and probably will do to you whatever He chooses to do for God wants you to be saved. Accordingly watch out therefore for those human angels of death that is those doctors of medicine and some family members as well who think that euthanasia is the best medicine for the sick and dying. It could very well be that the reason you are on your death bed and suffering so is because God is in the process of trying to woo you in the hopes you will repent for your life of sin and wickedness and that even on your final days or even hours. Be sure therefore to have the presence of mind to repent for your life of sin and wickedness rather than ending up doing what Elihu illustrates occurs with some individuals:

"The godless in heart harbor resentment; even when he fetters them they do not cry for help. They die in their youth, among male prostitutes of the shrines." {Job 36: 13-14}

So again more proof and more than enough of it! Accordingly faith and the existence of God is not just a matter of conjecture or theory. That is such utter nonsense and woefully dangerous as we see by what happened in West Virginia. Ignorance is not bliss where these snakes and scorpions are concerned. Rather one has to be well aware of what they are capable of and if only those in West Virginia had understood this, then the events of that fateful day would surely have been far, far different. Remember what the apostle said:

"...in order that no advantage be taken of us by Satan; for we are not ignorant of his schemes." {2 Corinthians 2:11}

"Submit yourselves, then to God. Resist the devil, and he will flee from you. Come near to God and he will come near to you." {James 4:7-8}

It is just that simple!!! Now if there are those though who would continue to think otherwise like for example the General Douglas McArthur's of the world well they had better look out for as Almighty God describes this life form will have such for dinner:

"Can you pull in the Leviathan with a fishhook or tie down his tongue with a rope?

Can you put a cord through his nose or pierce his jaw with a hook?

Will he keep begging you for mercy?

Will he speak to you with gentle words?

Will he make an agreement with you for you to take him as your slave for life?

Can you make a pet of him like a bird or put him on a leash for your girls?

Will traders barter for him? Will they divide him up among the merchants? Can you fill his hide with harpoons or his head with fishing spears?

If you lay a hand on him, you will remember the struggle and never do it again!

Any hope of subduing him is false; the mere site of him is overpowering.

No one is fierce enough to rouse him.

Who then is able to stand against me?

Who has a claim against me that I must pay?

Everything under heaven belongs to me.

I will not fail to speak of his limbs, his strength and his graceful form.

Who can strip off his outer coat?

Who would approach him with a bridle?

Who dares open the doors of his mouth, ringed about with his fearsome teeth?

His back has rows of shields and tightly sealed together; each so close to the next that no air can pass between.

They are joined fast one to another; they cling together and cannot be parted. His snorting throws out flashes of light; his eyes are like the rise of dawn.

Firebrands stream from his mouth; sparks of fire shoot out.

Smoke pours from his nostrils as from a boiling pot over a fire of reeds.

His breath test coals ablaze, and flames dart from his mouth.

Strength resides in his neck, dismay goes before him.

The folds of his flesh are tightly joined; they are firm and immovable.

His chest is hard as rock, hard as a lower millstone.

When he rises up, the mighty are terrified; they retreat before his thrashing. *The sword that reaches him has no effect, nor does the spear or the dart or the javelin.*

Iron he treats like straw and bronze like rotten wood.

Arrows do not make him flee; sling stones are like chaff to him.

A club seems to him but a piece of straw; he laughs at the rattling of the lance.

His under sides are jagged potsherds, leaving a trail in the mud like a threshing sledge.

He makes the depths churn like a boiling cauldron and stirs up the sea like a pot of ointment.

Behind him he leaves a glistening wake; one would think the deep had white hair.

Nothing on earth is his equal-a creature without
*   fear.*
He looks down on all that are haughty; he is king
*   over all that are proud."*
{Job Chapter 41}

No amount of military preparedness whatsoever is going to do anything against this Mothman. Nor is it a creature to be faced as it were alone that is without Christ Jesus at your side; for you can be sure of this it is only the Lord Jesus Christ and His Father who can put this creature down. Certainly not the U.S. Air Force and its generals who have actually looked at and studied what a war would look like against these so called extra-terrestrials. Unbelievable! You know the U.S. Air Force and its generals had better think twice about what they assume to believe is extra-terrestrials from another galaxy. Again what a ludicrous notion and do you know what is the most surprising thing of all where such encounters are concerned? Well the weather of course. For as one studies events such as that of West Virginia or for that matter the Roswell, New Mexico event and what one sees and learns is how it was all accompanied by severe weather. We find and hear everything from unimaginable thunder and lightning, to severe windstorms and hard rain and hail. It's rather astounding and for this particular writer it brings to mind well a man named Granger Taylor from Duncan, British Columbia who along with his truck vanished off the face of the earth back in 1980. {The very year this writer had his own encounters with the spiritual as was mentioned earlier!} A disappearance that he actually foretold to some friends would occur for he apparently had been in communication with these so-called aliens. The guy was all about flying saucers and what not and even built one in his backyard. On the night of his disappearance {Saturday, November 29, 1980} the city of Duncan along with most of the southern portion of Vancouver Island was hit with hurricane force winds and an enormous amount of rain. Surely not to an insignificant a matter given these words from the bible:

> "Rain will come in torrents, and I will send hailstones hurtling down and violent winds will burst forth... In my wrath I will unleash a violent wind, and in my anger hailstones and torrents of rain will fall with destructive fury." {Ezekiel 13:8-13}

Remember it all well I do! Accordingly it appears Almighty God was not far from what was going on in Duncan or West Virginia or Roswell, New Mexico for that matter which only makes sense given what evil was going on. A matter of which ultimately mankind can **be blamed for,** because as usual it is our faithlessness and sin to God's Laws and Commandments which so often provides Satan the power to do what he does. That is why God is so often provoked by us and though for the time being it appears that Almighty God is content to leave things the way they are the time is coming when God will bring all of this to an end. A time wherein His Majesty will sweep the heavens clean of these snakes and scorpions as well as the earth. A time that by all appearances could very well be at our doorstep now given what we see happening with **crop circles** which is only another form of <u>Divine Communication</u>. Again it is what Jesus said would happen along with all the natural disasters of course:

> *"There will be great earthquakes, famines and pestilences in various places, and fearful events and <u>**great signs from heaven**</u>."* {Luke 21:11}

As usual God looks to inform. The warnings are there and don't you just love the sense of humor that God interjects into some of what is going on. Like for example what occurred in a wheat field next to a giant radio telescope in England back in 2004 as described by this Wired magazine article:

"Glickman's "hard information" refers to a moment at the end of last summer's growing season when the crop circles turned away from the abstract. On August 14, an enigmatic human face, expertly executed in halftones, turned up next to a huge radio transmitter in Chilbotin, England. A few days later, a glyph appeared that many croppies believe to be an alien response to a SETI radio transmission sent into space almost 30 years ago. Formed out of expertly twisted wheat, the pattern shows a strand of DNA made with silicon instead of phosphorous, a transmission device of unknown design, an alternate solar system, and an extraterrestrial with a wide head.

One thing is for sure: The formation proves beyond a doubt that the life form responsible for it has a super-evolved sense of humor. In the words of Seth Shostak, senior astronomer of the SETI Institute, it's good fun and a nice example of grain graffiti - but not worth taking seriously. "If aliens wanted to communicate with us, why would they use such a low bandwidth method?" he asks. Why not just leave an Encyclopedia Galactica on our doorstep? He also noted that SETI's original signal was aimed at the star cluster M13, which means it, will not reach its target for 24,972 more years. The Institute he says "has no interest in investigating the phenomenon further."

Go here for the picture http://www.mightycompanions.org/cropcircles/wired/wheatgraffiti.html

WOW! What a truly fascinating God we serve and to think that this is something, 'not worth taking seriously?' You have got to be kidding?! What is wrong with people? To be faced with the very thing that mankind has been searching for should cause us all to jump up and down for joy not just glumly cast it aside as something extraneous. What has ignorance of the bible and religion really become such now that people have no way of recognizing the work of Almighty God when they see it? Or have people really become so dull in mind where the issue of sin and religion is concerned that they have just canceled it from their minds altogether? If so then one had better watch out for the God of the bible never does things for frivolous reasons. These crop circles are not coming as just a matter of fun but rather as a warning that the wickedness and sins of mankind are not going unnoticed. A matter of which could very well end in a very serious and bad way given what the writer of the book of Hebrews as well as Christ Jesus Himself had to say:

"See to it that you do not refuse Him who speaks. If they did not escape when they refused him who warned them on earth, how much less will we, if we turn away from Him who warns us from heaven? At that time His voice shook the earth, but now He has promised, 'Once more I will shake not only the earth but also the heavens.' The words 'once more' indicate the removing of what can be shaken -that is, created things-so that what cannot be shaken may remain. Therefore, since we are receiving a kingdom that cannot be shaken, let us be thankful, and so worship God acceptably with reverence and awe, for our God is a consuming fire." {Hebrews 12:25-29}

"Then Jesus began to denounce the cities in which most of the miracles had been performed, because they did not repent. '*Woe to you, Korazin! Woe to you Bethsaida! If the miracles that were performed in you had been performed in Tyre and Sidon, they would have repented long ago in sackcloth and ashes. But I tell you, it will be more bearable for Tyre and Sidon on the Day of Judgment than for you. And you, Capernaum, will you be lifted up to the skies? No, you will be brought down to the depths. If the miracles that were preformed in you had been performed in Sodom, it would have remained to this day. But I tell you that it will be more tolerable for Sodom on the Day of Judgment than for you.*" {Matthew 11:20-24}

The God of creation does not take rejection easily and for Him to throw some humor into it just goes to show and prove yet again His long, long-suffering ways with mankind. Accordingly consider; Woe unto you Britain? Woe unto you USA? Woe unto you France? Woe unto you Russia? Woe unto you Germany? Woe unto you China? Woe unto you Saudi Arabia etc. etc? Again religious faith is not just a theory. Proof there is and a considerable amount and if this so far doesn't suffice for the reader, well then perhaps what is needed is a good hard look at the world of money and banking and why that in particular? Well because that is where ultimately the deviousness of Satan's work really lies for money of course is where all of the power lies. A power that the bible describes Satan's avatar will ultimately use to control all commerce to the extent of even branding the human race accordingly. St. John makes this abundantly clear for us when he wrote...

"He also forced everyone, small and great, rich and poor, free and slave, to receive a mark on his right hand or on his forehead, so that no one could buy or sell unless he had the mark, which is the name of the beast or the number of his name.

This calls for wisdom. If anyone has insight, let him calculate the number of the beast, for it is man's number. His number is 666." {Revelation 13:16-18}

It is a rather stupefying kind of thing and for most people even laughable. Preposterous actually for how it is argued could the entire human race become subjected to such a thing? Looking at what those behind the scenes have to say however and it appears that there is something very fishy going on. Like for example...

Reginald McKenna, Chancellor of England's Exchequer, January, 1924...

"I am afraid that the ordinary citizen will not like to be told that banks can and do create money, and they who control the credit of a nation direct the policy of the governments and hold in their hands, the destiny of the people." (pg.1Cantelon)

Abraham Lincoln 1863...

"I see in the near future a crisis approaching that unnerves me, and causes me to tremble for the safety of my country...money power of the country will endeavor to prolong its reign...until wealth is aggregated into few hands, and the Republic is destroyed." {ibid pg. 31}

Thomas Jefferson...

"If the American people ever allow private banks to control the issue of their currency, first by inflation and then by deflation, the banks and the corporations that will grow up around them will deprive the people of all property until their children wake up

homeless on the continent their fathers conquered."
{pg. 30 Hellyer}

Curtis B. Dall April 1968 on the Federal Reserve
Bank...
"They are driving toward complete control of
the world's long-range monetary policy and prin-
cipal world markets for their own profit. They
foment foreign wars to aid this objective." {pg. 65
Cantelon}

John F. Hyland, mayor of New York, March the 22nd
1922...
"The real menace of our republic is the invisible
government which, like a giant octopus, sprawls its
slimy length over our city, state, and nation. At the
head is a small group of banking houses generally
referred to as international bankers." {ibid pg. 59}

Benjamin Disraeli before the British House of Commons
July 4, 1856...
"The world is governed by very different person-
ages from what is imagined by those who are not
behind the scenes." {ibid pg. 64-65}

President James Garfield, 1881...
"He who controls the money of a nation controls
the nation." {ibid pg. 2}

Vice-President John Garner in 1933...
"You see, gentlemen, who owns the United
States." {ibid pg. 2}

Congressman Charles Lindbergh of Minnesota, in 1920 who said...
"Financial panics are scientifically created."
{ibid pg. 1}

David Korten...
"The world is not, in fact, ruled by global corporations. It is ruled by the global financial system."
{pg. 96 Hellyer}

George Soros...
"The main enemy of the open society, I believe, is no longer the communist but the capitalist threat."
{ibid pg. 7}

Henry Ford, Sr....
"If the people of the nation understood our banking and monetary system, I believe there would be a revolution before tomorrow morning." {ibid pg.17}

Honorable Louis McFadden, chairman of Banking and Currency Committee March 4, 1933 to Congress:
"We know from assertions made here by the Honorable John Garner, Vice President of the United States, Paul Warburg did come here from Hamburg, Germany, for one purpose- to take over the treasury of the United States as the international bankers have done with the treasuries of Europe. And on June the 10th 1932 "It controls everything here, and it controls all our foreign relations. It makes and breaks governments at the will." {pg. 61-62Cantelon}

Karl Marx...
"Money plays the largest part in determining the course of history." {ibid pg. 58}

Meyer Amschel Rothschild...
"Give me control over a nations economy, and I care not who writes its laws." {ibid pg. 2}

Sir Josiah Stamp, Director of the Bank of England...
"Banking was conceived in iniquity and was born in sin. The bankers own the earth. Take it away from them, but leave them the power to create money, and with a flick of the pen they will create enough money to buy it back again. However, take that power away from them and all the great fortunes like mine will disappear, and they ought to disappear, for this would be a happier and better world to live in. But if you wish to remain the slaves of bankers, and pay the cost of your own slavery, let them continue to create money." {pg. 55 Hellyer}

So by all accounts the world of money and banking it appears is not a very moral institution and of course how could it be when it is based upon usury that is the taking of interest. In fact is it not the very foundation upon which the entire banking system is founded upon? The taking of interest is what has more or less built the great fortunes of the world next to war and of course slavery. It is something quite offensive and at one time the world apparently understood and realized this to the extant that kings made it quite clear that in their realms it would be forbidden. Like for example King Alfred the great in 901 who declared:

"If a man is found taking usury, his lands will be confiscated, and he will be banished from England." {pg. 32 Cantelon}

And King James 1566:

"If a man is found taking usury, his lands will be confiscated. It is like taking a mans life, and it must not be tolerated." {ibid}

These kings had apparently known and understood and paid attention interestingly and importantly enough to what Almighty God had said to the Jewish people thousands of years ago:

"Do not charge your brother interest, whether on money or food or anything else that may earn interest. You may charge a foreigner interest, but not a brother Israelite, so that the Lord your God may bless you in everything you put your hand to in the land you are going over to possess." {Deuteronomy 23:19-20}

This, however, today has all but been forgotten or rather forsaken to the extent that not only are we forced to pay interest on practically everything we do but we do this if you can imagine to members of our own families. It is something really quite unbelievable if not altogether shameful and people for the most part are completely oblivious to this to the extent that they actually think it preposterous that it would be any other way and look how it is taxing us to death. We have become indebted up to our bald spots with no way out and who are the beneficiaries of it all? Banks and get this, it apparently doesn't end here either for as Mr. Hellyer has observed the banks are looking to gobble up even insurance companies:

"At one time there were the "four pillars" of the financial world-banks, trust, securities and insurance companies. The banks have effectively bulldozed two of the other three pillars, trust companies and securities dealers, to the point where the few remaining independents are the notable exceptions. They are now working on the forth pillar, the insurance companies, and only an unmistakable government vote of disapproval will prevent the near total consolidation of the financial services industry under the banks umbrella." {pg. 57 Hellyer}

It appears something very odd is going on in the world of high finance and what is the explanation for it? Well it apparently has something to do with globalization which is just a fancy word for a new form of worldwide trade although if the truth really be told it probably has more to do with the continued creation of the welfare state but on a grander scale. A work of which the powers that be believe will ultimately lead mankind into a happier and better world which in some ways is not altogether wrong. For the truth of the matter here is that what they ultimately are trying to do with globalization is prevent another world war from occurring. This is what is really going on a matter of which can be traced historically right back to the events of the Treaty of Versailles in 1919 and why that in particular? Well because out of that conference was born World War Two and no one better understood the why and how of that occurring than the great British economist John Maynard Keynes. A man in whom William Sherdan in his book The Fortune Sellers sums up quite succinctly for us this way:

"After serving as an official representative to the Paris Peace Conference in 1919 during which the terms of settlement for World War 1 were set, Keynes came away shocked at the vengeful and shortsighted nature of the settlement. In his book The Economic Consequences of the Peace, Keynes warned of the dangers that would arise from the fact that "the Treaty includes no provision for the economic reha- bilitation of Europe-nothing to make the defeated Central Empires into good neighbors." He correctly predicted that a combination of starvation and hyper- inflation inflicted on Germany would ultimately lead to social upheaval throughout Europe: "Men will not always die quietly...In their distress [they] may overturn the remnants of organization, and submerge civilization itself." This is precisely what happened to Germany under the burden of paying war reparations and continuing to suffer the effects of its destroyed economy. Although he anticipated the potential for a dictator to emerge from such a desperate situation, Keynes, unlike more recent futurists, made no hard and fast predictions of what would happen, instead questioning, "But who can say... in what direction men will seek at last to escape their misfortunes." {pg. 213 Sherden}

As usual when it comes to the world of politics nobody bothers to learn or understand that the answers to the prob- lems of life lie first in the reconciliation of ours lives to God and to our fellow man. This is what has to happen first and then restitution and not the other way around. It is what the message of the bible is all about and why it is so vitally impor- tant. Again though no one bothers to pay much attention to that of course with everyone actually thinking it best that the Church and State remain separated which is most unfortu- nate. For if those in attendance at this Peace Conference had bothered to apply even a smidgen of such things as mercy, love, or even just a little forgiveness and one could make a

good case that World War Two would never have happened
and an interesting song by Elvis Presley sums it up quite
succinctly this way:

"As the snow flies
On a cold and gray Chicago mornin
A poor little baby child is born
In the ghetto
And his mama cries
cause if there's one thing that she don't need
It's another hungry mouth to feed
In the ghetto"

"People, don't you understand
The child needs a helping hand
Or he'll grow to be an angry young man some day
Take a look at you and me,
Are we to blind to see
Do we simply turn our heads
and look the other way"

"Well the world turns
And a hungry little boy with a runny nose
Plays in the streets as the cold wind blows
In the ghetto"

"And his hunger burns
So he starts to roam the streets at night
And he learns how to steal
And he learns how to fight
In the ghetto"

"Then one night in desperation
A young man breaks away
He buys a gun, steals a car,

Tries to run, but he don't get far
And his mama cries"

"As a crowd gathers round an angry young man
face down on the street with a gun in his hand
In the ghetto"
"As her young man dies,
on a cold and gray Chicago mornin,
Another little baby child is born
In the ghetto"

A song that Mr. Keynes I think would have surely been
quite taken by and looking back now is shockingly prophetic.
Mankind's inhumanity to man is something that should never
cease to shock and horrify any of us. Looking at what we do
to our own brothers and sisters is really something atrocious
and no where was this displayed more than in what came
out of Germany in 1940. The wickedness of mankind never
reached a more dreadful place and Mr. Keynes hit the nail
right square on the head about what would happen. Indeed
to the degree in fact that where Adolf Hitler was concerned
his rise to power was accomplished on the backs of this
very treaty with his ranting about the "thralldom of interest
payments." {Chernow pg. 225} Isn't that interesting? Interest
payments if you can believe it on some 33 billion dollars that
the Allies demanded of Germany which was a rather staggering amount of money for 1921 Germany. Something of
which left interestingly and importantly enough the bankers
of Europe, {Jews} in such a state of shock and horror that
they could see that this would never be repaid. How could it
and in that they could also see the coming of another war and
their own bankruptcy and try as they did to prevent it all no
body bothered to listen...

"On January the 15th 1920, the appeal authored by Keynes and Paul Warburg and signed by many luminaries was issued to the press. Herbert Hoover, William Howard Taft, and J.P. Morgan Jr., cosigned the American version with Paul. They stated that burdensome reparations could foster revolution in Germany and Austria as popular revulsion against unjust debt bred an ugly desperate mood. The affected governments would print money to pacify the populace, generating inflation. This prescient document had no effect, as Hoover had warned Paul. Indeed the U.S. Treasury Department thought its dire predictions overblown and resented Paul's involvement as possibly conveying an impression of official American favor. In April 1921, the Allies set the reparations tab at a stupendous 132 billion gold marks or 33 billion." {pg. 223 Chernow}

So apparently ignorance and emotions took the place of logic and reasoning and America was the one who pushed this through!? What did the bible for a nation that has stamped on its money 'In God We Trust' no longer become the standard by which a people are supposed to judge their actions? My word and get this, this banker {a Jew} who was pushed into trying to deal with the finances and politics of it all was left to deal with a world of finance on the brink of unimaginable disaster:

"In economics, Paul's prophetic powers were as unerring as Aby's in the cultural sphere, and he initiated a new phase as an embattled Cassandra. Whether from his Jewish background, personal sensitivity, or outsider status as an immigrant, he had a coldly detached vision of things. His Washington defeat had only sharpened his loathing for political folly and ineptitude. For the past five years, he thought, the world had consumed more than it produced, creating inflationary pressures. Now the governments were printing money instead of submitting to needed austerity. 'The world lives in a fool's paradise based upon fictitious wealth, rash promises, and mad illusions,' he said. 'We must beware of booms based upon false prosperity which has its roots in inflated credits and prices.'

Indeed global inflation crested in 1920, followed by a severe slump-the first confirmation of Paul's grim prophecies."

There was a moralistic dimension to his predictions. Paul saw wartime sacrifice giving way to intoxicated self-indulgence-a theme he would sound up to the 1929 crash. He criticized America's selfish retreat from global responsibility and the materialistic frivolity of the Jazz Age. He thought America morally obligated to assist European recovery by reducing German reparations and war debts owed to America by its Allies. Paul took on the stoic, unbending tone of a prophet who knew the world was weak, selfish, and deaf to his warnings." {ibid pg. 223-224}

Now how does that saying go, 'Nero fiddled while Rome burned.' Look again if the problem with everything doesn't come done to the issues of morality and ethics and of all of the people who understood the significance of it all it was a banker. A banker who just happened to be Jewish no less and a deeply religious one at that to and if that isn't something altogether intriguing if not altogether curious and why curious? Well because when it comes to the world of international finance and banking some of the ones who apparently dominate it all are the Jews, two of the most prominent of which were and are the Rothschild's and Warburg families. Two families who just happen to be extremely religious in character with Meyer Amschel Rothschild {1743-1812} originally studying to become a Rabbi of all things! Now how in the world did something like this happen especially occurring as it did during the Diaspora in which the Jewish people were looked upon as outsiders and intruders living spread out among the nations of Europe? Nations which just happened to be Christian no less? Well if the answer to that isn't as simple as the Law's of God for was it not Almighty God who taught them that when it comes to money they were to be lenders and not borrowers:

"For the Lord your God will bless you as he has promised, and you will lend too many nations but you will borrow from none. You will rule over many nations but none will rule over you." {Deuteronomy 15:6}

Taking their cue from the bible they ended up becoming the world's bankers, and look if it wasn't something that they were well placed and educated to do given how this actually started with something called money changing. A practice that in a Christian Europe was considered to be too sinful for one to be engaged in and yet for a number of the Jewish people became the only means of conducting any kind of business or commerce given their legal status as aliens and foreigners. It was one of the only things left open for many of them to do accordingly is it any wonder then that they would end up becoming the world's creditors? Wow if this isn't something utterly unbelievable a matter of which raises a number of astonishing questions. Like for example, how could a people and we are not talking here just about the Jews but about the entire European population along with

America's as well could go about justifying the taking of interest? Remember these words…

> "Do not charge your brother interest, whether on money or food or anything else that may earn interest. You may charge a foreigner interest, but not a brother Israelite, so that the Lord your God may bless you in everything you put your hand to in the land you are going over to possess." {Deuteronomy 23:19-20}

I mean what was and is applicable to the Jews should have been that much more applicable to the Christian {Gentiles} for is it not we who have the true knowledge of God? Most certainly we do but shamefully it appears that the bible in its entirety is not so serious a book for the Christian as it is for the Jews. Either that or people really do want to become selective about what they want to believe. Accepting only the good things that the bible has to say too many have ignored altogether the hard and difficult things that it has to say. Both Christian and Jew in fact have become more or less selective in what they want to accept and believe about the bible and religion and if that isn't a most serious and grave mistake to make? For remember was it not the Christ of God who said:

> "Do not think that I have come to abolish the Law and the Prophets; I have not come to abolish them but to fulfill them. I tell you the truth, until heaven and earth disappear, not the smallest letter, not the least stroke of a pen, will by any means disappear from the Law until everything is accomplished." {Matthew 5:17-18}

The Jews, the Jews!? If true aren't the words of St. Paul when he wrote:

"What then shall we say? That the Gentiles, who did not pursue righteousness, have obtained it, a righteousness that is by faith; but Israel, who pursued a law of righteousness, has not attained it. Why not? Because they pursued it not by faith but as it were by works. They stumbled over the stumbling stone.

As it is written:

See, I lay in Zion a stone that causes men to stumble and a rock that makes them fall, and the one who trusts in him will never be put to shame." {Romans 9:30-33}

They as usual are a people who constantly stumble over the cross of Christ. Pray we should for that blindness and hardening and even judgment to be removed that has for so many centuries blinded them to the work of their true savior Christ Jesus. {Romans 11:25-27} Pray we should also for all of those so-called Christian nations who though believing in Christ never bothered to pay serious attention to that admonishment of God's concerning the taking of interest. Remember well to the Christian should or rather have memorized is what St. Paul said concerning our relationship to the Jewish people:

"If some of the branches have been broken off, and you, though a wild olive shoot, have been grafted in among the others and now share in the nourishing sap from the olive root, do not boast over those branches. If you do, consider this: You do not support the root, but the root supports you. You will say then. Branches are broken off so that I could be grafted in. Granted. But they were broken off because of unbelief, and you stand by faith. Do not be arrogant, but be afraid.

For if God did not spare the natural branches, he will not spare you either. Consider therefore the kindness and sternness of God: Sternness to those who fell but kindness to you, provided that you continue in his kindness. Otherwise, you also will be cut off."
{Romans 11: 17-22}

The passing of judgment is reserved for God and God alone. The keeping of one's speech therefore to either a yes or a no is more than the correct and proper thing to do. Now what though has any of this possibly got to do with this matter of the 666? I mean how is that really going to be accomplished? Well, with the creation of the atomic bomb together with the history of the Treaty of Versailles and what one sees happening in the financial world is the near total amalgamation of the world's financial systems into a cohesive whole. The power brokers of the world after seeing and experiencing everything that happened in two world wars have come to realize that nothing short of a one world government is going to save planet earth and look how many are the voices calling for it:

Harold Urey: "The only escape from total destruction of civilization will be a world government, or we will perish in a war of the atom." {pg. 97 Cantelon}

Robert J. Oppenheimer: "In the field of atomic energy, there must be set up a world power." {ibid}

Arthur Compton: "World government has become inevitable." {ibid}

Dr. Ralph Barton Perry of Harvard: "One world Government is in the making. Whether we like it or not, we are moving toward a one-world government." {ibid}

Professor Hocking: "Therefore the alternative is that we rest all political power in one agency and resign that power ourselves." {ibid}

Raymond Swing to Albert Einstein: "Either we will find a way to establish world government, or we will perish in a war of the atom." {ibid pg. 132}

Albert Einstein: "The secret of the bomb should be committed to a world government, and the USA should immediately announce its readiness to give it to a world government." {ibid}

Professor Laski of Oxford, England: "Sovereignty must go, that means also the interests which sovereignty protects must be recognized as outmoded in character and dangerous in operation." {ibid pg. 133}

James Warburg, February 17, 1950 before the U.S. Senate said: "We shall have a world government whether or not we like it. The only question is, whether world government will be achieved by conquest or consent." {ibid pg. 62}

Dr. Charles Merriam, University of Chicago...

"I raise my voice to warn- human liberty may be lost." {ibid pg. 133}

This is where it all began. Rather unbelievable isn't it and yet understandable, for from their perspective mankind's ignorant and evil nature only makes this inevitable. With the end of the Second World War these power brokers of the world along with academics and government leaders realized that unless there is set up in our world a new kind of administration man is doomed. The issue of debt and taxes has become such a serious matter that look violence is again raising its ugly head throughout the entire world with Argentina surely being one the greatest examples of that. Closer to home though we have something called predatory lending which has practically crippled have the nations of the world! Then when you add to all of this the issues with health care and the environmental problems, increasing populations, famine and the lack of oil now and one can see that mankind is in grave trouble. Actually if there was ever an issue that could and probably will end up eclipsing the nuclear one in importance it would have to be the issue of oil and energy now and why? Well because our world the experts argue is some 3-5 years away from reaching that point wherein our need for oil is going to outstrip supply. We are running out of oil! Now if that isn't something altogether alarming? To the degree in fact that it probably and no doubt will add a whole new dimension and emphasis upon the need for a centralized world government and if you wish to learn more go here for some vital and important information regarding our worlds coming energy and oil crisis. www.lifeaftertheoilcrash.net

So accordingly then these power brokers are looking and hoping to do what then? Well they are looking at control of course which will ultimately result in the formation of the greatest of all *super welfare states.* The world has a term for it; Big Brother and how very interesting are the words of David Rockefeller regarding this:

"We are grateful to the Washington Post, the New York Times, Time magazine, and other great publications whose directors have attended our meetings and respected their promises of discretion for almost forty years. It would have been impossible for us to develop our plan for the world if we had been subject to the bright lights of publicity during these years. But the world is now more sophisticated and prepared to march towards a world government which will never again know war, but only peace and prosperity for the whole of humanity. The supranational sovereignty of an intellectual elite and world bankers is surely preferable to the national auto determination practiced in the past centuries. It is also our duty to inform the press of our convictions as to the historic future of the century." http://en.wikipedia. org/wiki/David_Rockefeller

Wow! So you see this is what is essentially happening. It is from their perspective the only answer which is not the case of course given the words of Almighty God to us from the bible. Again though, no one bothers to pay much attention to that in its totality and my how serious a matter is this given the creation of the atomic bomb now. I mean just imagine if you will what the likes of a Stalin or a Hitler would have done if they had access to such weapons? So you see its development changed everything, literally everything and you know if this right here isn't where we come across the *greatest single reason* as to why the bible does not go into providing any kind of scientific knowledge or explanations where life and the existence of God is concerned. In fact, not even Christ Jesus the Son of Almighty God if He had been born today which would have resulted in scientists the world over scrambling to have an audience with Him could He be convinced to give them any knowledge regarding the mysteries of life. In fact, Jesus would probably just look at them and say something to the effect of:

"...what is that to you? You must follow me."
{John 21:22} [Paraphrase mine]

For just consider that if a high moral being such as Almighty God were to knowingly give a lawless, sinful race of people the knowledge of how things actual exist and work in relation to scientific matters and they would have long ago destroyed not only themselves but planet Earth as well. That is principally why, by the way, we find within the bible a story such as the Tower of Babel that has God communicating:

> "If as one people speaking the same language they have begun to do this, then nothing they plan to do will be impossible for them. Come let us go down and confuse their language so they will not understand each other." {Genesis 11:6-7}

Can you imagine given at the time their long life spans together with their unity of mind and purpose and they could have discovered and unraveled the mysteries of science unlike any other generation. That tower of bricks would have evolved into a platform for the blasting off of rockets and space shuttles long before our own day and age. Nothing would have prevented them from penetrating the knowledge of everything from chemistry, to physics, astronomy, biology, the DNA molecule, and even the very heavens itself, especially if they were motivated by it for military reasons as we have been. An example of which in our present day generation can be seen with no greater consequences than in the work of J. Robert Oppenheimer {1904-1967} the scientist who after collaborating with his team of scientists learned what atomic power was capable of.

A knowledge that only after that fateful event occurred made him realize the scope of what they had actually done and moved him to utter those famous words from the Bhagavad-Gita:

"If the radiance of a thousand suns/Were to burst into the sky/That would be like/ The splendor of the Might One.../I am become death, the shatterer of worlds." www.quotationpage.com

Do you see or rather understand the horror of it? This knowledge of good and evil that our first parents bestowed us with connected together with scientific knowledge is a rather dangerous mix. A mix that as things continue to progress will quite literally place mankind into the position of playing god {Genesis 3:22} and who can be able to deal with the moral and ethical implications of that? To be sure no one will be able to, although of course many will try, for that is the nature of mankind. Indeed one need only look at what is beginning to transpire with genetic research and cloning, areas of science that could very well open up a Pandora's Box of horrors unlike anything we could ever imagine. It would be prudent here to remember what the science and business of pharmacology gave the world at one time {Thalidomide} with their development of the sleeping pill, deformed fetuses the drug having passed through the blood barrier and into the womb of the developing child. The scientific protocol of trial and error never had it so wrong or awful and is it not strange, or rather biblical, that whenever mankind discovers or develops something there is always an ethical dilemma attached to it? The more we learn the more trouble we end up getting ourselves into and a trouble that could very well end up being the most serious and dangerous of all given what is occurring now with scientists sending machines out into our solar system. Like for example one particular satellite that had been sent out to the sun. Called Genesis of all things and costing in the neighborhood of some 150 to

300 million dollars it was launched in August of 2001 and has traveled out some two million miles to a point in our solar system called the L1 Lagrangian Point which is where, according to our scientists, the gravitational and centrifugal forces of the Earth and Sun meet. Here the satellite thankfully stopped and has remained for 30 months where it has observed the sun and using specially designed tiles made from gold, sapphire, silicon and diamonds has it is hoped collected enough solar wind dust particles to determine what the sun is made of. Information that hopefully will provide insight into how our solar system developed along with an explanation and understanding of what is happening in relation to climate change. Now excuse me but what would happen if something were to go wrong with that spacecraft and it were to continue on towards the sun especially if it was nuclear powered or perhaps explode right there where it is sitting? Or let's consider what would happen if our scientists in studying those dust particles were to learn that our sun is dying? What are they going to try and do- play god by sending a team of astronauts out there to try and fix it? Or perhaps given what some scientists are being led to believe these days, and perhaps what they'll end up doing is just hooking up those huge radio telescopes to some extra juice of power in the hopes that their plea for immediate help will reach some alien's ears. My, what a foolish people! Mankind is playing with fire and a fire that could very well end up destroying all life as we know it! Something of which quite laughingly would probably reduce Satan to tears for it needs mankind to exist so that it can play god. Accordingly, is it any wonder then why the Creator put an end to how far the builders of the Tower of Babel could go and looking at how far our world is progressing one has to wonder how long before God decides to step into our affairs? ***Crop Circles***

We need to give our heads a shake and start understanding that ignoring the laws of God is not a healthy matter. We need to start understanding that it is the pollution of sin that exists within the human heart and character that is the more important matter, not where or how did life originate in the first place. O but we though are supposed to be talking about Satan and money and banking here and what has any of this got to do with that? Well ask yourself this, who is paying the interest on that 300 million dollars that it cost to build, develop and send the Genesis probe out to the sun? Who? You can bet it most certainly wouldn't be the bankers of the world!!! Wow, what a truly unbelievably faithless, evil and wicked world we live in. Truly it is really something to behold and what exactly are these politicians, academics, and/or specifically central bankers hoping to do about it all? Well again if they aren't looking at control of course which will ultimately lead mankind into the greatest of all <u>super welfare states and that on a global scale.</u> Again some interesting words by Mr. Rockefeller:

"For more than a century, ideological extremists at either end of the political spectrum have seized upon well-publicized incidents such as my encounter with Castro to attack the Rockefeller family for the inordinate influence they claim we wield over American political and economic institutions. Some even believe we are part of a secret cabal working against the best interests of the United States, characterizing my family and me as 'internationalists' and of conspiring with others around the world to build a more integrated global political and economic structure — one world, if you will. If that is the charge, I stand guilty, and I am proud of it."
— From Rockefeller's "Memoirs", (p.405). <u>http://en.wikipedia.org/wiki/David_Rockefeller</u>

You see since the end of the Second World War this is essentially what has been happening and if it wasn't a professor from Harvard, a Dr. Carroll Quigley, who summed it up perhaps the best and/or succinctly in his book Tragedy and Hope:

"I know of the operations of this network because I studied it for twenty years, and was permitted for two years in the early 1960's to examine its papers and its secret records. I have no aversion to it, nor to most of its aims, and have for much of my life been close to it, and many of its instruments." {pg. 64 Cantelon}

Studying the financial statements, history and records of entire nations this professor came to see and understand that something had to change and that internationally. It is why we find him apparently saying that they are the hope of the world as this Dr. Cantelon mentions in that book of his "The Day the Dollar Dies."

"He says in effect, that now it is too late for the little people to turn back the tide. In a spirit of kindness, he is therefore urging them not to fight a power that is already established. All through his book, Dr. Quigley assures us that we can trust these benevolent well-meaning men who are secretly operating behind the scenes. They he declares are the hope of the world. All who resist them represent tragedy hence the title of his book." {ibid}

The hope of the world!? Ah, no I don't think so, for the real truth of the matter here is that when the world's financial systems have finally been amalgamated into a cohesive whole this Mothman's avatar will arrive on the scene to assume control over it all. It is what the bible speaks about concerning the anti-Christ. Of course though these men {at one time Jews and now apparently a number of Gentiles as well} don't believe this and do you know if that don't play right into the hands of Satan and look at this!!

****For a centralized world government to succeed and actually work they need what to happen?****

Well they need someone with the *ability of a god* almost to handle or undertake the enormous responsibility of solving all of the problems facing mankind:

"It is necessary to discover a head capable of directing it, endowed with an intelligence surpassing the most elevated human level." H. G. Wells {ibid pg. 136}

"Let that man be a military man or a layman, it matters not."

Paul Henry Spaak, first president of the Council of Europe, planner of the European Common Market, president of the United Nations General Assembly, and one time Secretary-General of NATO {ibid pg.133-134}

"Strong, one-man civilian control of America's giant military establishment is vital to the nation's well being. The concentration of authority is inevitable." Roswell Gilpatrick, Deputy Secretary of Defense {ibid pg. 134}

Unbelievable! Look if the gigantic puzzle of history and prophetic knowledge isn't finally starting to come together. Everything is playing right into the hands of Satan, and look, is it not rather intriguing that of all of the places in the world where one finds the supposedly crash landing of a UFO it would be in a place called Roswell, New Mexico? A place that interestingly and significantly enough just happens to be not far from where the first <u>atomic bomb was developed and tested</u>. What knowing what Satan did about the way in which things are progressing did he just look to pull down the wool over the eyes of mankind even further? Yes, that I think is precisely the case. In fact, he probably found it quite useful if not altogether hilarious that there exists not only a man named Roswell in such a high position of power but a town named that as well. For me it makes sense given his character for he is the god of war ultimately. Really this can't be just some kind of a coincidence. Satan has to keep mankind preoccupied on other matters, if not full of fear; otherwise his plan for world domination will be severely jeopardized. Things do have to remain under his control and that of course can't happen if human beings realized what is actually going on. Humans may be blind and stupid but they can't be that stupid surely. Like for example the Marshall McLuhan, Malcolm Muggeridge and George Orwell's of the world next to a few in the Christian Church of course who could see and indeed foresaw where everything is going. In fact just take as an example the Russian writer Dostoevsky who unlike any other person in the whole history of mankind made what is the single most important statement ever about the way in which things have existed and are ultimately progressing from his book the Brothers Karamazov:

"Why hast Thou come now to hinder us?... We are working not with Thee but with him {Satan}...We took from him what Thou didst reject with scorn, that last gift he offered Thee, showing you all the kingdoms of the earth. We took from him Rome and the sword of Caesar, and proclaimed ourselves sole rulers of the earth...We shall triumph and shall be Caesar's, and then we shall plan the universal happiness of man...Hadst thou accepted that last counsel of the mighty spirit {Satan}, Thou wouldst have

221

accomplished all that man seeks on earth- that is, someone to worship... Who can rule men if not he who holds their conscience and their bread in their hands?" {ibid pg 137-138}

If this right here doesn't explain it all about what is happening in the world of banking and high finance and world politics? Dostoevsky hit the nail right square on the head with this statement that harks back interestingly and importantly enough to that encounter between Christ and Satan who made it quite clear who owns the kingdoms of the earth as we saw earlier but worth mentioning again:

"The devil led him up to a high place and showed him in an instant all the kingdoms of the world. And he said to him, 'I will give you all their authority and splendor, for it has been given to me, and I can give it to anyone I want to. So if you worship me, it will all be yours.'
Jesus answered, *'It is written: Worship the Lord your God and serve Him only.'* {Luke 4:5-8}

So accordingly then what exactly is the 666? Well the 666 is really nothing more than a plutocracy dovetailing into totalitarianism wherein a king {Satan's avatar} will have all of the wealth of the world and the rest of us will have nothing more than a mark based upon a personal number. This is essentially what it all boils down to, a system of which actually began of all places with the creation of the social insurance number "SIN" of all things back in the early part of 20th Century. The governments of the world in looking to govern a people and a nation set up a process by which a coming king will ultimately be able to exert total and complete control over mankind. It's simple enough to see isn't it especially given the technological wizardry that computerization has now brought to the world of government and banking? In fact for the world of banking the technology of it all was received as a kind of godsend given the enormous amount of accounting that goes on in their world. Data is no longer a slow cumbersome process but rather has taken on light speed dimensions. The transfer of data electronically has changed everything about the way in which we interact and that globally. With just a punch of the finger we can communicate with anyone anywhere in the entire world and even beyond no less. It is something really quite phenomenal if you stop to think about it long enough. Marshall McLuhan certainly did:

"Today in the electronic age of instantaneous communication, I believe that our survival, and at the very least our comfort and happiness is predicated on understanding the nature of our new environment, because unlike previous environmental changes, the electric media constitute a total and near instantaneous transformation of culture, values and attitudes. This upheaval generates great pain and identity loss, which can be ameliorated only through a consciousness of its dynamics. If we understand the revolutionary transformations caused by new media, we can anticipate and control them; but if we continue in our self-induced subliminal trance, we will be their slaves.

Because of today's terrific speed-up of information moving, we have a chance to apprehend, predict and influence the environmental forces shaping us- and thus win back control of our own destines. The new extensions of man and the environment they generate are the central manifestations of the evolutionary process, and yet we still cannot free ourselves of the delusion that it is how a medium is used that counts, rather than what it does to us and with us. This is the zombie stance of the technological idiot. It's to escape this Narcissus trance that I've tried to trace and reveal the impact of media on man, from the beginning of recorded time to present." www. vcsun.org/~battias/class/454/txt/mclpb.html

"TV is revolutionizing every political system in the Western world. For one thing, it's creating a totally new type of national leader, a man who is much more of a tribal chieftain than a politician. Castro is a good example of the new tribal chieftain who rules his country by a mass-participational TV dialogue and feedback; he governs his country on camera, by giving the Cuban people the experience of being directly and intimately involved in the process of collective decision making. Castro's adroit blend of political education, propaganda and avuncular guidance is the pattern for tribal chieftains in other countries. The new political showman has to literally as well as figuratively put on his audience as he would a suit of clothes and become a corporate tribal image-like Mussolini, Hitler, and F.D.R. in the days of radio, and Jack Kennedy in the television era. All these men were tribal emperors on a scale theretofore unknown in the world, because they all mastered their media." {ibid}

"The political candidate who understands TV-whatever his party, goals or beliefs-can gain power unknown in history. How he uses this power is, of course, quite another question. But the basic thing to remember about the electric media is that they inexorably transform every sense ratio and thus recondition all our values and institutions. The overhauling

of our traditional political system is only one mani-
festation of the retribalizing process wrought by the
electric media, which is turning the planet into a
global village." {ibid}

"The extensions of man's consciousness induced
by the electric media could conceivably usher in the
millennium, but it also holds the potential for realizing the Anti-Christ –Yeats' rough beast, its hour
come round at last, slouching toward Bethlehem to
be born." {ibid}

Significantly more important though is how it is leading
the nations of the world into a cashless society. Hasn't plastic
become the name of the game and look at how a small business owner describes what he sees himself as happening?

'Debit cards hit small business' bottom line'

"As the owner of a small retail business, it
concerns me that soon there will not be a single transaction in which money changes hands without the
banks handling that transaction and making money
from it.
Small-business owners are not a powerful bunch.
If anything, we spend more effort competing with
each other than we do joining forces to make positive change for ourselves as a group.
Consequently, we are often taken advantage of,
and I believe we have been taken advantage of by
the banks.
Why else would retailers accept debit cards? To
decrease their deposit and withdrawal costs, the banks
provide automatic teller machines, {ATMs} and give
their customers debit cards so they can do the work

themselves. They place the machines in convenient locations and make them a "free" service.

ATMs can be expensive, too, for retailers. Retailers already have convenient locations for our customers to shop. We have the goods to exchange for money, and we even have some cash in our tills if a customer needs it.

All banks need to do is tell their customers that they can use their ATM cards in our stores, and they can do away with the messy business of bills altogether. Our customers will soon demand this access to their accounts and we will be forced to please them.

The banks save millions on customer service, and for this added convenience we are delivering; they can now charge customers for using their cards in our stores.

The bank will tell retailers their benefit is that their customers will spend impulsively but how is it that a card with a service charge will make them more impulsive than roles of bills in their pockets?

It sure is convenient, and I am not one to suggest going back to the old ways. What I question as a business owner is why they charge me for giving their customers the convenience of having access to their account in my store.

We deliver a feature being offered to the bank's customers and then we are charged for the service.

I would have thought that the banks should pay me for serving their customers.

Soon there will be no cash, and what was once a system of payment in dollar bills provided by our government would be a system of payment provided by a group of private companies under one system called Interact.

Now, how did this happen?

Banks traditionally have been in the business of lending money {although a small-business owner would be quick to question that}, and today, the return is in digital pulses, virtual banking. These transactions cost a fraction of a cent to make, and if you own the system of exchange, the sky is the limit on what you can charge for them.

My company pays the bank many thousands of dollars in service charges. We have no alternative. We borrow from the banks, but now they also handle every transaction we make and we have no choice in the matter.

That's not to mention the fact that they know who our customers are, and all our vendors. It makes a little guy very uneasy.

The days when our federal government was responsible for printing cash as a medium of exchange for Canadians will soon pass and banks will own the payment system for all Canadians.

Then it will be too late to ask how did this happen?"

By Ed DesRoches co-owner The Plum Clothing Company and past chair of the Retail Merchants Association of British Columbia. As reported in The Vancouver Sun Newspaper, Monday, October 6, 1997.

As usual it is the small business owner who sees what is going on rather than the average Joe in the street. Imagine age old money-changing but with an electronic twist? Incredible! What they fail to understand however, is the biblical teaching surrounding how this debit card system is the final step in bringing about the actual implementation of a technology that will seek to tattoo us all. Again it's simple enough to see isn't it given the technological prowess that the computer brings to everything that it touches especially with something called biometrics now that can identify and control every living human being on the face of planet earth next to all of the animals as well. A biometric numbering system that coupled with computerization can ultimately and will eventually control everything from what we eat to what we buy and perhaps with the placing of a laser tattoo on our person even our consciences as well. A Dostoevsky and Marshall McLuhan's worst Orwellian nightmare coming true!!! This is what it is essentially all about and for those who are technologically savvy is it not rather intriguing that of all of the numbers that exist in the world of computer science and mathematics it is the number 6 that is the most important given its divisibility into so many parts. Now is that just a coincidence or do you think that maybe Almighty God knew what He was talking about? Certainly this writer has no problems believing God at His word and to pick up a newspaper and find an article of a professor from a local University {UBC} who by doing research on new kinds of identification had implanted between the thumb and fore-finger a computer chip that held all of her personal informa-tion was shocking! In fact slamming my fist into the desk I said to myself by God there you have it! The final begin-nings of the global super welfare state where ultimately a system of credit or rationing as Dr. Cantelon puts it {pg 145} will be the name of the game with one's conscience, if you can imagine being the ultimate payment and sacrifice. The exchange of which, this last king will demand ultimately to be worshiped and glorified as god. Frightening isn't it? Indeed and look if the word 'rationing' shouldn't be high-lighted here in particular and why? Well, with a world popu-lation reaching some 10 billion people and how long do you think we have before we start to experience serious short-ages of resources? Like energy for example which according too many experts nations are beginning to suffer from. It is why we are constantly hearing about going green and saving energy and looking for new technologies. Nothing though and I mean nothing can prepare anyone of us for what is spoken and written about in a documentary called Crude Awakening. www.lifeaftertheoilcrash.net. To think that we could actually see the end of oil is something utterly mind-blowing if not altogether frightening. The consequences of something like this would be utterly catastrophic. Indeed imagine the effects of little to no more gas for our cars, for our industries etc.etc? Our economies and communities and entire nations would implode almost overnight! Accordingly if that ultimately wouldn't or doesn't underscore how in trying to cope with these kinds of matters mankind will be forced into accepting the ultimate of all welfare states? Look if ones very survival should depend upon it they'll be lining up in droves to be implanted with or laser tattooed in some way. The survival of the economy or the entire world for that matter will more or less depend upon it. How difficult is it then to understand the ease of which a people will or may want to be a part of such a system? Taking the implantation of this number into your hand or forehead though will be the ultimate of all acts of sins and wickedness against Almighty God. It is one of only two of the unforgiveable sins in the bible. Actually is it not a very sin against life itself given the loss of all freedoms, liberties and privileges it brings with it. The ultimate abomination that the bible describes will bring about the final desolation and end of the world by the Creator. Wow, what a shocking display of biblical prophecy this was staring back at me and this, from of all places, the local newspaper. Again unbelievable and if you think that this is really mere science fiction just go to the website www.verichipcorp.com. There you will find even more of this desire to implement a new kind of "security" so called with the Verichip and /or the RFID. My word to think that a company that I would want to work for would actually demand that I be implanted with a microchip device so that they could feel secure about their vaults and money and what not is something really unbelievable if not truly despicable.

<u>Doesn't anyone bother to ask, think or understand that what an insult it is to one's character and dignity not to be trusted!!?</u>

In this brave new world of ours though it appears that ones word means little to nothing. Now how scary is that? That is the way it is though isn't it with our human nature {sin which is lawlessness} and because of it we are all being herded towards the ultimate of all totalitarian rule. {666}Our wars with the creation of the Atomic Bomb now along with our dwindling natural resources has and will only speed up the process that much more. This is the crux of it all folks and if you perchance want and /or need the technical data about where and how the 666 is actually imbedded in this elec-tronic system an interesting book that I highly recommend reading is Dr. Mary Stewart Relfe's book "The New Money System." You can find it by going here www.theleagueof-prayer.com; and so there you have it, the explanation of it all. Accordingly do you think it important that one should be well aware of and understand that Satan {this Mothman} is not a myth but a very real individual who needs to be taken seriously? For you can be sure of this he is the god of this present world ultimately. Ignorance accordingly is not bliss where this life form is concerned. Rather one has to be well aware of what he is capable of and that brings us now back to why this chapter was written in the first place and that is climate change. For as we saw in the last chapter Satan did use both a windstorm and a meteorite to inflict harm upon Job. It is something that far too many people including even those in positions of leadership within the Christian

Church no less use as the basis for what we see happening throughout the entire world. A matter of which can actually be reinforced and indeed is by scriptures which make it quite clear that Satan can and does possess a power almost equal to that of the Eternal Creator...

"And he performed great and miraculous signs, even causing fire to come down from heaven to earth in full view of men. Because of the signs he was given power to do on behalf of the first beast, he deceived the inhabitants of the earth. He ordered them to set up an image in honor of the beast who was wounded by the sword and yet lived." {Revelation 13:13-14}

"And then the lawless one will be revealed, whom the Lord Jesus will overthrow with the breath of his mouth and destroy by the splendor of his coming. The coming of the lawless one will be in accordance with the work of Satan displayed in all kinds of counterfeit miracles, signs and wonders, and in every sort of evil that deceives those who are perishing." {2 Thessalonians 2:8-10}

To apply this though in such a blanket form to everything that is going on without taking into consideration *all* that the bible has to say is an extremely grave mistake to make. Especially where the weather is concerned, for the bible makes it abundantly clear that it is Almighty God the Creator who controls the weather ultimately. Again we cannot be selective about what we want to believe about the bible as we shall see in our next chapter and as we go *please, please pay attention to, and or rather memorize these words:*

"It is written: Man does not live on bread alone but by 'every word' that comes from the mouth of God." {Matthew 4:4}

CHAPTER SEVEN

MAHAN AND FINNEY

Libraries are quite the interesting places especially when one knows what to look for. Certainly from the perspective of this writer his journey of discovery has led him into some utterly astounding places. Places which has filled him with an incredible amount of awe and excitement at how Almighty God works within the history of mankind. If it doesn't go back to those words of God's spoken through the prophet Jeremiah:

"Call to me and I will answer you and tell you great and unsearchable things you do not know." {Jeremiah 33:3}

Again it has certainly been quite the experience and one in which I had thought would have ended largely with what has been discovered and written so far. That however is not the case at all, but rather far from the truth for unbeknownst to me while browsing through some books at a bible college I happened to come across some other very interesting if not phenomenal works of Almighty God. Now what could possibly be more incredible than the Swan Quarter event you may be asking yourselves? Well it appears that while our blessed Lord and Savior Christ Jesus was busily moving that little church in Swan Quarter, North Carolina, {1876} He was apparently up to something entirely different over in Ohio {184?}. The account given to us is by a man named Asa Mahan:

"I had an appointment," he said, "during the season of afflictive drought, to preach in one of the churches of the city where I lived one Sabbath morning. As we came to our carriage, I said to my wife, 'There is not the remotest probability that it will rain today. I will, therefore, carry in the robe which we usually take with us,' and did so. "When

I kneeled before that congregation, I had no more expectation that it would rain that day outside than inside the house of God. When I began to pray about the drought, however a power came over me which rendered that prayer a wonder to myself and the congregation. The Monday's issue of our daily paper contained this statement: 'The preacher in one of our churches prayed very fervently yesterday morning that it might rain, and his congregation were drenched with rain on going home at the close of that service.'

"I can never tell when the 'spirit of grace and of supplication,' in that form, shall be poured upon me. Nor do I feel under obligation to have such experience whenever I pray. All that I can do, or feel bound to do, is leave my heart open, and let the Spirit intercede in it as and when He chooses. This I do say, however, that when the Spirit does thus intercede, I always obtain the specific object for which I pray. Nor can anyone pray under the intercessory power of the Spirit without the hearer, as well as himself, marking the peculiarity of prayer."

"Hence it is that, for many years past, my students, in times of drought, for example, have been accustomed to say, 'We shall have rain now. Did you mark our President's prayer?' Nor were they ever disappointed." {pg. 74-75 Harvey}

Now isn't this something utterly fascinating! Brings us back to the statement doesn't it of how we need to be hydrated both physically and spiritually? More significantly though would have to be how it reveals for us the incredible truth of what our Lord and Savior Christ Jesus said:

"I tell you the truth, anyone who has faith in me will do what I have been doing. He will do even greater things than these, because I am going to the Father." {John 14:12}

Wow if this didn't truly come to fruition in the life of this man Asa Mahan. In the annals of Church history it is again something really quite phenomenal if not utterly extraordinary. Who is this Asa Mahan though and why would Almighty God choose to do something like this through him particularly?

Born on November, 9, 1800, in the city of Vernon, New York, Asa Mahan was a man apparently of many talents. He was raised in an ultra Calvinistic home and learned early of the principles of religion and took to heart the faith and teachings of Christ. He was educated at Hamilton College and graduated from there in 1824. He then went on to Andover Theological Seminary where he graduated in 1827 and then became ordained in the Presbyterian Church in 1829. He served for a time as Pastor of a church in Cincinnati and then left to join the faculty of Lane Theological Seminary in Walnut Hills. This however did not last long for at that time there was a much heated debate over the issues of slavery and Lane was caught in the middle. A civil war was brewing and for some of the students as well as some of the faculty their view concerning the abolition of slavery outright was looked upon as far too radical. Accordingly this forced a number of both the students and the faculty including Asa Mahan to pack up and leave. Asa Mahan interestingly enough was against slavery and viewed it as a great sin against God. So as a result Oberlin College therefore became the new home for them all and given his credentials Asa Mahan became its first president. A position he would serve in for approximately 15 years {1835-1850} where he fought the good fight of faith. During his tenure there he would become known as a great reformer, philosopher and theologian as well as a revivalist. Vilified he was though for many of his views both theologically and politically. Indeed some of his views would shake up American Society to the core. Like for example his emancipation of the blacks as well as treating woman as equals to the degree of even offering them along with the blacks the equal opportunity of education. For the 1800's this was really quite shocking and radical and accordingly brought a great deal of scorn and condemnation upon them. Oberlin was not a school looked upon with much favor except by Almighty God that is! That we clearly see by way of God's use of Asa Mahan to bring to an end a drought. Imagine a mere human being used by Almighty God in that way? Inexplicably though like the Moravians and the Methodists before them he along with those under his care at Oberlin did not really understand the great significance of it. In fact to the astonishment of this writer there exists nothing in any of Asa Mahan's writings concerning the work of God in relation to Divine Communication and this whole issue of the weather. A matter of which is even more astounding if not altogether perplexing given what happened with Charles Finney. For he was used by Almighty God in the same sort of way as Asa Mahan was. Just look at this incredible report:

> "During the summer of 1853 Oberlin was struck with a severe drought. The hay fields were dried up so there was no feed for the cattle. The cattle soon must die and the harvest fail unless rain comes. Crops had withered, wells dried up, and the parched earth became powdery.
> On Sunday morning the church was filled. Not a cloud was in sight and no one expected a drop of water to fall from the skies that day. The situation was desperate. Finney arose from his chair walked to the pulpit and lifted his voice in prayer.

'O Lord! Send us rain. We pray for rain. Our harvests perish. There is not a drop for the thirsting birds. The ground is parched. The choking cattle lift their voices toward a brassy heaven and lowing, cry 'Lord give us water...We do not presume to dictate to Thee what is best for us, yet Thou dost invite us to come to Thee as children to a father and tell Thee all our wants. We want rain! Even the squirrels in the woods are suffering for want of it. Unless Thou givest us rain our cattle must die...O Lord, send us rain! and send it now! For Jesus sake! Amen.

"In the preachers voice," reports the California minister, "was the plaintiveness of a creatures cry. I do not know whether any pencil caught more of this wonderful prayer, but all who heard it had to tell of its bold importunity. It had the pathos and power of an Isaiah."

Then the pastor-revivalist poured out his soul in a searching sermon, 'hewing close to the line,' from the text, "I have somewhat against thee because thou hast left thy first love." "Not many minutes did the sermon go on before a cloud about the size of a man's hand came athwart the summer sky," says the California preacher, "It grew fast. The wind rattled the shutters of the old church. Darkness came on the air, joy aroused our anxious hearts as great raindrops pattered on the sun-scorched shingles of the monumental old church.

Finney's lithe figure, tall as a Sioux warrior, ruddy as a David, trembled. His clarion voice choked. God had heard his cry. The sermon was never finished, for torrents of water poured from the prayer-unlocked heavens. The preacher bowed over the pulpit and said, Let us thank the Lord for the rain."

He gave out the hymn, When all they mercies, O my God my rising soul surveys, Transported with the view, I'm lost in wonder, love and praise."

The congregation could not sing for weeping. Then Finney lifted heavenward a prayer of thanksgiving and praise. "I can remember not a word of the closing prayer, but the reverent and relaxed figure, the pathetic voice, the pallid and awe-struck countenance, are vivid as if it was yesterday; the plank sidewalks of the dear old town splashed our garments as we walked home from a short service, of which life's memory must be lasting." This is the testimony of the student who sat in the gallery and saw and heard Finney that morning." {pg. 126-128 Miller}

Now again if this isn't something utterly astounding?! Look not only was Asa Mahan used by Almighty God to bring to an end a drought {184?} but also Charles Finney {1853}. Now what could have possibly been going through the mind of Almighty God to have done this through both of these men? Well if it doesn't ultimately go back to what He said to the Jewish people millennia ago:

"Observe therefore all the commands I am giving you today, so that you may live long in the land that the Lord swore to your forefathers to give them and their descendants, a land flowing with milk and honey. The land you are entering to take over is not like the land of Egypt, from which you have come, where you planted your seed and irrigated it by foot as in a vegetable garden. But the land you are crossing the Jordan to take possession of is a land of mountains and valleys that drinks rain from heaven. It is a land that the Lord your God cares for; the eyes

239

of the Lord your God are continually on it from the beginning of the year to its end.

So if you faithfully obey the commands I am giving you today to love the Lord your God and to serve him with all your heart and with all your soul – then I will send rain on your land in its season, both autumn and spring rains, so that you may gather in your grain, new wine and oil. I will provide grass in the fields for your cattle, and you will eat and be satisfied.

Be careful, or you will be enticed to turn away and worship other gods and bow down to them. Then the Lord's anger will burn against you, and he will shut the heavens so that it will not rain and the ground will yield no produce, and you will soon perish from the good land the Lord is giving you. Fix these words of mine in your hearts and minds!" {Deuteronomy 11:8-18}

Like the Jewish people before them God looked with much favor upon these people at Oberlin and if it isn't something again utterly phenomenal! Why Oberlin though and why through these two individuals particularly? Well, can't help but wonder if it didn't have something to do with the making of America herself? Looking at the history of it all and wasn't Ohio specifically the Ohio Valley and the forks of the Ohio where the major battles for the new land took place? Most certainly it was and if all of that bloodshed wasn't enough, yet another war was looming on the horizon. This time though it was over slavery of all things that would determine once and for all just what kind of a nation was going to emerge from it. So if that isn't something altogether important, and to look at the life and work of Charles Finney and if we haven't got a prophet here? In fact known as the father of revivalism, and wasn't it he who reshaped much of

American Christian thought and beliefs? Most certainly he did accordingly if he isn't therefore someone that we need to have a closer look at as well.

Born August 29th, 1792 in Warren, Connecticut Charles Finney came from an old and well established New England family. At the age of two his family moved to New York State where he spent most of his childhood finally settling in Henderson which is near Lake Ontario. As a child he, unlike Asa Mahan, received no religious education though later was exposed to a great deal of it especially as a lawyer, his chosen profession. He even ended up becoming a Freemason which for many in his position was apparently the looked upon and expected thing to do. What is there a recruitment center at law schools wherein people are expected to become members of this organization? This however did not last long given the praying of his soon to be wife Lydia Andrews as well as a minister and friend George W. Gale. A pastor of the Adams Street Presbyterian Church in New York City of which Charles Finney attended and was the choir director of. The two men would spend many a night discussing the many issues of theology and religion even ending up arguing over the issues of Calvinism. Charles Finney interestingly enough disagreed with many of Calvin's ideas and this led at times to a great deal of friction between both men. Nevertheless it was because of George Gale's work and endeavors that Charles Finney would end up being converted and ultimately enter into the ministry. It wasn't an easy transformation though for him. Indeed being the proud man that he was he struggled greatly with it. The more he read the bible though and the more he reflected over everything the more the conviction came until finally locking himself away in the forest one night he makes the important decision:

"I...found a place where some large trees had fallen across each other, leaving an opening between.

There I saw I could make a kind of closet. I crept into this place and knelt down for prayer." {pg. 21 Basil Miller}

Here he becomes an entirely new kind of man and this is where it gets very interesting; for he finds himself coming face to face with Christ Himself. He makes the confession that after returning to his office and entering into some back room to again pray he testifies to the receiving of a very special blessing...

"There was...no light in the room; nevertheless, it appeared to me as if it were perfectly light. As I went in and shut the door...it seemed as if I met the Lord Jesus Christ face to face...as I would see any other man. He said nothing, but looked at me in such a manner as to break me right down at his feet...it seemed to me a reality that He stood before me and I fell down at His feet and poured out my soul to Him. I wept like a child...I bathed his feet with my tears." {ibid pg 23}

Then if this wasn't enough he goes on to describe the anointing that he further received from our Lord and Savior Christ Jesus:

"But as I turned and was about to take a seat by the fire I received a mighty baptism of the Holy Ghost. Without expecting it...the Holy Spirit descended upon me in a manner that seemed to go through me body and soul. I could feel the impression like a wave of electricity going through and through me. Indeed it seemed to come in waves and waves of liquid love... like the very breath of God...and seemed to fan me like immense wings."

"No words can express the wonderful love that was shed abroad in my heart. I wept aloud with joy and love; and...I bellowed out the unutterable gushings of my heart. These waves came over me and over me and over me one after the other until I recollect I cried out, 'I shall die if these waves continue to pass over me...Lord I cannot bear any more." {ibid}

Now imagine this then Charles Finney goes from being a proud and timid man to a chosen vessel of Almighty God. He ends up being baptized into the Spirit of our Lord and so begins a new chapter in his life. Indeed giving up the lawyer profession he immediately enters the ministry which begins interestingly enough at the invitation of George Gale his former pastor to preach in his church one morning. It was a service that to the astonishment of Mr. Gale and others was unusually successful. Then in what would become known as the 'Burned over District' which was an area of Rome, New York that had seen a great deal of religious fervor his career would really take flight. The area had apparently seen everything from the formation of new religions and cults to revivalism and all types of spiritism. This is why it was and is referred to as the 'Burned over District.' Finney's work there was again unusually successful and this caused him to become noticed by many as well as garnering him much talk in the newspapers of the day. His success in turning people to the truth in that perplexing place caused his former leaders to see in him more than just a mere lawyer and accordingly set about helping to further his ministry. It would be a ministry that would take Finney far and wide but not without a great deal of controversy. Apparently Finney's modification to Calvinism wasn't something particularly favorable to the Old Guard Presbyterians. For this idea that the will has no place in salvation because everything depends upon predestination was to Finney nonsense. Hallelujah! Thankfully

Finney saw through this nonsense. Calvinism, Calvinism and with Finney constantly warning his hearers of the hell to come, and is it any wonder that the establishment would have more and more problems with him? Finney carried on though through it all having firmly established within himself through his own readings of the bible a new perspective to the Gospel of Christ. A gospel that came to be referred to as New Light Theology which contrary to the old emphasized such things as the conviction of sin and the need for a conversion experience that would lead to moral obedience and holiness. Astonishingly it was comparable in fact to Methodism and isn't that interesting. Finney along with Mahan in fact would come to espouse a kind of theology that was in many ways Methodist in nature. They like the Moravians and the Methodists before them came to see and experience the truth of those words from the bible concerning the work of the Holy Spirit of Almighty God. {Joel 2:28] Now isn't that interesting! Accordingly no wonder then that they conflicted with the Old School Presbyterians even charging them of Arminianism and Antinomianism? Charging Finney with that though was really quite ridiculous for Finney was a lawyer and the interesting thing about that is how he used that in his ministry. Like a lawyer making his case before a jury he presented the gospel in such a way as to prick the very conscience and hearts of the people. It is no doubt why he was particularly successful in the pulpit. Everything begins with law doesn't it; and if that doesn't underscore or put aside the argument that law is no longer important or relevant to the gospel of Christ? I mean how in heavens sakes is one to live a holy and righteous life if one is not educated in the laws of God to begin with? Accordingly it can't be just about grace and faith and if this doesn't bring us back to the whole issue of God's reputation and the issue of perfection. Again if God doesn't want and or even demand perfection on our part and so any argument against that should surely be seen for what it is? A desire on the part of men to go beyond what is written in the Word of God and one need only look at the whole slavery issue to see the truth of that. In fact to learn of Christians or rather so-called Christians in the Deep South going to church armed with guns in fear of their slaves taking revenge is something that totally flabbergasts this writer. Why or rather how could something like this happen? Well if again it doesn't come down to the whole issue of selectivity? That is the taking of what is good in the bible while rejecting the hard and difficult issues that it has to say. Instead of obeying everything that the bible has to say {the full gospel} there were those who chose to take from it what they wanted to believe while ignoring and rejecting the hard and difficult things. Again just take the whole issue of slavery. When it came to trying to deal with emancipation no one bothered to pay attention to the Old Testament record and God's Laws concerning it. They instead came up with their own laws and what not. Yes, got to keep power under ones their own thumbs and wishes, right? O, if only the political and religious leaders of the day had bothered to pay even a smidgen of attention and time including the Old Guard Calvinists to what the Talmud had to teach and command, the entire civil war I think one can make a good argument for could have been prevented. O, but as the argument often goes that is the Old Testament and we are under the New. What rubbish and if this isn't the reason as to why no one understands the truth that climate change is the work of Almighty God including even droughts. Whatever we know concerning the work of Almighty God and the weather comes to us by way of the Old Testament record. In the New Testament there exists little to nothing except that is by way of the book of Revelation. There we find a great deal on the subject of climate change as we shall see in a following chapter. Other than that the only other thing we find in the New are just a few references to the rain as we saw in our last chapter. Beyond that all we further have are these words from St. Paul who mentioned in the book of Romans:

> "The wrath of God is being revealed from heaven against all the godlessness and wickedness of men who suppress the truth by their wickedness, since what may be known about God is plain to them, because God has made it plain to them. For since the creation of the world God's invisible qualities-his eternal power and divine nature –have been clearly seen, being understood from what has been made, so that men are without excuse." {Romans 1:18-23}

As a Jew and a former Pharisee, St. Paul would have known that this had everything to do with the weather. In fact, if the weather wasn't affected by this mans life!? Any argument therefore that the Old Testament is not for our day and age is nonsense. I mean how in heavens sakes are we to understand the New without the Old and vice versa? Moreover according to such a statement as St. Paul's and wouldn't it be interesting to know what the weather was doing over the estates of many a slave owner in the Deep South? Certainly makes for some interesting questions especially if one had been able to speak with a man named Frederick Douglass on the subject. I mean just consider:

> "Nor did the outpoured rain close the story of those opened heavens. That afternoon, the congregation packed the building once again, so the minister 'could comfort the slain of the Lord.'
> 'I have never witnessed so solemn a scene, says the minister in his Advance story. 'He continued with added force and directness until his shafts struck home...From the galleries, the side seats and the choir they filed solemnly to the front seats. If the

old church seats fifteen hundred, then there were a thousand penitents at her altar that day.'

Among the weeping throng an impressive black man arose way in the back of the audience to speak. Said an usher to Finney, 'Frederick Douglass has something to say to the people.'

The great colored orator, now gray-haired and form-bent, came forward for forgiveness. He said, 'When I was young and a slave, Mr. Finney, when my back quivered under the master's lash, I clung close to God and felt the comfort of true religion. But prosperity has been too much for me, and I have come under the dominion of the world, and have lost my first love.'

Finney, the soul stirred preacher, wept aloud and cried, 'God bless you, Brother Douglas! God bless you!' So the evangelist comforted his colored brother." {pg. 128 Miller}

America, America what you had in Oberlin and in these two men Asa Mahan and Charles Finney was something utterly and truly unique. Sadly however, it appears that what Almighty God and His Son Christ Jesus tried to do there and through these two men turned into a terrible debacle of sorts. For some inexplicable reason there was a falling out between Asa Mahan and Charles Finney which ultimately ended this schools experiment with religion. Actually if it didn't have everything to do with theology for in trying to come to grips over the question of whether, 'one can look to Christ to be sanctified wholly or not' and it led to quite a schism. The question actually came as quite a shock to both Asa Mahan and Charles Finney in fact because of the implications it had for their theology. Could a Christian actually attain a perfect sinless state? It was a question they had a hard time with and after a considerable amount of thought and reflection they both came out as saying yes to the question. One of their chief arguments based upon the fact of what Christ Jesus Himself said concerning how the believer should become perfect as God is perfect. {Matthew 5:48} If the Son of God was of the opinion that mankind could become such then surely it could be attainable. It was a doctrine that Asa Mahan would fully develop and unfortunately take to such an extreme that it resulted in a great deal of friction and schisms at Oberlin. Even between him and Charles Finney it would lead to some unfortunate battles culminating ultimately in the very removal of Asa Mahan from the Oberlin presidency. A dismissal that was none to graceful and one in which embittered permanently Asa Mahan against Charles Finney and an interesting account of it is described this way:

> "His behavior became offensive and harsh, and he was considered by most of the staff to be unfairly critical and arrogant-a rotten example of the holy lifestyle he promoted. In 1850, after an extended and unpleasant ordeal in which Mahan refused to accept a graceful dismissal, and became permanently embittered toward Finney, he resigned and took some sympathetic staff and students to Cleveland to found a new school. Lewis Tappan wrote to him... 'you are so self conceited-so sensitive to your reputation-so idolatrous to your influence that you have, I fain believe, done immense injustice to Mr. Finney and to yourself.'" {pg 18 Christian History}

So here we go again more divisions within the body of Christ and for what an argument over the means and modes of Christian Perfection? Isn't that something incredible!? Better that though I guess than over something like an adulterous affair with prostitutes and what not as we have come to see in the Charismatic Movement. If Asa Mahan and Charles Finney were around today they would be utterly dumbfounded if not traumatized by the goings on. Indeed to the degree that maybe their views would have changed some with the question of not whether 'one can look to Christ to be sanctified wholly or not' but rather why God's people especially and specifically those who are in leadership committing sin? In fact if that shouldn't be the answer to the question surrounding whether 'one can look to Christ to be sanctified wholly or not.' Surely that it seems to this writer anyway is the real issue and if it isn't one that is much on the mind of God and on His Son Christ Jesus as well. Remember those words of God from the Old Testament:

> *"See I have refined you, though not as silver; I have tested you in the furnace of affliction. For my own sake I do this. How can I let myself be defamed? I will not yield my glory to another."* {Isaiah 48: 10-11}

It is part and parcel of what we find written in the New Testament concerning discipline, isn't it?

> "And you have forgotten that word of encouragement that addresses you as sons: 'My son, do not make light of the Lord's discipline, and do not lose heart when He rebukes you, because the Lord disciplines those He loves, and He punishes everyone He accepts as a son.'
> Endure hardship as discipline; God is testing you as sons. For what son is not disciplined by his father? If you are not disciplined {and everyone undergoes discipline}, then you are illegitimate children and not true sons. Moreover, we have all had human fathers who disciplined us and we respected them for it. How much more should we submit to the Father of our spirits and live! Our fathers disciplined us for a

little while as they thought best; but God disciplines us for our good, that we may share in His holiness. No discipline seems pleasant at the time, but painful. Later on, however, it produces a harvest of righteousness and peace for those who have been trained by it." {Hebrews 12:5-11}

Now why neither Asa Mahan nor Charles Finney paid particular attention to this is really quite odd and yet if it doesn't have something to do with Calvinism! Calvinism, Calvinism? Truly if everything confusing about theology doesn't stem from the foundation of John Calvin. My word he should never have begun with predestination, but rather with the history and foreknowledge of God and an interesting quote sums it up quite succinctly this way:

"The enlightened spiritual mind will accept predestination as a result of the foreknowledge of God and not exclusive unconditional election." {Jay Atkinson www.latter-rain/theology/armen.com}

If there is one thing about the theology of God it is that He knows exactly how everything is going to unfold beforehand. If it isn't one of the enigmas about Almighty God as God Himself quite astonishingly declared through his prophets:

"*I am God, and there is no other; I am God, and there is none like me. I make known the end from the beginning, from ancient times, what is still to come. I say: My purpose will stand and I will do all that I please.*" {Isaiah 46:9-10}

It is something that was quite evident as well in Christ Jesus God's Son...

*"I have told you now before it happens, so that when
it does happen you will believe."* {John 14:29}

In the bible you will find that there exists an interesting
example of this by way of a people called Gog and Magog who
apparently are going to be destroyed by Almighty God and
the reason for it? Well according to what the book of Ezekiel
{38} and the book of Revelation {20} say it is because they
will look to attack the nation of Israel and this during peace-
able times. That is during or rather after the millennial reign
of Christ on this planet. That is not for another one thousand
years from our perspective and this significantly enough will
coincide with the release of Satan from his prison. {Rev.
20:7} So God it appears is in need of again testing a people
for their faith and obedience and if this doesn't take us back
to these words of His from the book of Jeremiah:

*"I the Lord search the heart and examine the mind,
to reward a man according to his conduct, according
to what his deeds deserve."* {Jeremiah 17:10}

Now what has this got to do with anything? Well, let's
ask ourselves did Almighty God 'predestine' this to happen?
No, that certainly can't be but rather 'foreknowing' what
they would do in disobeying Him and that at a time such as
this wherein Christ will be a living reality right before their
very eyes will be the ultimate of grave mistakes to make.
You see the issue here is not that they will attack the nation
of Israel per se as the reason for their destruction but rather
that they will have committed the ultimate of all treasonous
acts of sin against Almighty God. It will be a rebellion of the
most serious and dreadful kind. Delight yourself in the Lord
and in His Laws the scriptures teach {Ps. 1:2 & 37:11} and
why people don't is something that God always looks to get
to the bottom of! Accordingly where Calvinism is concerned

then if true therefore aren't the words of the late and great Arthur Wallis who wrote in that immortal book of his:

"It is a mistake to view the sovereignty of God, as some Calvinists seem to do, as the hub of the Deity, with all of God's other attribute's radiating like spokes from the hub. God's sovereignty {or ability to do what He wills} is clearly subordinate to His character of holiness and love. Because He is a moral being and has constituted man as a moral being, He cannot act without reference to His moral principles. Even a sovereign God cannot forgive the unrepentant or bless the disobedient.

Though man may be influenced from within and from without, God still holds him responsible for his moral choices. This is the consistent teaching of scripture, and we must not weaken the grasp on conscience that this provides by suggesting that since the fall man is no longer a free agent, no longer with a will of his own. This view, carried to its logical conclusion, not only has a tendency to absolve the unconverted person from his moral responsibility towards God, but by the same token to relieve the believer of his responsibility in terms of obedience and submission. Both could be tempted to take up a passive attitude and leave it to God who 'works all things according to the purpose of His will.'" {pg. 37-38 Wallis}

When St. Paul spoke to the Ephesians about election and predestination he makes an interesting statement:

"And you also were included in Christ when you heard the word of truth, the gospel of your salvation. Having believed, you were marked in him with a seal, the promised Holy Spirit, who is a deposit guaranteeing our inheritance until the redemption of those who are God's possession-to the praise of his glory." {Ephesians 1:13}

The key word here is 'having believed' which is a choice, isn't it? The issue therefore ultimately is one of submission. That and for some inexplicable reason the world is truly made up of two different kinds of individuals those who have the seeds of righteousness and faith within them and those who do not. {Cain & Abel for example} God therefore is simply the ultimate visionary and to look at what St. Paul further speaks about in the book of Thessalonians and won't it be shocking if not altogether frightening to see what will be left of the church Calvinist or otherwise when that rebellion occurs:

"Don't let anyone deceive you by any means for that day will not come until the rebellion occurs and the man of lawlessness is revealed, the man doomed to destruction." {2 Thessalonians 2:3-4}

Apparently it's not just about Gog and Magog and if they could so easily fall to the influences of Satan what does that say about what is happening today? Brings a whole new dimension doesn't it to those words from our brother St. Paul:

"Land that drinks in the rain often falling on it and that produces a crop useful to those for whom it is farmed receives the blessing of God. But land that produces thorns and thistles is worthless and is in danger of being cursed. In the end it will be burned." {Hebrews 6:7-8}

Accordingly election it appears isn't about God's choice so much as it is that which exists within our own hearts. It all begins with us doesn't it and if all of this doesn't bring to mind also these words of Christ Jesus concerning the wheat and the tares:

"The kingdom of heaven is like a man who sowed good seed in his field. But while everyone was sleeping, his enemy came and sowed weeds among the wheat, and went away. When the wheat sprouted and formed heads, then the weeds also appeared. The owner's servants came to him and said, 'Sir, didn't you sow good seed in your field? Where then did the weeds come from?' 'An enemy did this,' he replied. The servants asked him, 'Do you want us to go and pull them up?' No he answered, 'because while you are pulling up the weeds, you may root up the wheat with them. Let both grow together until the harvest. At that time I will tell the harvesters; First collect the weeds and tie them in bundles to be burned; then gather the wheat and bring it into my barn.'" {Matthew 13:24-30}

Wheat and tare's people, wheat and tares! Accordingly if the kingdom of God isn't a mixed multitude as Christ Jesus said. Now John Calvin where was his understanding of all of this? More significantly surely though is if only Asa Mahan had understood this along with bringing to the attention of others these words of Almighty God from the Old Testament:

"See I have refined you, though not as silver; I have tested you in the furnace of affliction. For my own sake I do this. How can I let myself be defamed? I will not yield my glory to another." {Isaiah 48:10-11}

I'm sure that he along with Charles Finney never would have been faced with the kind of onslaught against their perfectionist teaching. According to God's reputation and that of His Son perfection is exactly what they are after in our lives. Asa was right therefore in following what Christ said! "Be perfect, therefore, as your heavenly Father is perfect." {Matthew 5:48} Sadly however for Asa Mahan he apparently needed himself to come to a place of refinement. Like St. Paul it appears he could have used a thorn in the flesh to humble him a little and O if only!? If only for his Calvinistic ways and attitudes and that desire of his for a school that would be unmatched even for an Athens would have come to fruition. The world would have lived to see a Christianity unlike anything that either a Constantinople or a Rome could have ever envisioned especially over something like climate change. Imagine if only Asa Mahan and Charles Finney had understood what this book has to teach about climate change and the story and history of Oberlin if not America herself would have looked much different. Truly and look if what happened between these two men doesn't bring clarity to these words from the bible:

"Not many of you should presume to be teachers, my brothers, because you know that we who teach will be judged more strictly. We all stumble in many ways. If anyone is never at fault in what he says, he is a perfect man, able to keep his whole body in check." {James 3:1-2}

Wouldn't it be interesting to know what occurred with Asa Mahan and Charles Finney there in heaven before Christ Jesus? What would they have to say to each other with Jesus summoning both of them to give account for their stumbling ways? As for John Calvin well who cares! Isn't it enough that what after some 400 hundred years since his birth and we today in the church are still divided by this man's teaching? One would think that with our access to so much of the bible and that with just a few presses of a button {plug and play} and we today would be much farther ahead in our understanding of the bible. Truly don't we have anyone today who can explain the bible better than him? As for leadership well what pray tell about that? I mean where does the authority actually lie? Yes 'Sola Scriptura' may very well be the name of the game but look if one doesn't pay attention to all that it says and moreover makes mistakes as to its interpretation what pray tell are we to do? Again just take as an example Jim Bakker and the ridiculousness of his interpretations of the bible. His views of it were totally and completely wrong and look where it ended. Are we to follow that!? I would think certainly not and so again where does the authority lie? Then again if the answer doesn't lie in one simple and all important sentence which again comes from the bible:

"Anyone who welcomes him shares in his wicked work" {2 John 11}

Never ever will the blessings of Almighty God accompany the work of iniquity in whatever format it exists? To look at the church therefore or any religious movement for that matter and one has to ask the question *of who really is the called of God and who is not?* Certainly makes for some serious questions doesn't it especially if one applies the word Ichabod? Accordingly if Jesus wasn't right, "do not be deceived" {Luke 21:8} which ultimately means look well to what you are being told people and that by anyone and everyone. Indeed don't end up in the shoes of this particular writer who as a young Christian was so taken up in the things of Almighty God that he foolishly opened his wallet to the tune of a thousand dollars to support the work of some evangelist. An evangelist who just happened to be caught using a secret microphone to find out what people were hoping for from Almighty God and using that for his own purposes. It is something that I to this day still find really quite astounding for what a way to make a living for one self? It must take a great deal of courage if not outright stupidity to go about living one's life in the public eye like that? Moreover to find how such individuals go about using what God did through St. Paul with handkerchiefs and pieces of his clothing being used to heal and bless people is utterly unbelievable if not truly scandalous and deceiving. Doesn't anyone understand what the scripture say and mean when it says that God did such things through St. Paul -*meaning it wasn't for everyone including the very apostles who walked, lived and suffered with Christ.* {Acts 19:12} Remember St. Peter, St. John, St. Matthew, etc. etc. None of these men were used by God like that and they certainly wouldn't have gone around looking to copy the same. That would be like putting the cart before the horse. That would have been presumptuous on their part. Almighty God does not submit to us? Rather we are supposed to submit to Him! It is His choice ultimately what is to be done and through whom! Many of these so called evangelists today however, seem to think that they are in the same league as St. Paul. They think its okay for them to do the same and get this they don't stop there either! Rather they go even further by actually merchandising this by selling their own handkerchiefs and even holy water/oil with the promise that God will bless you? Holy water that came from of all places the Jordan River which is ludicrous to say the least given the scarcity of water in that land. The government of Israel along with her neighbors would be mortified to think and find people actually looking to bottle the water from the Jordan to sell it overseas. There isn't enough water for them there! So again what a presumption this is on the part of some who actually have the courage to put themselves in

257

league with St. Paul who was a saint! These people however are something altogether different surely!?

Getting back to Mahan and Finney though and how any of the Old Guard Calvinists if any that is are still around today could criticize and shake their heads at a Charles Finney or an Asa Mahan is really quite pathetic. Look like St. Paul before them the defense of their ministry could come done to what he said in the book of Hebrews:

> "God also testified to it by signs, wonders and various miracles, and gifts of the Holy Spirit distributed according to *his will*." {Hebrews 2:4}

No one can argue that God was on the side of Asa Mahan and Charles Finney. So again how any Old Guard Calvinists could shake their heads at them or their particular theology is quite incredible and wow if they haven't got some explaining to do. For to the utter disbelief of this writer I came to learn while taking a course at a Bible College that there are Calvinists who actually believe that the signs, wonders and miracles of God are no longer for today. What I said, how can that be? To that the teacher replied that for some the argument stands that they are no longer needed or neces-sary because the Revelation of God was made complete by the writing of the New Testament. The church therefore was no longer in need of any miracles but simply needed to pay attention to the scriptures and theology and what not. How convenient. Flabbergasted by this I for years have struggled with wondering how a church could believe this and of course if it doesn't come done to election and predestination. O good grief. Again it begins with us doesn't it? Calvinism, Calvinism and isn't the infighting among Christians over this one issue really pathetic? Since when was Jacob Arminius ever a threat to the faith? Look shouldn't our attention be drawn towards other more important battles like for example against the many cults that have arisen in our world? In fact, just take Freemasonry as an example which interestingly enough was what Charles Finney was engaged in? As a former member of that organization he came to see and learn of its dangers and what dangers would that be? http://www. isaiah54.org/finney.htm Well given its apparent political nature and its desire to amalgamate all of the religions of the world into a cohesive whole under the banner of the great architect whoever 'he is' is something that Satan will surely take full advantage of. We should all find it most disturbing that Christ Jesus is not the hero of their faith but rather a man named Hiram, one of the chief 'architects' and builders of King Solomon's Temple. Taking him as the foundation of their faith they along with the Jewish people are looking to rebuild that very temple in Jerusalem. A Temple and belief system of which they think is going to somehow usher in a utopian society for all of mankind. The history of it all is really quite a perplexing mess beginning apparently of all places with the formation under Roman Catholicism no less of the Knights Templar's. O good grief another Roman idea. More shocking however, was what was learned by way of a TV documentary on the Masonic Lodge and their sacred use of a word that revolves around 'here is the builder.' It actually sent shivers through me. What I thought to myself are these people actually looking and hoping for that 'someone' who will be able to rebuild King Solomon's Temple in the city of Jerusalem? If so watch out or rather look out for that is not going to go over well with the "great architect of the universe." That is not going to go over well at all as we have clearly seen. Remember that earthquake from May 20, 363 AD!!? Wow! Furthermore to learn that they refer to the divine being by way of an acronym that mixes the profane with the holy 'jahbulon' which is apparently a mix of the names Jehovah, Baal and Osiris is something truly and utterly unbelievable. Frightening actually! Don't these people understand that the bible calls this idolatry and what did the Creator do with those who were involved in such things? {Chapter 3}Understand that a Temple is irrelevant, Jesus of Nazareth having replaced it and its procedures with His own sacrifice! The temple was removed therefore from being located in some vicinity in the city of Jerusalem to or rather *within the human heart*. The Word of God makes this abundantly clear and that by way of the book of Corinthians specifically:

"For we are God's fellow workers; you are God's field, God's building. By the grace God has given me, I laid a foundation as an expert builder, and someone else is building on it. But each one should be careful how he builds. *For no one can lay any foundation other than the one already laid, which is Christ Jesus*. If any man builds on this foundation using gold, silver, costly stones, wood, hay or straw, his work will be shown for what it is, because the Day will bring it to light. It will be revealed with fire, and fire will test the quality of each man's work. If what he has built survives, he will receive his reward. If it is burned up, he will suffer loss; he himself will be saved, but only as one escaping through the flames. Don't you know that you yourselves are God's temple and that God's Spirit lives in you? If anyone destroys God's temple, God will destroy him; for God's temple is sacred, *and you are that temple*." {1Corinthians 3:3-17}

This is what the true religion of Almighty God is all about and if there are those who would balk at this well then perhaps what they should look at paying attention to is again earthquakes and/or better yet climate change. Look no one can argue that Almighty God was on the side of those who belonged to the work and teachings of John Wesley. That the

Swan Quarter Methodist Church proves out well enough. To find though that is also included the work and teachings of Asa Mahan and Charles Finney is surely even more fascinating and how utterly intriguing if not altogether important are the dates involved here. Asa Mahan 184? Charles Finney 1853. The Swan Quarter event 1876. Wow, what a fascinating God we serve.

WHAT A TRULY FASCIANTING GOD WE SERVE!!!

Where has the church been though all these years that they have failed to understand the great significance of all of this? Again looking for answers this writer has certainly been at a loss to understand it all. One thing though that does come across is how utterly divisive the church has and is and continues to be over such issues as Calvinism and a whole host of other theological issues as well. Actually looking into the history of the Methodist church fifty years after the death of its founder and leader and what do we find? Divisions! Methodism they actually broke up into different branches by arguing over the means and modes of Christian Perfection, Calvinism, Entire Sanctification, issues of slavery{which John Wesley bitterly opposed} etc. etc. etc. Astonishingly even John Wesley himself wasn't immune to the controversy of it all having between him and George Whitefield many heated debates and arguments over the issue of Calvinism. Now how utterly unbelievable is that? So is it any wonder then that a topic like Divine Communication and its relationship to the weather specifically as taught in the book of Job gets largely ignored? Things are changing though aren't they? Most certainly they are with these words of God surely being the most serious and dramatic:

> "See the storm of the Lord will burst out in wrath, a driving wind swirling down on the heads of the wicked. The fierce anger of the Lord will not turn back until He fully accomplishes the purposes of His heart. In days to come you will fully understand this." {Jeremiah 30:23-24}

If those days haven't ultimately come upon us now and with that we bring this chapter to a close? Oberlin, Oberlin though what happened to you, what happened to you? As for the rest of the church well wasn't St. Paul correct regarding that admonishment of his?

> "Keep watch over yourselves and all the flock of which the Holy Spirit has made you overseers. Be shepherds of the Church of God, which he bought with his own blood. I know that after I leave, savage wolves will come in among you and will not spare the flock. Even from your own number men will arise and distort the truth in order to draw away disciples after them. So be on your guard! Remember that for three years I never stopped warning each of you night and day with tears." {Acts 20:28-31}

With tears people, with tears!!!!

CHAPTER EIGHT

LEADERSHIP, LEADERSHIP!

Of all of the questions to plague mankind where religion is concerned and it would have to be the question of why are there so many different types of churches and religions. That and of course the question which one is the right one for me? Certainly from the perspective of this writer these are the two questions that have been constantly asked of him over the last 25 years. In fact, such has been the questioning that well I remember do a friend of mine who was having some serious problems with his fiancés parents. They were Protestants and he was of a Catholic background so the wedding for them was going to be held in their church. This of course though did not go well with his parents and so an argument ensued between everyone. The poor girl was reduced to tears and Dave knowing my faith at the time came seeking my counsel about all of this. What I gave him though was of little help and why is because though brought up a Roman Catholic I jumped ship for the Foursquare Church. So you see the predicament that everyone is in. Accordingly before we can move on in our study at looking at climate change from the religious perspective and what we need to do here is surely pause for a moment and consider this question of why are there so many different types of churches? Somewhere the confusion has to end doesn't it?

Shortly after the church was born and it began to grow throughout the Mediterranean world St. Paul was faced with a peculiar problem and that is leadership. What I mean by this is that as St. Paul travelled and visited the numerous churches under his care he began to see the development of divisions between established churches. It is something that he became quite concerned about and we can see this by way of what he wrote to the Corinthians on this particular matter:

"I appeal to you, brothers, in the name of our Lord Jesus Christ, that all of you agree with one another so that there be no divisions among you and that you may be perfectly united in mind and thought. My brothers, some from Chloe's household have informed me that there are quarrels among you. What I mean is this: One of you says, 'I follow Paul'; another, 'I follow Apollos'; another, 'I follow Cephas'; still another, 'I follow Christ.' Is Christ divided? Was Paul crucified for you? Were you baptized into the name of Paul? I am thankful that I did not baptize any of you except Crispus and Gaius, so no one can say that you were baptized into my name. {Yes, I also baptized the household of Stephanas; beyond that, I don't remember if I baptized anyone else.} For Christ did not send me to baptize, but to preach the gospel-not with words of human wisdom, lest the cross of Christ be emptied of its power." {1Corinthinas 1:10-17}

Apparently what we find today in the world of religion with all of its divisions is nothing really knew for St. Paul was himself faced with the same kind of dilemma. In fact just replace the names of Paul, Cephas, Apollos with names like Luther, Roman Catholicism, Foursquare, Southern Baptist and what not and what you have is a rather remarkable comparison between the two ages. You will even find people today who like those with St. Paul are actually going around saying that they belong to and follow no one but Christ? It is something really quite astounding and for St. Paul it was quite ridiculous and even wrong and how did he deal with it? Well of course by trying to teach these people first and foremost that Christ is not divided. Being Jewish that certainly would have had great meaning for him, indeed to the degree that if his nation had accepted Christ they would never have divided Him up into belligerent sects as the Gentiles have done. A family is a family no matter what the size of a nation is. So for St. Paul the ridiculousness of such divisions was evidence that they lacked knowledge in the things of Christ and religion and how does he go about trying to heal the rifts as it were? Well he begins by first explaining the peculiarity surrounding Christ and His gospel:

> "For the message of the cross is foolishness to those who are perishing, but to us who are being saved it is the power of God. For it is written:
> 'I will destroy the wisdom of the wise; the intelligence of the intelligent I will frustrate.'
> Where is the wise man? Where is the scholar? Where is the philosopher of this age? Has not God made foolish the wisdom of the world? For since in the wisdom of God the world through its wisdom did not know him, God was pleased through the foolishness of what was preached to save those who believe. Jews demand miraculous signs and Greeks look for wisdom, but we preach Christ crucified; a stumbling block to Jews and foolishness to Gentiles, but to those whom God has called, both Jews and Greeks, Christ the power of God and the wisdom of God. For the foolishness of God is wiser than man's wisdom, and the weakness of God is stronger than man's strength." {1Corinthians 1:18-25}

Here we find that of all of the different kinds of knowledge and philosophies that exist in the world the one that supersedes everything it is Christ Jesus. Accordingly that is where everything begins and ends! He then goes on to explai:

> "Brothers, think of what you were when you were called. Not many of you were wise by human standards; not many were influential; not many were of noble birth. But God chose the foolish things of the

world to shame the wise; God chose the weak things of the world to shame the strong. He chose the lowly things of this world and the despised things-and the things that are not-to nullify the things that are, so that no one may boast before him. It is because of him that you are in Christ Jesus, who has become for us wisdom, from God-that is, our righteousness, holiness and redemption. Therefore, as it is written: 'Let him who boasts boast in the Lord.'" {1Corinthians 1:26-31}

When it comes to leadership St. Paul says the issue is not about us but about the one who calls us and empowers us for service. Accordingly therefore whatever we are and whoever we are it is because of Christ and His gifts ultimately. To set oneself up against another and so forth therefore is not a very wise or smart thing to do nor is it proper to go about boasting. Selfishness with God is not part of the game here, so whatever boasting does occur it had better be done in Christ that is in what Christ has done for the particular individual. However, having said that though it appears that there could come a time in some leader's lives where such boasting can have its own detrimental effects as evidenced by what St. Paul said to the Corinthians when defending his own ministry:

"To keep me from becoming conceited because of these surpassing great revelations, there was given to me a thorn in my flesh, a messenger of Satan, to torment me. Three times, I pleaded with the Lord to take it away from me. But he said to me, 'My grace is sufficient for you, for my power is made perfect in weakness.' Therefore I will boast all the more gladly about my weaknesses, so that Christ's power may rest on me. That is why, for Christ's sake, I delight in weaknesses, in insults, in hardships, in persecutions, in difficulties. For when I am weak, then I am strong." {2 Corinthians 12:7}

Apparently for some particular leaders the work and gifts of God in ones life can become such that it could lead a person to think of oneself more than they ought and for St. Paul that it appears became true. Just goes to show and prove how truly insidious this whole nature of sin really is within the human heart of mankind and the difficulty of trying to bring it under control. Like a weed it always makes its presence known. That is no doubt why we find St. Paul saying that he enjoys the weaker times because that is when God's power becomes most manifest of all. It is in those times that the presence of Christ really comes through. It is what the Christian life ultimately depends upon! Now as for him being conceited well certainly at the beginning of his ministry that could have been the case given his enormous education and learning and how it put him almost immediately above the other apostles.

"Paul was the only scholar among the apostles... Peter and John had natural genius, but no scholastic education; Paul had both, and thus became the founder of Christian theology and philosophy." {Pg. 228 Schaff}

That and of course his apparent need for a thorn! Humbleness, I don't think though was ever really a problem for St. Paul. Leadership however was even for him a difficulty as evidenced by what happened to him with the Corinthians. That is no doubt why in the next part of his discourse with the issue of divisions he says this:

"When I came to you, brothers, I did not come with eloquence or superior wisdom as I proclaimed to you the testimony about God. For I resolved to know nothing while I was with you except Jesus Christ and him crucified. I came to you in weakness and fear, and with much trembling. {go to Acts 18:9 for an interesting insight on this} My message and my preaching were not with wise and persuasive words, but with a demonstration of the Spirit's power, so that your faith may not rest on men's wisdom, but on God's power." {1 Corinthians 2:1-5}

Here we find an interesting statement that surely goes to the very heart of everything! Faith for St. Paul was never something that was too based upon just mere words but with an actual demonstration of the Spirit's power. For him fighting the fight of faith was never about having the best sermon or the most and better education but rather with a demonstration of God's power. In fact, it appears the last thing that God ever wanted was for His people to base everything upon just words. "For the kingdom of God is not a matter of talk but of power?" {1 Corinthians 4:20} How sad and unfortunate it is though that this is what it has more or less come down too in so much of religion today. Faith seems to rest on just that- words, words and more words. Scripture gets quoted, gets taken out of context, gets distorted etc. etc. etc. As for Christ well He is more or less presented as just some kind of a philosophy that needs to be studied and poked for truth. The Christian life however is not about this but rather it is all about having a "spirit of power, of love and of self-discipline." {2 Timothy 1:7} It is what makes the Christian life so exciting and on this point I would like too mention something that happened to me regarding the power of God. However, before we go there it would be helpful to continue for a moment with what St. Paul next says in his discourse:

"We do, however, speak a message of wisdom among the mature, but not the wisdom of this age or of the rulers of this age, who are coming to nothing. No, we speak of God's secret wisdom, a wisdom that has been hidden and that God destined for our glory before time began. None of the rulers of this age understood it, for if they had, they would not have crucified the Lord of glory. However, as it is written:

'No eye has seen, no ear has heard, no mind has conceived what God has prepared for those that love Him.'
but God has revealed it to us by his Spirit. The Spirit searches all things, even the deep things of God. For who among men knows the thoughts of a man except the man's spirit within him? In the same way no one knows the thoughts of God except the Spirit of God. We have not received the spirit of the world but the Spirit who is from God, that we may understand what God has freely given us. This is what we speak, not in words taught us by human wisdom but in words taught by the Spirit, expressing spiritual truths in spiritual words. The man without the Spirit does not accept the things that come from God, for they are foolishness to him, and he cannot understand them, because they are spiritually discerned. The spiritual man makes judgments about all things, but he himself is not subject to any man's judgment:
'For who has known the mind of the Lord that he may instruct him?'
But we have the mind of Christ." {1Corinthians 2:6-16}

Here St. Paul continues by making a distinction between the carnal and spiritual nature by saying simply that when it comes to the work of God it cannot really be understood apart from the work of the Spirit of God in ones life. For St. Paul everything goes back to and depends upon the posses- sion of this blessed Spirit of God's in ones life. It is some- thing that even the other Apostles of Christ were themselves well aware of and constantly emphasized as well:

> "I am writing these things to you about those who are trying to lead you astray. As for you, the anointing you received from him remains in you, and you do not need anyone to teach you. But as his anointing teaches you about all things and as that anointing is real, not counterfeit-just as it has taught you, remain in him." {1John 2:26-27}

Basically St. John is saying the same thing here as St. Paul is trying to get across and that is this need for the Spirit of God in ones life and if this ultimately doesn't reveal some important insights as to why there are so many divisions within the Christian Church. I mean look with all of the divi- sions and doesn't it appear that for many this Spirit of God is missing within many of our leaders? Certainly it appears that way doesn't it with our last chapter surely providing more than enough proof of it all and if all that wasn't enough well then consider these intriguing testimonies. First concerning one Dr. Francis C. Lembke a professor in Strasborg and assistant preacher in the Church of St. Peter:

> "The more he prepared his sermons, the less warmth and life they had. Of this he was himself keenly conscious. His congregations decreased every Sunday until at last he preached to empty benches. He felt that he was not fitted for the pulpit, and on one occasion became so utterly discouraged while preparing, that he secured a substitute for the next day, late on Saturday night. He now made his

preaching the subject of special prayer, beseeching the Lord, either to relieve him of this duty, or loose his tongue and give him grace to proclaim the gospel. The wonderful answer to these prayers we will set forth in Lembke's own words: 'One day, when I entered the pulpit in great fear, crying for aid, the Lord suddenly spoke to me His omnipotent word Ephphatha.' Pentecostal power was given to me, and to the astonishment of my hearers as well as my own, I proclaimed the free grace of God in Christ with an overflowing heart and with utmost freedom of speech.'

From that day he preached sermons that caused a sensation throughout the city. The Church of St. Peter was crowded, whenever he appeared in the pulpit. In a little while the aisles and even the pulpit steps were filled with hearers, until the building could not contain the multitude which flocked together." {pg. 88-89 Greenfield}

Then to a Dr. Samuel Chadwick, of Cliff College, England:

"I have written and preached much on the Holy Spirit, for the knowledge of Him has been the most vital fact of my experience. I owe everything to the gift of Pentecost. ***I came across a prophet, heard a testimony, and set out to seek I knew not what. I knew that it was a bigger thing and a deeper need than I had ever known. It came along the line of duty, and I entered in through a crisis of obedience. When it came I could not explain what had happened, but I was aware of things unspeakable and full of glory. Some results were immediate. There came into my soul a deep peace, a thrilling joy, and a new sense of power. My mind was quickened. I felt that I had received a new faculty of understanding. Every power was alert. Either illumination took the place of logic, or reason became intuitive. My bodily powers also were quickened. There was a new sense of spring and vitality, a new power of endurance, and a strong man's exhilaration in big things. Things began to happen. What we had failed to do by strenuous endeavor came to pass without labor. It was as when the Lord Jesus stepped into the boat that with all their rowing had made no progress; immediately the ship was at the land whither they went. It was gloriously wonderful" {ibid pg. 56}

So working under their own power and understanding and reading of the scriptures too many have all but confused themselves and everyone else with their interpretations. In fact look wasn't it something that St. Paul was himself afflicted with given his persecution of 'the Way' in the days before Christ finally got a hold of him? He misunderstood everything about Almighty God and so is it any wonder then that he would go about placing such an emphasis here upon this need for the Spirit of God within the believer. If he needed this blessed Spirit with his enormous learning and education then certainly everyone else was as well and so if that doesn't go to show and prove that something has gone wrong terribly, terribly wrong with the entire Christian Church? Most certainly and as St. Paul continues on with his discourse how does he next deal with it all? Well he goes on by saying this:

"Brothers, I could not address you as spiritual but as worldly-mere infants in Christ. I gave you milk, not solid food, for you were not yet ready. Indeed, you are still not ready. You are still worldly. For since there is jealously and quarreling among you, are you not acting like mere men? For when one says, 'I follow Paul,' and another, 'I follow Apollos.' are you not mere men?

What after all is Apollos? And what is Paul? Only servants, through whom you came to believe-as the Lord has assigned to each his task." {1Corinthians 3:1-5}

Here St. Paul makes an interesting analogy to milk and why that of all things? Well, if it isn't because the issue of learning and education is such a difficult and complex process that it often takes an enormous amount of repetitive work to get across the message of the bible to its hearers. Just look at what happened to Christ and how He was constantly found saying to His disciples:

"Are you still so dull?" {Matthew15:16}

"Do you still not see or understand?"{Mark 8:17 &21}

"Why is my language not clear to you?" {John 8:43}

We never learn do we? Nope hardly ever and if it isn't something that can be altogether maddening when you consider what St. Paul further mentions on this some time later to another group of people:

"We have much to say about this, but it is hard to explain because you are slow to learn. In fact, though by this time you ought to be teachers, you need someone to teach you the elementary truths of God's word all over again. You need milk not solid food.

Anyone who lives on milk, being still an infant, is not acquainted with the teaching about righteousness. But solid food is for the mature, who by constant use have trained themselves to distinguish good from evil." {Hebrews 5:11-14}

Slow learners all aren't we? Indeed we are and if this isn't why we find in the Old Testament that admonishment about 'here a little, and there a little.' {Isa. 28:10} We need to take things slowly don't we and so you see how the analogy works? We like babes need to be fed the word of God like babes do their milk and if on this point I haven't got an astounding testimony to share here. A testimony that reflects exactly upon what St. Paul said earlier about our faith being placed not on men's wisdom but upon the power of God.

It occurred when I was just a mere 18 years old and at a time in my life wherein I was seeking some truth regarding the Church and Christ. You see at that time I was full of animosity towards the church if not everything religious being brought up the way I was and that as a Catholic. Even those who knew me from school knew that I would be the last one ever to step into a church though I did have a belief about Christ nevertheless. This however didn't prevent some Christians from the local Foursquare Gospel Church from trying to minister to me the gospel of Christ. I was amused but listened to them anyway and eventually told them that though I believed in Christ I wanted nothing to do with them or church. One of their group though didn't give up on me and after a few weeks of getting to know each other we ended up praying together after which Jim then told me that I should find a church to begin attending. To that I of course had a great deal of trouble with and told him after much consternation look if God does indeed exist He can show me Himself whether I needed to go to church and/or for that matter which one I should attend. To that I also muttered to myself why moreover could He explain to me why are there so many different types of churches? I was myself filled with the questions of the why of so many different types of churches and what not and so began my search. It was a search though that unlike most people didn't revolve around going to a priest or the bible for answers but rather I took the matter to God Himself in prayer. I thought that if God does indeed exist He can show me and answer me Himself and so I pursued God in prayer for my answers, prayer that didn't last for just a couple of minutes but rather took many hours over many, many days. Actually it took about five weeks in fact after which I was asked if I would like to attend a Wednesday night church service. It was a bible study night and to this I said yes but was quite apprehensive. I found the courage to go though and upon arriving at the Foursquare Church I found myself sitting among a small group and after some singing the Pastor, one Ross Fox stood up and to my astonishment began to teach upon this subject of why are there so many different types of churches and what not. I thought it quite strange that of all of the things to be hearing it was a message concerning the very things I was praying about! I sat there quite intrigued by what I was hearing concerning the why of so many different types of churches and denominations and then to my utter surprise this Pastor Ross Fox bless his memory reads this from chapter three as we saw earlier but worth noting again:

> "Brothers, I could not address you as spiritual but as worldly-mere infants in Christ. I gave you milk, not solid food, for you were not yet ready. Indeed, you are still not ready. You are still worldly. For since there is jealously and quarreling among you, are you not acting like mere men? For when one says, 'I follow Paul,' and another, 'I follow Apollos.' are you not mere men?

What after all is Apollos? And what is Paul? Only servants, through whom you came to believe-as the Lord has assigned to each his task." {1Corinthians 3:1-5}

To this my attention was now riveted to this Pastor and to this message and why is because all I was eating and drinking for the last five weeks was milk! Now you have to understand here I hated milk with a passion. I wouldn't touch the stuff let alone even look at it and here I was drinking it by the glass full's? At the time I didn't think much of it and a waitress at work said to me that I probably needed some calcium. Sitting here in Church however and seeing and hearing this come from the bible by Pastor Ross Fox left me with an astounding answer to prayer. It was as though God was literally speaking to me as it were through this man and the bible. I was dumbfounded! Almighty God in looking to answer my questions brought to pass a fascinating and unique way of doing it. He used milk of all things to communicate to me and why milk? Well, because as we saw it represents an analogy of the way things are between us and the Word of God. Milk is for infants and so God accordingly fed me His words as a parent would and does their own children. I was astounded and do you know if this desire to drink milk didn't begin almost to the day that I began to seek God for answers. Wow, I thought to myself, this is something fantastic and after church I shared this with my friend and guess what he told me. Well, Jerry I believe that message was directly and explicitly for you because to the surprise of everyone Pastor Fox never changes or jumps around from a particular message or study of the bible mid way until he finishes it. We were supposed to be in the book of Ephesians tonight not Corinthians! At that I smiled and wondered later to myself what the pastor must have been going through for doing this. Did he realize or rather recognize God's Spirit working within him that night? If not just wait till this man hears about my story I mumbled to myself on my way home.

Wow, and so with that then I made my choice that the Foursquare Church would become my church home. Let me tell you that though this was an easy transition for me to make personally it caused me a great deal of grief and pain and why is because of family. Indeed after I decided to get baptized my mother was livid with me for having thrown away as it were our families faith. In fact, after reflecting over what I did she screamed at me; I would never do something like that! Don't you understand you spit on our families name and history! Don't ever let your father find out about what you did for he will give you a beating! Even my brother got into the act by threatening to find those responsible and beat them as well. I argued back that Jesus now lives in my heart and no one is going to take that away from me. Some time later too as I began to reflect over this I wondered why God would choose to use someone from the Foursquare Church rather than someone from the Roman Catholic denomination to speak to me the way He did. It is something that after some 25 years I still have no answers to and whatever the case may be one thing just continues and that is how this change of mine has continued to be a struggle between all of us and though my family has accepted my change of heart and faith as it were there have been some trying times. Like for example when I travelled with my mom back to Slovenia and Croatia her homeland she made it quite clear to me not to engage our family there with religious preaching or talk. More heart breaking however is what occurred at the funeral of my father which of course was held in the Catholic Church. To my surprise my sister had sought counsel from the priest there and poured out her heart to him concerning everything about our family's history including my change of churches. At that the priest said to her not to worry that I would eventually return. At the funeral I became well aware of peoples distaste for what I had done and when my family went up for communion I followed but was refused communion and the look on the priests face was well, I shall never forget it. Later when I spoke to my mother on this she looked at me and said it was because of the way you folded your arms which meant that you were only looking for a blessing from God and not being in communion with Him. At this I later realized no wonder the priest glared at me the way he did, the very thought that here stood a man who walks away from the church and now here he was wanting me to bless him. It was like an insult to him. Moreover to think that here stood a convert to Protestantism and he's looking to receive the bread and wine from me? Later when I was alone and in tears and angry I thought to myself wow if only they knew what God has done in my life. If only they really knew everything and get this no matter how much I try to tell them about what God has done it just doesn't register or sink in! Culture and pride I guess really does take precedence over the work of God and the bible and so if all of this didn't bring me back to this issue of divisions. Yes I said to myself if divisions are going to cause problems anywhere it is going to be within families. In fact looking at what others are going through and what I have become increasingly aware of is that churches are going to be faced with some serious and difficult problems if their not already. Immigration is changing everything where one's culture and practices are concerned. Like for example what I have witnessed working with the Greek people. Being immigrants as my parents were their sons and daughters are now looking to marry and to try and keep things the way they are culturally and religiously they are being forced to marry within their own kind. This for some though is not very conducive to their well being or happiness and many are marrying others thus bringing into the church a mixed bag so to speak. Now of course this can all be solved readily enough by simply paying attention to what St. Paul had to say on the subject:

"Do not be yoked together with unbelievers. For what do righteousness and wickedness have in common? Or what fellowship can light have with darkness? What harmony is there between Christ and Belial? What does a believer have in common with an unbeliever? What agreement is there between the temple of God and idols? For we are the temple of the living God. As God had said: 'I will live in them and walk among them and I will be their God, and they will be my people.'
'Therefore come out from among them and be separate, says the Lord. Touch no unclean thing, and I will receive you. I will be a father to you, and you will be my sons and daughters, says the Lord Almighty." {2 Corinthians 6:14-18}

How many do you find though are really taking their faith and relationship to God this seriously? Accordingly how these old historic churches in particular are going to deal with this is none to important especially in view of the theological issues. For some of their sons and daughters are marrying those who have little to no faith as well as marrying those of entirely different religious views and backgrounds altogether. {Just go and mention the Jehovah's Witnesses to the Greek Orthodox Fathers and see what kind of response you will be in for} Now how this mixed bag is going to affect the church is surely causing many of their leaders to become quite concerned. Multiculturalism may be a wonderful thing in one way but on the other hand it will and is leading to the dissolution entirely of ones own culture. As for religious faith well people I find are more or less just ignoring and or throwing it aside altogether and why is because they simply can't be bothered to deal with it. Emotional speaking it has become a bone of contention. Theologically speaking it opens a can of worms. So everyone is lost as it were and if all of this doesn't bring me back to these teachings of St. Paul. It is why these particular chapters from the bible are so important to me and why I have chosen to spend an entire chapter on the subject and look what you are learning here comes from a man never having had any formal education in biblical theology or for that matter a graduate from any bible college or seminary. What I learned I learned from God Himself and of course by way of His servant Ross Fox and if true haven't therefore been these words of St. Paul or rather Almighty God's to me.

"My message and my preaching were not with wise and persuasive words, but with a demonstration of the Spirit's power, so that your faith may not rest on men's wisdom, but on God's power." {1Corinthians 2:1-5}

Milk! Imagine Almighty God used something as mundane as milk to speak to me and teach me. Accordingly you see how faith then was never meant to be just about words, words and more words but rather with a demonstration of the Spirit's power and believe me that is where my faith lies. It doesn't nor will it ever lie in or around the persona of individuals no matter how gifted they supposedly are from God. Look that is just so ridiculous and even childish as St. Paul clearly teaches and no doubt even dangerous given how it can and does lead to the formation of cults. In fact just take a look at the victims of the polygamous communities who are bound under terrible and bizarre circumstances and that to so-called prophets of God. Wow, do we ever need to be careful and if ever we truly needed the work of the Holy Spirit of God in our lives and churches it is surely us today along with unity of course. How though is this possibly going to be accomplished? Well with St. Paul that of course began first with an understanding of why these divisions occurred in the first place and as he begins to conclude that message of his he says this:

"For since there is jealously and quarreling among you, are you not acting like mere men? For when one says, 'I follow Paul,' {Foursquare} and another, 'I follow Apollos.' {Roman Catholicism} are you not mere men? What, after all, is Apollos? And what is Paul? Only servants, through whom you came to believe-as the Lord has assigned to each his task. I planted the seed, Apollos watered it, but God made it grow. So neither he who plants nor he who waters is anything, but only God, who makes things grow. The man who plants and the man who waters have one purpose, and each will be rewarded according to his labor. For we are God's fellow workers; you are God's field, God's building. By the grace God has given me, I laid a foundation as an expert builder, and someone else is building on it. But each one should be careful how he builds. For no one can lay any foundation other than the one already laid, which is Christ Jesus. If any man builds on this foundation using gold, silver, costly stones, wood, hay or straw, his work will be shown for what it is, because the Day will bring it to light. It will be revealed with fire, and fire will test the quality of each man's work. If what he has built survives, he will receive his reward. If it is burned up, he will suffer loss; he himself will be saved, but only as one escaping through the flames. Don't you know that you your-selves are God's temple and that God's Spirit lives in you? If anyone destroys God's temple, God will destroy him; for God's temple is sacred, and you are that temple." {1Corinthians 3:3-17}

And...

"Do not go beyond what is written. Then you will not take pride in one man over against another. For who makes you different from anyone else? What do you have that you did not receive? And if you did receive it, why then do you boast as though you did not?" {1 Corinthians 4:6-7}

So here is the answer to everything. Mankind is simply a victim of their own desires when it comes to leadership and if this doesn't explain the entire history of the Christian Church if not every single religious cult that exist out there as well! Unfortunately men have looked at the church as being *their work and not God's and have accordingly tried to control it!* They have therefore misjudged everything about the way in which the Church is supposed to function especially where the gifts of God are concerned. Going beyond what was written mankind has filled the church with all kinds of manmade ideas and nonsense. Following the example of the world they have all but forgotten what is taught in the Word of God. Like for example the very words of Christ Jesus. Words that Christ spoke after watching his disciples interestingly enough debate and argue among themselves about which one of them was going to be the greatest:

"The kings of the Gentiles lord it over them, and those who exercise authority over them call themselves Benefactors. But you are not to be like that. Instead, the greatest among you should be like the youngest, and the one who rules like the one who serves. For who is greater, the one who is at the table or the one who serves? Is it not the one who is at the table? But I am among you as one who serves. You are those who have stood by me in my trials. And I confer on you a kingdom, just as my Father conferred one on me, so that you may eat and drink at my table in my kingdom and sit on thrones, judging the twelve tribes of Israel." {Luke 22:24-32}

And...

"When he had finished washing their feet, he put on his clothes and returned to his place, 'Do you understand what I have done? He asked them. You call me Teacher and Lord, and rightly so, for that is what I am. Now that I, your Lord and Teacher, have washed your feet, you also should wash one another's feet. I have set you an example that you should do as I have done for you. I tell you the truth, no servant is greater than his master, nor is a messenger greater than the one who sent him. Now that you know these things, you will be blessed if you do them." {John 13:12-17}

If this doesn't explain everything as well! With Almighty God things are truly the direct opposite of what they are in the world. Power wasn't to be used for ones own benefit or yet to rule {lord it over} people but to serve. This is the crux of everything! That and of course the possession of God's gifts which is the result of our being baptized into that Spirit. By all accounts it appears though that many in the Church do not have this Spirit, nor are looking or even care to have him within their lives. If they did then surely we would be witnessing the result of it by way of what St. Paul again spoke about:

'When He ascended on high, he led captives in his train and gave gifts to men.'" {Ephesians 4:1-8}

{What does 'he ascended mean except that he also descended to the lower, earthly regions? He who descended is the very one who ascended higher than all of the heavens, in order to fill the whole universe.} It was he who gave some to be apostles, some to be prophets, some to be evangelists, and some to be pastors and teachers, to prepare God's people for works of service, so that the body of Christ may be built up until we all reach the unity of the faith and in the knowledge of the Son of God and become mature, attaining to the whole measure of the fullness of Christ.

Then we will no longer be infants, tossed back and forth by the waves, and blown here and there by every wind of teaching and by the cunning and craftiness of men in their deceitful scheming. Instead, speaking the truth in love, we will in all things grow up into him who is the Head that is Christ. From him the whole body, joined and held together by every supporting ligament, grows and builds itself up in love, as each part does its work." {Ephesians 4:9-16}

Here we find how Almighty God never wanted his people to be nothing but hearers and followers. Rather everyone has a part to play in one way or another. That is everyone in some aspect or another was to fulfill the role of the priesthood. Again though going beyond what was written mankind has filled the church with all kinds of nonsense. Becoming selective in what they wanted to believe about God and the bible they have all but thrown the baby out with the bath water so to speak. So truly if something hasn't gone wrong!

If something hasn't gone terribly, terribly wrong with the entire Christian Church in this whole world of ours. Now of course it goes much, much farther than just this alone for one cannot forget about the other side of the coin to all of this and that is the matter of Satan. That fallen angel who as an enemy of God has looked to try and destroy the Church of God by any means necessary. In fact if divide and conquer hasn't been one of his most useful weapons and how did he accomplish that? Well as many of the New Testament writers have warned about by infiltrating the church:

First by way of St. Peter...

"But there were also false prophets among the people, just as there will be false teachers among you. They will secretly introduce destructive heresies, even denying the sovereign Lord, who bought them-bringing swift destruction on themselves. Many will follow their shameful ways and will bring the way of truth into disrepute. In their greed these teachers will exploit you with stories they have made up. Their condemnation has long been hanging over them, and their destruction has not been sleeping."{2 Peter 2:1-3}

"His letters contain some things that are hard to understand, which ignorant and unstable people distort, as they do the other Scriptures, to their own destruction." {2 Peter 3:16}

St. John...

"Dear friends, do not believe every spirit, but test the spirits to see whether they are from God, because many false prophets have gone out into the world.

This is how you can recognize the Spirit of God: Every spirit that acknowledges that Jesus Christ has come in the flesh is from God, but every spirit that does not acknowledge Jesus is not from God. This is the spirit of the antichrist, which you have heard is coming and even now is already in the world. You, dear children, are from God and have overcome them, because the one who is in you is greater than the one who is in the world. They are from the world and therefore speak from the viewpoint of the world, and the world listens to them. We are from God, and whoever knows God listens to us; but whoever is not from God does not listen to us. This is how we recognize the Spirit of truth and the spirit of falsehood" {1 John 4:1-6}

"Dear children, this is the last hour; and as you have heard that the antichrist is coming, even now many antichrists have come. This is how we know it is the last hour. They went out from us, but they did not really belong to us. For if they had belonged to us, they would have remained with us; but their going showed that none of them belonged to us" {1 John 2:18-19}

St. Jude...

"For certain men whose condemnation was written about long ago have secretly slipped in among you. They are godless men, who change the grace of our God into license for immorality and deny Jesus Christ our only sovereign and Lord." {Jude 4}

And St. Paul…

"Evidently some people are throwing you into confusion and are trying to pervert the gospel of Christ. But even if we or an angel from heaven should preach a gospel other than the one we preached to you, let him be eternally condemned! As we have already said, so now I say again: If anybody is preaching to you a gospel other than what you accepted, let him be eternally condemned!" {Galatians 1:7-9}

"If anyone teaches false doctrine and does not agree to the sound instruction of our Lord Jesus Christ and to godly teaching, he is conceited and understands nothing. He has an unhealthy interest in controversies and quarrels about words that result in envy, strife, malicious talk, evil suspicions and constant friction between men of corrupt mind, who have been robbed of the truth and who think that godliness is a means to financial gain." {1Timothy 6:3-5}

"For if someone comes to you and preaches a Jesus other than the Jesus we preached, or if you receive a different spirit from the one you received, or a different gospel from the one you accepted, you put up what with it easily enough….For such men are false apostles, deceitful workman, masquerading as apostles of Christ. And no wonder, for Satan himself masquerades as an angel of light. It is not surprising, then, if his servants masquerade as servants of righteousness. Their end will be what their actions deserve." {2 Corinthians 11:4 & 13 to 15}

Now wow do you think that the Church of Christ is stuck between a rock and a hard place or what? No wonder we are in so much conflict and divided as we are and so full of scandals to boot. What we are up against from both respects is something unbelievable and given what we have seen over the last few decades specifically and do we find or is there any response from the Spirit of Almighty God, that great counselor and comforter to help us to deal with it all? Or are we to just use the scriptures to beat each other over the head with it all? Well that can't be and one need only look at a message like Anton Sawyer's - Ichabod or Revival {page 332} to see the truth of it! There you will find how Almighty God spoke about sending preachers and teachers to warn His people about the dangers of what was happening and for this particular writer if one of those teachers didn't revolve around the work and teachings of the late Dr. Walter Martin? That Southern Baptist Pentecostal theologian was one of the few leaders in the North American Church sent from God to try and deal with all of the issues plaguing the church. No one I don't think was more divinely inspired by God to deal with the many issues facing the church during the 1980's and early 1990's. It wasn't just about education and what not in his case but rather the Holy Spirit empowered him to undertake Christ's work. Vilified was he though by not only those within his own convention but especially by those within the Charismatic Movement who thought of themselves as being the called of God? My how that turned out to be a joke and if that doesn't bring to mind something that God did to me. It occurred late one afternoon when I was about to sit down for dinner when my mind became flooded with some scriptures from St. Paul. It was a message that so penetrated my mind that I literally memorized the gist of it in what the space of about ten seconds. Not only that but I couldn't eat dinner because of it; the desire for the word of God having taken away from me at that moment the pangs of hunger. Opening a bible instead it was as though I had received an entire sermon on the subject and what was it that I was given by God? Well the context of it came from 1 Corinthians 6:1-11 which speaks about Christians suing each other:

"If any of you has a dispute with another, dare he take it before the ungodly for judgment instead of before the saints? Do you not know that the saints will judge the world? And if you are to judge the world, are you not competent to judge trivial cases? Do you not know that we will judge angels? How much more the things of this life? Therefore, if you have disputes about such matters, appoint as judges even men of little account in the church! I say this to shame you. Is it possible that there is nobody among you wise enough to judge between believers? But instead, one brother goes to law against another-and this in front of unbelievers! The very fact that you have lawsuits among you means you have been completely defeated already. Why not rather be wronged? Why not rather be cheated? Instead, you yourselves cheat and do wrong, and you do this to your own brothers. Do you not know that the wicked will not inherit the kingdom of God? Do not be deceived: Neither the sexually immoral, nor idolaters, nor adulterers nor, nor male prostitutes, nor homosexual offenders, nor thieves, nor the greedy, nor drunkards, nor slanderers, nor swindlers will inherit the kingdom of god. And that was what some of you were. But you were washed, you were sanctified, you were justified in the name of the Lord Jesus Christ and by the Spirit of our God."

Being spoon fed again by Almighty God it was a message that I mulled and reflected over for a few days after which I then took it to my Pastor to ask why would God do this to me and he just shrugged his shoulders? A few days later though as I sat down to watch some evening news and what were the headlines of the day? Jimmy Swaggart, Jim Bakker, Marvin Gorman, Oral Roberts etc, etc, etc. Wow, I said to myself, now I perhaps know why! God apparently wanted me to know something about all of this from His words and for me it became something even more incredible and significant. For after travelling to Montgomery, Alabama for a prayer conference under the leadership of a dear lady named Dr. Mary Stewart Relfe I was given a most astonishing and blessed experience. For to my utter shock and surprise she asked me to join her on an evening television program where I would speak about this. She took the first 45 minutes speaking on true revival and I the last 15 on this issue of law suits among the churched. It was something that I will never forget and indeed will always treasure. In fact after returning home guess what I came across? Yet another newscast except this time it had something to do with Tammy Fay actually wanting to get the proceedings removed from the courts of the state and into the courts of the church? What I said wondering to myself, was she watching my episode with Dr. Relfe and thought that a prudent thing to do? Now the State of course wasn't about to allow that to occur given what happened and the enormous amount of money involved. So again my word if something hasn't gone wrong? If something hasn't gone terribly, terribly wrong with the entire Christian Church in North America if not the entire world and look if this doesn't bring to mind or take us back to the teachings from the book of Job. Again isn't character the name of the game? Remember how our actions can affect God and His reputation and that when it comes to His Son Christ Jesus can have some serious implications if not grave consequences. To bring shame upon Him and His Son is a dreadful, dreadful matter. Again look at what St. Paul said on this:

"It is impossible for those who have once been enlightened, who have tasted the heavenly gift, who have shared in the Holy Spirit, who have tasted the goodness of God and the powers of the coming age, if they fall away, to be brought back to repentance, because to their loss they are crucifying the Son of God all over again and subjecting Him to public disgrace." {Hebrews 6:4-7}

My word if this isn't what happened?! You won't find many speaking on this though will you. No and why? Well because we are under a new dispensation. A dispensation of grace wherein everyone thinks that God's grace is going to see them through everything. What unbelievable nonsense! If this Darbyism shouldn't be questioned in light of the revelations put forth in this book. Thrown in the garbage ultimately! How can this be correct? Again looking to take from the bible what they want to believe they have all but forgotten some of the most important and vital teachings in the bible. Like for example the above passages which make it quite clear about what it takes to get into heaven and on that note I surely want to bring to everyone's remembrance also these words of Christ Jesus Himself on this:

"Not everyone who says to me, Lord, Lord, will enter the kingdom of heaven, but only those who do the will of my Father who is in heaven. Many will say to me on that day, Lord, Lord, did we not prophesy in thy name, and in your name drive out demons and perform many miracles? Then I will tell them plainly, I never knew you. Away from me, you evildoers!" {Matthew 7:21-23}

I like what follows this though perhaps the best:

"Therefore everyone who hears these words of mine and puts them into practice is like a wise man who built his house on the rock. The rain came down, the streams rose, and the winds blew against that house; yet it did not fall, because it had its foundation on the rock. But everyone who hears these words of mine and does not put them into practice is like a foolish man who built his house on sand. The rain came down, the streams rose, and the winds blew and beat against that house, and it fell with a great crash." {Matthew 7:24-27}

A 'great crash' has certainly been the outcome hasn't it for many of our supposedly leaders? Moreover to look at what is happening with other denominations like the Catholic Church for example and the sins of many of its 'fathers' and look out I think is the name of the game here! The harm, the sins, the wickedness, the lawsuits, the closing of churches and schools? I am deeply afraid that this kind of wickedness being perpetrated and that on children is not going unnoticed by their heavenly Father! What is surely more mind-blowing though is what we see happening now with these polygamous communities. Why children? Why? You know if there are men today who truly want to live as polygamists hey all the power to them, but why children? Why don't they go and find women their own age to engage in such activities? I suppose though that given are day and age women are far too smart to put themselves under such stupidity. Most twenty, thirty or forty year old women that I am aware of would be laughing their heads off at the thought of being forced to become one of numerous wives and that constantly pregnant to a fifty or sixty year old man while being told to 'keep sweet.' Unbelievable and if this doesn't bring to remembrance a fellow co-worker and friend who while working together at a restaurant she related to me how she ran into a black bear while out hiking one day alone. I gasped at that and then to my reply to her aren't you afraid to go out hiking alone? To that she said; Jerry its not bears that I am afraid of its men. After laughing about that I couldn't help but give her statement some thought and reflection and then replied back to her; well said, Marcie, well said! So mothers look out for your daughters and to find or think that such men do these kinds of things in the name of and/or authority of Almighty God? Of course under the authority of God for how else could they possibly justify and get away with what their doing? Use religion right? LOOK OUT!!! Believe me if the wind isn't going to kick up and the clouds roll in over these people! No amount of concrete or bars of steel is going to stand between Almighty God and the likes of the Warren Jeffs of the world. It won't just be; '*the rain came down, the streams rose, and the winds blew*' but rather full blown anything that God has in his arsenal of weapons! Like for example what St. Paul added to that message of his from two paragraphs ago which quite astonishingly reflects exactly upon what Jesus said Himself:

> "Land that drinks in the rain often falling on it and that produces a crop useful to those for whom it is farmed receives the blessing of God. But land that produces thorns and thistles is worthless and is in danger of being cursed. In the end it will be burned." {Hebrews 6:7-8}

The land that Paul was and is talking about here isn't just the earth but our hearts people. So how close do you think people especially those who take on positions of leadership within His church and/or use His name are to be being cursed and thrown into hell? Alarming isn't it? Indeed and look didn't we here something about a tornado hitting Salt Lake City some time ago? Wow!

Furthermore given what St. Paul said in 1Timothy 3:2 "Now the overseer must be above reproach, *the husband of but one wife*" and why is it that no one bothers to pay much attention to the one person who understood everything about Jewish history and life? Look if anyone's teaching should be followed to the letter it should be this man St. Paul. Accordingly what does this tell us then? Well it tells us doesn't it the truth of what Christ Jesus said: '**by their fruit you will know them**.' {Matthew 7:16}

You know I don't think it's going to be much longer before we approach that day wherein His Majesty is not going to put up at all with His name being applied to anything and everything where mankind's desires are concerned and why is it? Why is it that when it comes to the ministry of God and the church too many people end up treating it as some kind of a career choice? Isn't it supposed to be a calling? It reminds this writer of something that he saw I'm not sure exactly where now. Either it was on television or in a magazine somewhere which I feel is the most likely case of a billboard advertising the priesthood. It was a Catholic advertisement and it so flabbergasted me that at the time I could hardly speak. In fact staring at the picture I later said to everyone I met and talked to that day wow what a way to fill positions in the Church. Advertise it on the highway and byways of America's thorough fares. You have got to be kidding and looking back now some 25 years later I find myself saying no wonder. No wonder one can't read a newspaper without coming across almost weekly now of some scandal involving the Catholic priesthood?

Now where all of these divisions are concerned, will any of this ever change? Well that is a very difficult question to ask. I mean how in the world does one go about healing the rifts between Calvinism, Arminianism, Lutheranism, Popism, Covenantalism, Dispensationalism, Presbyterianism, Pentecostalism, Jehovah's Witnessism,

Mormonism etc. etc. etc? Surely something has to change though for if things continue down the road the way they do I am afraid the church 'the true church' will cease to exist altogether. Actually how the church can still exist and even function for that matter in this unbelievably wicked world of ours is something astonishing especially given so many wars. Wars that actually caused me to ask a dear pastor friend of mine if a member of the Foursquare Church ever ended up killing another member on the other side of the battle-field? To that he snapped back at me 'well I'm sure something would be done to prevent that from happening don't you think?' To that I later balked at going over in my mind the European conflicts, the American civil war, the British wars and countless others. In fact, watching a documentary on the American Civil War I was flabbergasted to hear that during particular battles soldiers made a mockery of religion by lauding how a Presbyterian rainfall was a mere spring shower and a Southern Baptists was a Texas downpour? Sitting there I was speechless by what I was hearing and seeing and talk about bringing to remembrance those words from the Old Testament:

> "Rain will come in torrents, and I will send hailstones hurtling done and violent winds will burst forth...In my wrath I will unleash a violent wind, and in my anger hailstones and torrents of rain will fall with destructive fury." {Ezekiel 13: 8-13}

Significantly more important though is how these words from our Lord and Savior Christ Jesus resounded loudly in my mind:

> *"Every kingdom divided against itself will be ruined, and every city or household divided against itself will not stand. If Satan drives out Satan, he is divided*

*against himself. How then can his kingdom stand?
And if I drive out demons by Beelzebub, by whom
do your people drive them out? So then, they will be
your judges. But if I drive out demons by the Spirit of
God, then the kingdom of God has come upon you."*
{Matthew 12:25-28}

A scripture that by the way Abraham Lincoln apparently
used but sadly went largely ignored. Later to as I reflected
more and more over all of this history I began to wonder what
many of the religious and military leaders like Stonewall
Jackson and so many others ever going to do and say at the
judgment seat of Christ? Everything, literally everything is
recorded on God's video machines and it will all be played
back while we are there in Christ's very presence. Now if
that isn't something alarming to think about? Moreover to
find how many so called believers treated African Americans
sent shivers up my spine. Indeed turning my attention again
to the words of God from the Song of Solomon and if it
didn't reduce me to tears:

"I am black but lovely, O daughters of Jerusalem,
Like the tents of Kedar, Like the curtains of Solomon.
Do not stare at me because I am swarthy, for the sun
has burned me. My mother's sons were angry with
me; They made me caretaker of the vineyards, but I
have not taken care of my own vineyard." {1:5-7}

That a hell exists thank Almighty God, is surely going to
serve a great many people extremely well. Turning my attention also to the words of Hosea, I wondered to unbelievable
isn't it how a people could so easily be destroyed and for
what a lack of knowledge:

"My people are destroyed from a lack of knowledge. Because you have rejected knowledge, I also reject you as my priests; because you have ignored the law of your God, I also will ignore your children. The more the priests increased, the more they sinned against me; they exchanged their Glory for something disgraceful. They feed on the sins of my people and it will be: Like people, like priests. I will punish both of them for their ways and repay them for their deeds." {Hosea 4:6-9}

To think that this was written 2400 hundred years ago and for the last two hundred years this is still so applicable to the entire Christian Church and entire nations is utterly astounding if not altogether sad and shameful. If ever there existed a people who should be totally and completely educated on everything regarding biblical theology and religion it should be us today. *Especially where technology is concerned?* I mean look with just a few presses of a button and a world of knowledge is displayed before us. Even the television for heavens sakes has it own merits! So how is that possible? To this I am often left in total disbelief and as I look for answers I find myself thinking well if people aren't simply content with the status quo. Looking and or wanting to trust what they hear from their leaders they never bother to question anything and why is essentially because of laziness. The reading and studying of the Word of God is simply not important or rather is esteemed in much the same way as dishwashing is a mere chore. Most won't even bother to learn passively by using their cars music system to listen to the bible by way of cassettes, CD's, and/or DVD's on the way to and from work or shopping. Look with today's astounding technology {plug and play} reading isn't even that necessary anymore. So we really are without any kind of excuse. If it isn't a sad and unfortunate mess with most people actually knowing more about Darwinian evolutionism than anything revolving around Christ indoctrinated as they are in the public school system! It reminds me of something that happened to me many years ago when I was trying to minster to a girl the gospel she said to me that she believes in both God and Darwinian evolution. Imagine that! What a contradiction but I guess you have to keep everyone happy right? O good grief and so if Oswald Chambers wasn't totally and completely correct about what he said:

"The reason why the average Christian worker is only the average Christian worker is that he or she will remain grossly ignorant about what he does not see any need for. The majority of us have been brought up on 'spooned meat.' We will only take the truths we see immediate practical use for, consequently the average Christian worker knows nothing about Bible Theology or Bible Psychology, and cannot therefore push the battle for God on any of those domains." {Pg. 180 McCasland}

It was about fifteen years ago that I came across the story of a man who had been at one time the pastor of the Church of the Nazarene. A Methodist affiliate! He was apparently let go and the reason for his dismissal had something to do with his teachings regarding demonology and Satan and spiritual warfare. I suppose after having travelled to Romania and adopting some children from there and seeing the horrors first hand he decided that would be the important and prudent thing to do. It is a teaching though that the church apparently didn't care to hear or even bother with and this Pastor who tried to open their understanding to what the bible teaches on the subject was vilified for it. They wanted nothing to do with the issues of Satanism and what not and the pastor paid for it by becoming unemployed. To this I was quite intrigued by and wondered to myself how is it that a people could reject one of the most foundational doctrines in the entire bible? If God as well as His Son Christ Jesus takes Satan seriously shouldn't the church as well? To this I thought as well, if a man has been called by Almighty God into the ministry shouldn't there be or exist an authority that those under his care would recognize and respect? I mean how many people would go about questioning and or vilifying the likes of a St. Peter or a St. Paul? Or imagine John Wesley showing up in a Methodist Church and summarily being told to stop talking about a particular subject because they didn't like it? Unbelievable! So again if Oswald Chambers wasn't correct? He doesn't stop there though but rather goes on to mention something else about the way in which things sometimes exist within some churches:

"More than half the side-tracks and all the hysterical phenomena that seize whole communities of people, like a pestiferous epidemic, from time to time, arise from spiritual laziness and intellectual sloth on the part of so-called religious teachers. There are a host of Holiness adventurers, whose careers would suddenly end, if vigorous sanctified saints were abroad." {ibid pg. 106}

What was it that Malcolm Muggeridge referred to them as-'trendy clergymen' wasn't it? Is this not the truth and my how the church has suffered because of it in the eyes of the world? Indeed if the world doesn't look at us and just shake their heads in disbelief while exclaiming to themselves and each other who can understand. Even the church herself has suffered from this kind of 'who can understand' an excellent example of which would have to be what ultimately became of the Latter Rain Revival of 1948. Whatever Almighty

God tried to do there sadly ended in failure if not outright disaster:

"In a letter to his daughter, Faith Campbell {May 7, 1949}, he wrote that it was inappropriate to associate 'this new revival which God is so graciously sending, where so many souls are being saved, where so many lives are being transformed, where God is so graciously restoring the gifts of the Spirit with the fanatical movements of the past 40 years.' In 1949, under pressure and eligible to retire, Frodsham resigned from the editorship of the Pentecostal Evangel and withdrew his name as an ordained minster of the AG." {pg. 533 R.M. Riss}

Moving closer to our own day and age though and look wasn't it Jim Bakker who said in that book of his I Was Wrong {pg. 532} something to the effect of having never gotten around to studying the bible until after he ended up in prison. Unbelievable! What weren't these words of any importance?

"Do your best to present yourself to God as one approved, a workman who does not need to be ashamed and who correctly handles the word of truth." {2 Timothy 2:15}

When St. Paul spoke to the Galatians about the law being a schoolmaster {Galatians 3:24-25} as it were that was certainly true for him. Being raised Jewish and that for the purposes of becoming a Pharisee meant that the law was everything for him. Even for the early church which was made up essentially of Jewish people the law was something that everyone knew and understood to a very high degree. Where pray tell though will you find that being applicable to anyone among the Gentiles then or now? You won't find anyone no matter the leader who could possibly say in the same context as St. Paul said, that the law was our schoolmaster except perhaps maybe a Rousas John Rushdoony bless his memory. To live everyday, every moment, every turn of the road with the laws of God stuck to ones forehead as it were doesn't exist and if you want some idea of just how serious this was and is to the people of the bible consider what this writer found in the daily paper:

JUDAISM Studying the massive book on Jewish life takes 7 ½ years using the 'daf yomi' system.

Ottawa: "An estimated 120,000 Jews will take part in celebrations across the globe Tuesday after turning the last page on the 11th reading of the Talmud under a daily study calendar invented by a Polish Rabbi in the 1920s.

Under the two-sided page-a day calendar-known as the 'daf yomi' in Hebrew -it takes people, such as Arthur Sheffield, 7 ½ years to read the massive compendium of rabbinical wisdom and religious law, the study of which is the foundation of Jewish life.

'It's a big accomplishment,' said Sheffield from Ottawa. 'I never thought I would have done this.'

The epicenter of celebrations will be in at Madison Square Gardens in New York and an arena in New Jersey, where 47,000 tickets sold out weeks in advance. Those events will be broadcast live to 70 satellite hook-ups spanning six continents in countries including Hong Kong, Israel, the United States and Australia as well as venues in Edmonton, Toronto, Montreal, and Ottawa.

'You can't get much more universal than that,' said Rabbi Binyonin Holland, head of the Kollel of Ottawa, a center for Jewish learning. 'It's going to be unifying the whole Jewish world together through Talmud study.'

Rabbi Holland will join 16 other Ottawa men in New York, where they have box seats at Madison Square Garden, to hear speeches by some of the world's greatest Jewish scholars. During a special part of the ceremony, they will join scholars and ordinary Jews to read the final page of the Talmud together.

And then, because Jewish learning is a lifelong pursuit, they will begin the cycle again with page 1.

Such a unified expression of faith would have satisfied Rabbi Meir Shapiro, who proposed the daf yomi program in 1923. Traditionally, Talmudic study was a training ground for scholars, but Shapiro saw it as a way to bring ordinary Jews closer to their faith and to unify Jews around the world. And by starting on the same day, participants would literally be on the same page as they study the ancient script of the Talmud...

Participants usually devote at least an hour a day to their studies, which can happen anywhere- on a train, at lunchtime, privately, in groups, via the Internet, or even by using the 'Dial A Daf' telephone network.

Scholars can spend a lifetime studying the laws and rabbinical wisdom contained within its pages. Youth begin studying the text in Jewish schools at age 10, and studies can progress all the way to Talmudic institutes. {By Hayley Mick the Vancouver Sun Saturday, February 26, 2005}

Shortly after I became a new believer in Christ and not long after that event of the milk Almighty God decided to discipline me with some suffering. I came to experience something similar to what Job went through and given to me was Psalms 77 and 88. I lived or rather suffered with what was written therein for many months and was beside myself with grief looking for answers. Praying as I did though it only resulted in more of the same affliction from God and then one day I ended up listening to a man named George Belobaba. He was a guest speaker at the Foursquare Church and was a close friend of Pastor Ross Fox. In his message he said that while serving the Lord back in Oregon he was afflicted by God and it became such that he even ended up in the hospital. The more he prayed he said the more afflicted he became and inquiring of the Lord on this particular matter given to him was Psalm 77 and 88! Upon hearing this I as you could well imagine was rendered totally and completely speechless and flabbergasted. I couldn't believe what I was hearing and I became so agitated sitting there I could hardly keep myself from screaming out. Composing myself however I waited for the service to end and then immediately grabbed this man and pulling him aside I spilled my entire story to him. He looked at me kind of puzzled and stunned and then smiled and then to my reply to him about what was to become of me he said well to just continue praying and God will answer. To that I did of course and taking his message that night which interestingly revolved around Job I pondered much of it in my heart. Unfortunately though I did not pay as much attention to that message as I should have and for some time afterwards continued to struggle with what God did to me. A slow learner I guess. Questioning God however, 'He told me that in good time I will come to understand everything.' Later that is a few years after this as I was still perplexed looking back on the matter God immediately answered me by simply telling me that it all comes down to this. 'My people, they will accept all of the good things that exist in my word while ignoring and even rejecting the hard and difficult things that it has to say.' To this I thought and mumbled to myself some time later while looking at the state of affairs in the Church that truly if the whole counsel of God isn't sorely missing among God's people. In fact as I sit here writing this I have often wondered when was the last time you ever heard a sermon on Law? When a sermon on discipline? When a sermon on judgment? When a sermon on hell bells? When a sermon on demonology etc. etc? When a sermon on climate change for heavens sakes!!? Astonished I find myself actually quite shocked by it all. So true to God's words and actions His people have more or less become selective in what they want to accept and believe. This is the gist of it all and with that guess what further happened to me regarding Psalm 77 & 88? While attending as a guest recently the Alliance Church I came across the story of a dear black woman who was dying of kidney failure. She had apparently only a week to live and after the service the Pastor offered that if any one wanted to stay afterwards and pray for this lady that would be good. To this I felt quite oddly that I should stay and pray and as a number of people began gathering down near the front of the church I remained in the balcony and prayed along with everyone else for this dear lady. Being a visitor I didn't want to take away or interfere with peoples prayers by wondering who I was.

Now after a week had passed I was again back at this same church and to the surprise of everyone we had a guest speaker that morning. It was this dear lady who we had prayed for the week before. Jesus had apparently decided to answer ours prayers for her and after telling everyone about her astounding story of being healed guess what she did? She opened her bible and told us that God had given her a Psalm regarding what she had been through and proceeded to read Psalm 88! Upon hearing this I as you could well imagine was totally and completely blown away and no less reduced to tears. Wow, bless God I said to myself, bless Almighty

God! What a truly divine communicator He is! Moreover I mumbled to myself, God truly isn't finished with anyone of us by any stretch of the imagination and if all of this doesn't go back to those words of His through the prophet Isaiah:

> "See, I have refined you, though not as silver, I have tested you in the furnace of affliction. For my own sake, for my own sake I do this. How can I let myself be defamed? I will not yield my glory to another." {Isaiah 48:10-11}

So His Majesty accordingly then was correct to teach and discipline me as it were along with George Belobaba all those years ago. He had our and His own best interests in mind praise be His glorious name and that forever and forever! Again though what a slow learner I turned out to be. It all comes down to character and faith of course which with Almighty God is what everything stands on. Interestingly enough when we pray therefore and do not receive answers to our prayers I think maybe we need to start being aware that the problem is not with Almighty God but rather the problem most likely lies right at our own feet. This moreover and alarmingly is no doubt why you will find in many churches God's presence and power sorely missing. Indeed if the word Ichabod doesn't come to mind. My glory has departed. God takes His character and reputation very, very seriously as evidenced by what Job had to go through and it is no less different with any of us. Again just take the words of God to the Jewish people on this through His prophet Jeremiah:

> "Therefore this is what the Lord Almighty says: *See, I will refine them, for what else can I do because of the sin of my people? Their tongue is a deadly arrow; it speaks with deceit. With his mouth each speaks*

cordially with his neighbor, but in his heart he sets a trap for him. Should I not punish them for this? Declares the Lord. Should I not avenge myself on such a nation as this?" {Jeremiah 9:7-9}

So accordingly what took place then at the Alliance Church was for me of far reaching importance and significance. Then later to as I began to listen to another guest speaker at this particular church that summer, a one Darrel Shultz who blessed us all with his teachings he turned out to be a lawyer. To this I was quite intrigued by and immensely interested in for I had for quite some time become aware of lawyers in the church. What I mean by this is that of all of the ministers of Almighty God who have become great successes in the church and have finished their ministries well it has been those who have had legal training. When you look at leaders like Charles Finney, Walter Martin, Charles Price, John Chrysostom, St. Paul and a number of others one thing comes across in them all. They were all either lawyers or had or began their ministries with legal training. So of them it can be said the truth that the law was a kind of schoolmaster. So, yes I said to myself sitting there while being none to jealous here you have it in all its glory a minister of Almighty God! Then to further perk my interest he said something to the effect that before becoming a lawyer his interest was in science and proceeded to end his message that morning with a most intriguing illustration. I drove home that morning so excited hardly waiting to get into his hands something of peculiar importance and the rest I'll leave for him to explain.

So law I said to myself is not irrelevant after all. Not for a people like us who have never had it as a schoolmaster! As for grace well I think we all had better start taking into account God's disciplining ways and stop going around thinking that its all about forgiveness, forgiveness, and more forgiveness as though God were already finished with us. That's absurd and you know why is it that only the business world and its corporations understand this by way of removing and or firing entirely those employees who turn out to be thieves and bring disrepute upon their characters and businesses? Shouldn't this be even more applicable to the Christian Church? Not so though. Rather, leaders either remain in or return to or get posted to other ministries and my what courage or rather folly is this? Indeed if not especially so for those 'evil priests' as the late pope called them! God sees everything people, absolutely everything and He don't care at all about what denomination one is a part of! Accordingly watch out!!! Remember the words of Christ Jesus:

> "And if anyone causes one of these little ones who believe in me to sin, it would be better for him to be thrown into the sea with a large millstone tied around his neck. If your hand causes you to sin, cut it off. It is better for you to enter life maimed than with two hands to go into hell, where the fire never goes out." {Mark 9:42-43}

Now one other thing I should share here which I feel is important. George Belobaba has a brother named Mitch and to my utter surprise heard him speak one morning about attending a conference in Switzerland I believe. It was a conference between the Roman Catholic Church and the Pentecostal denominations that sprung up in the early part of the Twentieth Century. Apparently the conference was to try and bring an understanding between our two faiths. Too this I was immensely interested in as you could well imagine given my own background and was utterly intrigued by what he had to say. More important to me though at the time was what he said concerning his families background. They were from the same country as my parents were from that is at the time Yugoslavia. They though were further south than my parents were that is Serbia and partly Russian. I was surprised and excited and quite intrigued by this because here I was coming from a country and family similar in background to these two men and here was God using them to speak to me and that in the Foursquare Church no less. It was just another blessing in a long list of blessings for me. Wow I said to myself at the time this is surely something fantastic. I love God and the way He works I further said to myself as I made my way home from another most interesting day in church.

Now as for what Mitch said regarding the conference well it was quite interesting for me for it more or less goes to what is written in this chapter regarding divisions and unity. Yes as I look back now on everything I find myself wondering if only? If only Roman Catholicism had applied the kind of activity that the Jews are doing today with their 'daf yomi' system. That and adding of course to that the teachings of Christ to the European Continent during the Middle Ages and beyond and there would surely never have been the need for a Luther or for that matter the entire Reformation and all the wars that followed in its train. As it stood though they deemed the bible as so sacred a text that they locked it up in their libraries allowing no one access to its wealth of information but themselves. That was argued was reserved only for the priests and for those who spoke Latin that sacred language of the Roman Empire? Accordingly what do you think here? Have men not in their own selfish desires looked at the church as being their work and not God's? Have men not in their own selfish ambitions looked at controlling the work of Almighty God themselves? Have they not ignored some of the most vital and important teachings in the entire bible? Have they not changed and that universally the Gospel of Christ to fit their own theological agendas and presuppositions? Have they not ignored the very Law of God? Have they not ignored the priesthood of all believers? Have they not ignored the teaching about the Baptism of the Holy Spirit? Have they not ignored what St. Paul said?

"For we are God's fellow workers; you are God's field, God's building. By the grace God has given me, I laid a foundation as an expert builder, and someone else is building on it. But each one should be careful how he builds. For no one can lay any foundation other than the one already laid, which is Christ Jesus. If any man builds on this foundation using gold, silver, costly stones, wood, hay or straw, his work will be shown for what it is, because the Day will bring it to light. It will be revealed with fire, and fire will test the quality of each man's work. If what he has built survives, he will receive his reward. If it is burned up, he will suffer loss; he himself will be saved, but only as one escaping through the flames. Don't you know that you yourselves are God's temple and that God's Spirit lives in you? If anyone destroys God's temple, God will destroy him; for God's temple is sacred, and you are that temple." {1Corinthians 3:3-17}

These are surely the important questions that need to be asked. At one time it was all about, *'faith cometh by hearing and hearing by the word of God.'* {Romans 10:17} Sadly however, that was changed to faith cometh by hearing and hearing by the word of our scientists. Thank you and congratulations Roman Catholicism for that! Thank you so very, very much and with that this chapter comes to an end but again not before mentioning this. When it comes to the tradition of some Western Churches there exist a peculiar interpretation of God's words regarding the elect and how the end time's events are to unfold. That is there are some that believe that the elect has nothing to do with the Gentiles

310

but rather the Jewish people. Accordingly when it comes to a statement like the one below it is taken to be in reference to the Jews and not the Gentile believers who it is believed will be raptured out before the great tribulation begins.

"If those days had not been cut short, no one would survive, but for the sake of the elect those days will be shortened." {Matthew 24:22}

Now let's ask ourselves how would St. Paul ever be able to agree with that and still teach what he taught in the book of Romans? I mean it appears to this writer by way of that book that the elect has got nothing whatsoever to do with the Jewish people. Rather it has got everything to do with both the Jews and the Gentile people and this is surely in accordance with what the bible teaches regarding the Lambs Book of Life. You will find many passages from Genesis right through to the Book of Revelation that bears out the truth of this but it is in Daniel who says:

"At that time Michael, the great prince who protects your people will arise. There will be a time of distress such as has not happened from the beginning of nations until then. But at that time your people- *everyone whose name is found written in the book will be delivered.*" {Daniel 12:1}

It appears the foreknowledge of Almighty God has taken into account everything and everybody. Now isn't that something interesting to think about? Furthermore according to what follows this and what we find is again only more proof that Almighty God is by no means finished with anyone of us where faith, character and salvation is concerned:

311

"When the power of the Holy people has been finally broken, all these things will be completed"... "Many will be purified, made spotless and refined, but the wicked will continue to be wicked. None of the wicked will understand, but those who are wise will understand." {Daniel 12: 7 & 10}

Again if this isn't something interesting to think about, in fact, to the degree that for this writer it brings well to mind some rather interesting and surely none too important words from St. Peter:

"Bear in mind our Lord's patience means salvation, just as our dear brother Paul also wrote you with the wisdom God gave him. He writes the same way in all his letters, speaking in them of these matters. His letters contain some things that are hard to understand, which ignorant and unstable people distort, as they do the other Scriptures, to their own destruction." {2 Peter 3:16}

If the problems exist anywhere it is in the book of Romans isn't it? Let's try therefore to focus on Christ and His Wounds while remembering ultimately people these dear words from our brother Paul:

"As a prisoner for the Lord, then, I urge you to live a life worthy of the calling you have received. Be completely humble and gentle; be patient, bearing with one another in love. Make every effort to keep the unity of the Spirit through the bond of peace. There is one body and one Spirit- just as you were called to one hope when you were called- one Lord, one faith, one baptism; one God and Father of all, who is over all and through all and in all. But to each one of us grace has been given as Christ apportioned it. This is why it says:

'When He ascended on high, he led captives in his train and gave gifts to men.'" {Ephesians 4:1-8}

{What does 'he ascended mean except that he also descended to the lower, earthly regions? He who descended is the very one who ascended higher than all of the heavens, in order to fill the whole universe.} It was he who gave some to be apostles, some to be prophets, some to be evangelists, and some to be pastors and teachers, to prepare God's people for works of service, so that the body of Christ may be built up until we all reach the unity of the faith and in the knowledge of the Son of God and become mature, attaining to the whole measure of the fullness of Christ.

Then we will no longer be infants, tossed back and forth by the waves, and blown here and there by every wind of teaching and by the cunning and craftiness of men in their deceitful scheming. Instead, speaking the truth in love, we will in all things grow up into him who is the Head, that is Christ. From him the whole body, joined and held together by every supporting ligament, grows and builds itself up in love, as each part does its work." {Ephesians 4:1-16}

O and if there isn't just one more thing to mention. For those who are at a loss to understand the 'Trinity' of Almighty God well there is a very easy and interesting way of understanding it in all its glory. It comes to us by way of a prayer doesn't it and that by Christ Jesus interestingly enough:

"My prayer is not for them alone. I pray also for those who will believe in me through their message, that all of them may be one, Father, just as you are in me and I am in you. May they also be in us so that the world may believe that you have sent me. I have given them the glory that you gave me, that they *may be one as we are one: I in them and you in me. May they be brought to complete unity* to let the world know that you sent me and have loved them even as you have loved me." {John 17:20-23}

CHAPTER NINE

THE LATTER RAIN

To continue now with what will be our final look into climate change and its history within the church specifically and what we come to is something called the Latter Rain Movement? Not a church denomination in the normal sense of the word but rather a movement that began in the year 1948 in North Battleford, Saskatchewan as well as in a number of other places. Apparently it was a spiritual awakening of some kind that led the church out of its dry and lifeless state and into an entirely new dynamic. A dynamic that from all outward appearances has it seems something to do with the weather. Now could a branch of the church finally understand the importance of the work of God in relation to Divine Communication and the weather?

It was during a season of prayer that a small community of believers at Sharon Orphanage and Schools in North, Battleford, Saskatchewan came to experience the presence of Almighty God in a very unique way. The account written comes to us by a man named Ern Hawtin:

> "...on February 12, 1948, God moved into their midst in a strange new manner. Some students were under the power of God on the floor, others were kneeling in adoration and worship before the Lord. The anointing deepened until the awe of God was upon everyone. The Lord spoke to one of the brethren. 'Go and lay hands upon a certain student and pray for him.' While he was in doubt and contemplation, one of the sisters who had been under the power of God, went to the brother saying the same words, and naming the identical student he was to pray for. He went in obedience and a revelation was given concerning the student's life and future ministry. After this a long prophecy was given with minute details, concerning the great thing God was about to do. The pattern

for the revival and many details concerning it were given." {pg. 532 R. M. Riss}

Then if this wasn't enough he goes on to describe that this was followed two days later by an even more tremendous outpouring of the Spirit of Almighty God. The event was apparently so wonderful and intense that it was as though heaven literally came down to greet one and all. It was a revival or spiritual awakening of some kind that awakened the church that had more or less become dry and lifeless. After two world wars and the enormous amount of upheaval it caused left the church in a sad state of affairs leaving what was left of the prior outpourings of 1904 to be swept away. In looking to gain more details though of what exactly occurred there along with an understanding of it all and sadly there exists little to nothing. Unfortunately those involved never bothered or got around to keeping good records. It reminds this writer of a teacher who while taking a course under her on the Latter Rain Movement at the Glad Tidings Church in Vancouver she lamented that very fact and admonished everyone to keep a diary. Sadly the church doesn't have much on the events of those years and this to this writer is especially woeful given what occurred under one Reg Layzell. Founder and Pastor of the Glad Tidings Church and one of the leaders of the Latter Rain he after praying fervently for years to God for a revival received exactly that in 1948. It was similar apparently to what occurred in North Battleford, Saskatchewan which is surely not to an insignificant a matter. Again though looking for more details and sadly no one among the blessed bothered to ask the important questions or for that matter were sufficiently academically minded. That shouldn't stop us though from understanding some of what possibly occurred there by way of looking back at other outpourings. Like for example what we saw under the Moravians and Methodists as well as

Finney and Mahan and if that doesn't suffice or is enough well then perhaps something like these will:

Ireland A.D. 1859:
> Reverend William Magill of Dundrod, Ireland...
> "The revival commenced here on the 10th of June. On the morning of that day, I rose from my bed impressed with the thought that something strange and wonderful was about to happen in Dundrod.
> I had been in Belfast the day previous and had leaned over the prostrate bodies of men and women laboring under strong conviction of sin. I had heard, for the first time in my life, the sighs and groans of breaking hearts and witnessed with a feeling of wonder and awe the mental agony and the terrible struggle of souls wrestling with the 'principalities and powers of darkness,' and 'contending earnestly' for life and liberty; and when the battle was won, I heard with almost equal wonder the shout of victory, like the pealing of a trumpet on the field from which the enemy had fled. I came home filled with strange thoughts, cherishing high hopes and breathing earnest prayers that the Lord would come over the mountains and visit my people." {pg. 54-55 Relfe}

Rev. John Stuart:
> "After more than seven months experience, I can boldly and fearlessly bear my testimony to the blessed fruits and marvelous results of this mighty movement. I have not confined my labors to my own locality. I have preached and delivered addresses in many a town and village, and in many a country parish, of several counties; and when I gaze on the hundreds and sometimes the thousands of whom I was surrounded, I could not but exclaim, 'Who are

these that fly as a cloud and as the doves to their windows?' Society appeared to be stirred up its lowest depths.

Never was there such a summer as the last; never such an autumn; never such a winter, so far as it has gone. Many have been savingly converted to the Lord; some 'stricken' down when the Spirit came upon them like a rushing mighty wind; others convinced and converted whilst He spake to their consciences by the 'still small voice.' {ibid pg. 53}

India A.D. 1860:

"In 1860 revival broke out in Tinevily, South India. The man whom God used in the movement was a national evangelist called Aroolappen, and the movement began {Tell it not in Gath} in the Brethren assemblies in which A. N. Groves, one of the early Brethren leaders, had labored. Aroolappen described the beginnings of the movement:

'From the 4th of May to the 7th the Holy Spirit was poured out openly and wonderfully. Some prophesied and rebuked the people: some beat themselves on their breasts severely, and trembled and fell down through shaking of their bodies and souls...They saw some signs in the air. They were much pleased to praise God. Some ignorant {i.e. uninstructed} people gave out some songs and hymns that we never heard before...All the heathen marveled, and came and saw and heard us with fearful minds...

In the month of June, some of our people praised the Lord by unknown tongues, with their interpretations. In the month of July, the Spirit was poured out upon our congregation at Oleikollam, and above twenty-five persons were baptized. They are steadfast in prayers...Some missionaries admit the truth of the gifts of the Holy Spirit. The Lord meets every-where one after another, though some tried to quench the Spirit.

Henry Groves, a son of A.N. Groves, writing in the Indian watchman for July 1860, takes up the story:

The spirit of prophecy was given to some there, and a little boy said in a certain village which he named, about a mile distant, the Spirit of God had been poured out. Within a quarter of an hour, some men and women came from that village beating their breasts in great fear and alarm of conscience. They fell down and rolled on the ground. This continued a short time. They all asked to have prayer made for them after which they said with great joy, the Lord Jesus has forgiven our sins, and clapping their hands together in the fullness of their hearts gladness, they embraced one another.

For nearly three days this ecstatic joy appears to have lasted. They ate nothing except a little food taken in the evening, and passing sleepless nights they continued the whole time in reading of the word, in prayer and in singing praises to the Lord. Of some it is said, 'they lifted up their eyes to heaven and saw blood and fire and pillars of smoke, and speaking loudly they told what they had seen. {pg. 62-63 Wallis}

Wales, England 1904 as reported in the Ram's Horn:

"A wonderful revival is sweeping over Wales. The whole country, from city to the colliery under-ground, is aflame with gospel glory. Police courts are hardly necessary, public houses are being deserted, old debts are being paid to satisfy awakened consciences and definite and unmistakable answers to prayer are recorded.

The leader in this great religious movement is a young man twenty-six years of age, Evan Roberts. He was a collier boy, then an apprentice in the forge, then a student for the ministry. But all his life he has yearned to preach the gospel. He is no orator, he is not widely read. The only book he knows from cover to cover is the Bible. He has in his possession a Bible which he values above anything else he has belonging to him. It is a Bible slightly scorched in a collier explosion." {pg. 82 Relfe}

America, Massachusetts A.D. 1735 by Jonathan Edwards:

"There was scarcely a single person in the town, either old or young, that was left unconcerned about the great things of the eternal world. Those that were wont to be the vainest and loosest, and those that had been the most disposed to think and speak slightly of vital and experimental religion, were now generally subject to great awakenings. And the work of conversion was carried on in a most astonishing manner, and increased more and more; souls did, as it were, come by flocks to Jesus Christ." {pg. 78 Wallace}

David Brainerd 1745:

"The power of God seemed to descend upon the assembly like a mighty rushing wind and with an astonishing energy bore down all before it. I stood amazed at the influence that seized the audience almost universally, and could compare it to nothing more aptly than the irresistible force of a mighty torrent." {ibid pg. 16-17}

If anything gives us some kind of an idea of what occurred in North Battleford, Saskatchewan and at Glad Tidings in Vancouver it would be these! As for any accompanying climate change that followed such outpourings well sadly we really don't know what if anything occurred. Again though given what we have seen from previous outpourings with perhaps the Singapore event being the most significant here and surely something must have occurred. It wouldn't have been the rain though that is for sure occurring as it did in the north of Saskatchewan and that during the month of February no less. Saskatchewan is a very cold province so if anything meteorologically occurred with this outpouring and it would probably have had something to do with the snow perhaps or even thunder. The prophet Joel does mention that such phenomena will accompany the work of Almighty God:

"The Lord thunders at the head of his army; his forces are beyond number, and mighty are those who obey his command. The day of the Lord is great; it is dreadful. Who can endure it?" {Joel 2:11}

Whatever the case though we are left with only the wonder of it all which is quite perplexing in a way given their use of the rain as a picture of the outpouring of God's Holy Spirit. From all outward appearances this movement it appears does have some kind of an understanding of the work of Almighty God in relation to Divine Communication and the weather. Sadly though upon further investigation and what we find is that this has really got nothing whatsoever to do with the weather at all but rather revolves entirely around the spiritual. Their use of the rain is only used allegorically to symbolize the outpouring of the Spirit of Almighty God and why do they do this? Well proceeding as they do from the book of Joel chapter 2 they have apparently mistakenly mixed together two different works of Almighty God {2:23 and 2:28} to form essentially one.

"Be glad, o people of Zion, rejoice in the Lord your God, for he has given you the autumn rains in righteousness. He sends you abundant showers, both autumn and spring rains as before. The threshing floors will be filled with grain; the vats will overflow with new wine and oil." {Joel 2:23}

"And afterward, I will pour out My Spirit on all people. Your sons and daughters will prophesy, your old men will dream dreams, your young men will see visions. Even on my servants both men and women, I will pour out my Spirit in those days." {Joel 2:28}

Emphasizing the spiritual more than the physical attributes of the work of Almighty God they have mistaken one aspect of God's work against the other and why or rather how did this happen? Well ultimately if it wasn't because of a lack of knowledge regarding biblical history and Divine Communication specifically? In fact looking at George Warnock's thesis on the Feast of Tabernacles which came to espouse everything concerning the Latter Rain and we can see this readily enough. www.georgewarnock.com/feast10.html

His interpretation of this feast fails miserably to take into account this whole issue of Divine Communication and the weather. Rather taking what the Word of God says and applying it typologically he has come to imply that it has more to do with the coming harvest of souls for the kingdom of God. He seems to think that God's use of the rain is only used as a kind of metaphor to represent the work of God's Spirit specifically which is clearly not the case. It's a kind of half truth and if this sadly isn't the reason as to why this movement has gone on to cause and indeed create a great amount of confusion and friction within the Christian Church. In fact proceeding as they do from the book of Joel instead of the book of Job and their emphasis if not entire theology revolves mostly around prophecy and the end-times. An end times ministry of the church which they believe began in 1948 and why is essentially because of the rebirth of the nation of Israel. To many it wasn't a coincidence that both events would occur the way they did. Accordingly taking what they saw happening around them together with the teachings from the book of Joel along with this so called new revelation of the Feast of Tabernacles and they proceeded with an interpretation of the bible that was entirely different from the norm. Like for example their interpretation and belief that through this outpouring was going to be restored the offices of the apostle and prophet as well as the fulfillment entirely of the five-fold ministry of the church as spoken in Ephesians 4:11. A matter of which was to occur by way of the laying on of hands which contrary to the old way came about by a tarrying or waiting for the work of the Spirit of God. It was something that for all intents and purposes was going to change the church into an entirely new and different entity. It was to be a kind of restoration of sorts that would finally bring the fulfillment as illustrated in Ephesians 4:11 in its entirety. This is what they ultimately came to believe and espouse, and it was something that for a time grabbed a great many believers with a new found hope and faith. Indeed looking for a word from God everyone involved were hoping that the apostles and prophets that came out of this movement would somehow bestow upon them some word leading to their placement within the five-fold ministry. This is where ultimately the modern day use of, 'Thus Saith the Lord' came from and if this didn't go on to spark quite a controversy. Indeed looking at it all today, and many in church leadership are beside themselves with grief and anger over it all and why? Well as Dr. Riss explains:

"This "blaze of prophetic light" was not restricted to the penetration of mysteries within the bible but included the "unveiling of peoples' lives and hearts through the agency of the Spirit of God working through the laying on of the hands of "prophets and apostles of His choosing." While many people received renewed faith and hope with respect to their gifts and calling as a result of prophetic ministry of this type, there were a few people whose faith had become shipwrecked, perhaps after receiving the laying on of hands with prophecy from inexperienced people or from others who may have engaged in these practices with mixed motives. The controversy that raged as a result of these problems served to discredit the entire movement in the eyes of most of the major Pentecostal denominations including the PAOC, the AG in the US, the PHC, and the Apostolic Church. Many experienced pastors were dropped from the rolls of these churches for their involvement in the Latter Rain movement." {pg. 532 Riss}

"Stanley Frodsham was also active in the movement. In a letter to his daughter, Faith Campbell {May 7, 1949}, he wrote that it was inappropriate to associate 'this new revival which God is so graciously sending, where so many souls are being saved, where so many lives are being transformed, where God is so graciously restoring the gifts of the Spirit with the fanatical movements of the past 40 years.' In 1949, under pressure and eligible to retire, Frodsham resigned from the editorship of the Pentecostal Evangel and withdrew his name as an ordained minster of the AG." {ibid pg. 533}

So what a sad thing this is. The genuine apparently ended up being filled with the counterfeit. Brings well to mind some rather interesting and important words from Arthur Wallis in that immortal book of his Revival the Rain from Heaven:

"Revival is recognized as clearly 'heaven sent,' when men cannot account for what is happening in terms of human personality or organization, and when the work continues unabated without human control. When a movement becomes organized or controlled by man, it has ceased to be spontaneous – it is no longer revival. The course of the 1904 Welsh Revival has been outlined thus:

God commenced to work.
Then the devil began to work in opposition.
Then God worked all the harder.
Finally man began to work, and the revival came to an end.

It is of course necessary that leaders ensure that the work of the Spirit is not infiltrated by false doctrine or practice, but great care needs to be taken that we do not take things out of the control of the Holy Spirit. When God has put His hand on the helm we do well to keep ours off." {pg. 47 Wallis}

If this doesn't explain what ultimately happened to this movement? Men apparently decided to add something more to the work of Almighty God and to find that this involved prophecy on a personal basis is quite troubling and why? Well because of this of course:

"Dr. Willard Cantelon called me a few days back. In the conversation he was addressing the fall of television's superstars. I am taking the liberty of attempting to recap his words:

'All this brings to mind a most unusual man, Dr. Price. I was privileged to be with him in a service in Pasadena. The year was 1949. The Holy Spirit began to speak to him prophetically about a time when it would appear that the Church was in renewal, from which era would emerge dazzling personalities, and multitudes would follow them. But after many days, it would be discovered that there was glitter, not glory, upon these men, and one by one they would sink into oblivion."

"As their decline was being witnessed, God would raise up an army of humble 'unknowns,' on whom He would pour out His Spirit and through whom He would move to send a genuine, mighty Revival to America.'

"Dr. Cantelon continued, 'Have we not lived to see it, Dr. Mary?' He added:

'This Dr. Price was my mentor... O what a humble man of God! Allow me to illustrate this man's contrition. It was my privilege to be with Dr. Price during a subsequent meeting in Calgary. The services were extraordinary. The supernatural was manifested in just outstanding healings and miracles. On a Tuesday as we were exiting the building, Dr. Price began to visibly weep. He leaned over to me and said: 'The people, did you hear them? They were saying, Isn't he wonderful! I have failed my Lord; I must decrease; Jesus must increase. Dr. Price went to his room and prayed with strong crying and tears for two hours.

A couple of nights later, as we were leaving the meeting where skeptics and unbelievers were made obedient by Word and deed through mighty signs and wonders, Dr. Price was smiling, He said to me, 'Son, tonight I heard the people saying, Isn't Jesus wonderful! I got through to God, and He got through to the people." {Mary Stewart Relfe The League of Prayer}

It appears that 'Thus Saith the Lord' became more a work of man than the work of Almighty God and my how serious and dreadful a matter is this? Too many people it appears came to think or believe that they were actually hearing from God when in fact they weren't at all. It is interesting if not altogether significant to note here as well what Reg Layzell had to say about what he saw happening in the years following the outpouring:

"At the first camp meeting you were made a member of the body of Christ by the Spirit of God. And even if you said you were not in the body you still were. No man could put you in or take you out. Now the error: They claim you are only put in by them and can be put out by them." http://www.apologetic-sindex.org/l08.html

Now what a penetrating insight this is and surely not an altogether incorrect one at that too! Here we find an educated individual in the things of God who could see what was happening. He hit the nail right square on the head for sure on this and if it doesn't cast an interesting light upon a question this writer came across some time ago of what would an apostle or prophet look like? If anyone gives us an interesting insight into how to tell the genuine from the counterfeit it would be this man Reg Layzell!

Leadership, leadership truly nothing ever causes mankind more trouble and heartaches that this one issue. That and of course how the bible in its entirety is never perused thoroughly and completely enough. It should never cease to amaze anyone of us that from one generation to the next nothing ever really changes. Looking to be spoon fed rather than seeking and doing the work for themselves too many have all but shipwrecked their faith along with the faith of others. It's one of Almighty God's requirements that a people judge carefully what they hear but for most people they truly never bother to go into the bible to see for themselves whether the minister is telling them the truth or not. My word if the words of the late Dr. Walter Martin bless his memory doesn't come screaming back at us about the need for a centralized clearing house!!! Some place where a candidate's faith and theology can be thoroughly examined and analyzed before going out and entering into the pulpit. Truly if this isn't the case and if only this had been applied to the Latter Rain by those who were a part of it in the beginning! Let's however not throw the baby out with the bath water though but rather as the scriptures teach lets try to extract the precious from the worthless shall we where this movement is concerned:

"If you extract the precious from the worthless, you will become my spokesman." {Jeremiah 15:19}

For it appears to this writer anyway that there is some truth to what these people came to espouse originally. Look the church does need to be unified doesn't it and if ever a people needed the leadership and guidance of an apostle or prophet in the train of either a St. Paul or a St. Peter it would have to be us today! This is surely without question and given the teachings of books like Ephesians and something has to change! In fact they have to change for heavens sakes for things cannot continue to exist the way they do especially if we are heading in to the final days before the return of our Lord and Savior Christ Jesus and /or the unveiling of the antichrist. It certainly makes for some serious and intriguing questions which given the teachings within this book will surely engender a great many discussions within the body of Christ and that universally! What is of far more interest to this writer though is what I came across in a church service one morning. It occurred by way of a song and that in a Foursquare Church no less which for this writer is not an altogether insignificant matter given how the North Battleford outpouring was originally a Foursquare work!

"Here in this moment of time
We search for wonders for miracles and signs
Something to satisfy the hunger in us all
A human rage from deep within the soul

Like a machine in pursuit
On the horizon like a raging fire we move
Driven by questions in an endless search for truth
There is a stirring in us a great awakening begins

I believe there's a mighty power I believe it's a latter
    rain
I believe there's a move of God calling us all higher
Oh, I believe these are the days of the great awakening
Days of the great awakening

More than our hearts can contain
It is an overflow of God's amazing grace
Coming to reconcile a world that's lost its way
Oh, all consuming fire come purify us once again

There's no containing this great move of restoration
It knows no walls, no boundaries or lines
Without a doubt I do believe if we'll just get down
On our knees the latter rain is gonna fall
It's just a matter of time" {Mark Harris]

O if only George Warnock had understood the significance of the weather to the work of Almighty God in relation to Divine Communication and their history would have been much different than what it is. If the Feast of Tabernacles has got anything to do with anything it is the weather specifically and no where was and is this explained more than in Zechariah chapter 14:16-19.

"Then the survivors from all the nations that have attacked Jerusalem will go up year after year to worship the King, the Lord Almighty, and to celebrate the Feast of Tabernacles. If any of the peoples of the earth do not go up to Jerusalem to worship the King, the Lord Almighty, they will have no rain. If the Egyptian people do not go up and take part, they will have no rain. The Lord will bring on them the plague he inflicts on the nations that do not go up to celebrate the Feast of Tabernacles."

It all comes down to faith and obedience ultimately with the warning that if a people do not honor Almighty God with a celebration of thankfulness they will receive nothing but a drought and a famine. Just go back to the chapter on the history of Israel for an in-depth analysis of that! This is the crux of it all and so what a sad and unfortunate thing this is but as we see things are a changing and with that we come to the conclusion now of looking at climate change and its history within the church. As for Joel chapter 2 and the Latter Rain's use of it in their particular hermeneutic well if anything prophetically gives us any kind of an exegesis of who and what that entails exactly and it would have to be what a South African housewife by the name of Anton Sawyer prophesied about. In her God given prophecy Ichabod or Revival she sums up by the Spirit of Almighty God some very interesting details. Details that reflect quite astonishingly upon what was testified earlier by Dr. Charles Price and yes it is quite lengthy but ultimately extremely important!

Ichabod or Revival
By

Anton Sawyer

"God takes the most unlikely characters to do his work. He says He will take the foolish things to confound the wise. And I'm a foolish thing. God began to speak to me in visions. And when God gave me these visions I thought, "Lord, am I hallucinating?" And then God said, "I want you to go to America and tell them to repent." I said, "You must be joking." I said, "God, who will believe a housewife." I said, "What options do I have?" He said, "Jonah." I said, "God, I have no intentions of being in the whale's belly. I'll go the first time around but speak to me and confirm in Scripture that you are on My side." He said, "I'm going to give you a forehead like flint. You will speak to the people and you'll speak what I put into your mouth. There will be times when I tell you to be silent and you be silent. But when I tell you to speak you open up your mouth and you give the Word that I have put into your mouth. Because if you don't I will make a fool of you publicly." Then God said, "Don't look at their faces, just give the Word; don't look for results, just give the Word. Whether they hear or whether they hear not, don't let that worry you. Just give the Word because I am about to bring a divine visitation to this country. And this country is not ready to have Me in the divine visitation that I intend, when My glory is seen. My glory and sin cannot be in the same place together. My glory consumes sin and if I were to visit the church in the condition that she's in now, my people would be consumed like Ananias and Sapphire.'

God spoke to me concerning the believer, the army of God, and the church.

The one about the believer, this is how the picture came to me. I saw, as it were, a people lying across the face of the earth in a drugged state, unable to get up; just lying in a sick, apathetic condition. And then I noticed, every now and then, there was someone standing upright covered with a sheet of Shekinah glory that penetrated right into the throne room of God. I said, "God, what am I seeing?" And then I noticed a thick, jet black layer of darkness, like a blanket pressing down on these people. I said, "Father what am I seeing?" He said, "The people that you see lying in this sick condition are my people the church." I said, 'God who are these standing upright?' He said, "Do you notice how few?" I said, "God who are they?" He said, "They are the FEW INTERCESSORS that dare to stand in the gap. It is their prayers that are going to move my arm to rescue My people in this sick condition." I said, "God, what is that blanket of blackness?" And it's almost like God's voice changed and He said, "Those are the sins of my people." I said, "What do you mean, Lord?" He said, "Outwardly righteous but inwardly filled with corruption.' And the Holy Spirit said, "I cannot live in this corruption. This bride is being prepared to meet the Father. She cannot come before the Father's face in this condition." He said, "So I'm going to purify my church."

Next I saw a pair of hands, so sharp, pierce into this blackness and just push it aside. The darkness changed into the most grotesque, demonic figures and they began to fall backwards on each other. And they were yelling with a loud voice and they said, "Our time is short, we've got to work quickly." You know, as these demons were falling over, the Holy Spirit said, "There's a tidal wave of deception flooding into the church and my people do not know the difference between truth and error anymore. They are eating any bait that is thrown out. There are hirelings standing behind the pulpit and they lead people astray." God said, "I will bring a judgment on them."And I want to say to preachers, if you're not called of God, get out from the pulpit because judgment is going to come upon you for standing in that position and leading God's people astray. Wake up before it's too late. There is still time to repent.

Suddenly God pushed the blackness aside and I noticed a wind just came blowing down on God's people. God's people began to rise and next they were standing upright, and I said, "Lord what's happening?" He said; "Tell the believer who has been a pew-warmer all this time, I'm going to breath a new fire upon them. I'm going to release them in the innermost being. Out of them is going to flow a river of living water. I am going to be set free in my people who have held Me captive." God said, "I'm going to revive them. I'm going to restore them. I am going to renew them. I am going to make up the years that the locusts have eaten."

"But listen," God said, "there is going to be a choice. There are going to be people of God who only want to play church, who will not hear the call, who will not heed the Word, and there are going to be those who are crying out." God says, "In those who will listen, I will do a new thing. I will do this, they will speak to the blind and the blind will see. It won't be left to the hierarchy. The pew-warriors are going to discover the power of God like they've never known it before." As a matter of fact God said, "The names of great evangelists written in lights and the mere pew-warmer, the gap is closing. There is going to be one name that is going to be elevated and that name is JESUS."

The next vision God gave me concerned the army of God. I saw, as it were, an enormous crowd of people walking through the most barren territory you have ever seen- like a wilderness. As I looked I noticed there wasn't one person that wasn't damaged. Everyone had a scar. And I said, "God who are these weak, weary, crippled people?' He said, "My army." I said; "God, that looks like an emergency ward, you call that your army?" He said, "Behold what I am about to do." With that I noticed shadows hovering above God's people. And I noticed them walking, some of them were stumbling, some were on crutches, some were bandaged. There wasn't one that wasn't wounded. They were hurting and they were useless. Someone fell and as they fell I noticed these shadows. Suddenly a vulture swooped down as this victim fell and took a huge chunk of flesh out of that person. And I said, "God, your army doesn't have a chance. They are so weak, so depleted, in such a useless condition and when they fall, down come the vultures to eat them."

He said, "Behold what I do." An angel with the speed of lightning, moved through the entire army and placed a mirror on everyone's forehead. When everyone had the mirror on the angel yelled, "Look up for your redemption draweth nigh!" As these weak, weary people lifted their heads and looked heavenward-that's where we should look towards higher ground –up came the sun from behind the clouds. And the glory was reflected from off those mirrors with such awesomeness that the vultures backed off and could no longer harm God's people. And you know what the Lord said? He said, "Tell my people, I'm the glory and the lifter of their heads. In Joel, Chapter 2, you're going to see the army I am going to raise up. Fire will go before them; fire behind them. They'll scale the heights; they'll run on the walls. Even when they fall on the floor they will not be wounded." The world has looked at this army and they've pointed their finger and they've been shaking their heads and saying, "I don't understand." But I tell you what they are going to see a difference. You know why this army is so chaotic? We're the only army that is stabbing our own people. We kill our own people.

And why is this army in such chaos? No one knows their job description. God said there are too many heads moving in too many different directions and bringing such division in the army. You know what Joel, Chapter 2 says? They will know their rank. They will know their positions and no one will crowd anybody. We are not anywhere near what that army should be. And God said, "I am going to be the leader of this army and with My voice, I will speak and my people will hear what I have to say and each one will know His job description." I want to encourage people, if your job description is smaller than someone else's job description, if you fulfill your job description you'll get the same reward as someone with a bigger job description. You see God says, 'All I want from you is total obedience. I'm tired of your sacrifices. I want your obedience.' If you fulfill your job description, that's all that matters.

People have said to me, "Surely your husband should be the preacher." When you come to salvation, if God's people would realize this, we become divinely owned property. You no longer have any rights other than the authority God gives you over the enemy. We have no rights but to report for duty to be instructed by the Most High God.

God's people no longer fear Him. They treat Him with disrespect. And God said, "My people need to come back to the place where they realize who they are dealing with." We think of God as some Santa Claus and we say, "Jump here, do this, go here, fix this." God said, "My people need to get their priorities right! They need to know who is God and who is the servant. Who is at whose feet?" God said, "I'm going to lead this army and they're going to be champions! The enemy will come but because of the glory reflected from their lives, he will back off because he will not be able to touch them."

In the third vision the first thing took place in heaven. I saw what looked like angels carrying a guided missile. They placed the missile into the bow, stepped aside and there was a silence that you could hear. Uncanny. Next I saw a garment moving and I saw the feet of Jesus and realized that the Lord was walking towards the bow. He walked up, took His awesome arm {I saw the nail prints and I knew it was Jesus}, and He directed the bow towards Him. He pulled it towards Him and then let it go, and it came hurtling towards the face of the earth. As it reached the earth's surface, the atmosphere, it divided into splinters, thousands upon thousands of thousands, all over the entire face of the earth. And I said, "God, what are you doing?"

The next thing took place on earth. I saw a church building completely burnt out and I found the people walking around the church, weeping and wailing and crying. And I said, "Oh God look how they mourn." Then God's voice changed. He said, "Mourn? They are crying over buildings that they've erected and now are brought to naught. But did they even cry for the souls that were entering into the caverns of hell while they built palaces?" And God said, "I've heard day and night the cries of men and women and young people, crying out to be delivered from the caverns of hell." Do you know what the Bible says? Hell has opened up its mouth and enlarged itself and swallowed. I hear their screams and you say, "My people weep?"

I said, "God what have you done?" He said, "Go to the front door." When I got to the front door there was one of the splinter arrows right through a scroll and He said, "What do you read?" I said, "God I read the word, ICHABOD." He said, "Yes. My glory has departed." I said, "Why God?" God said, "My people have pushed me out of my sanctuary and they've made the idol of entertainment their god!" He said, "I am a jealous God and I will share my glory with no one! I have warned my people that it is a terrifying thing to fall into the hands of the living God! I spoke to my people through the Word! I spoke to my people through prophecy! I brought preachers, teachers, layman but my people didn't hear my instructions! They were to busy playing church." I said, "God when are you going to do this?" He said, "I have already begun."

I want to tell you in our travels I have seen "Ichabod" written across some of the churches.

God said, "When man begins to think the church is his work and he tries to monopolize it, he is treading on dangerous ground. When the people come to church to be entertained and to have concerts they have forgotten that my house is a house of prayer. They have forgotten that they come to the house of God to hear from God. My people are playing around the golden calf and they think they're hearing God." It's time God's people woke up. God says, "I'm bringing judgment because they refuse to listen." But He is giving a choice. God says, "That's why I'm sending you and many others to tell this nation to get ready for a divine visitation."

The next scene moved and I came and saw a building that was again on fire. And I heard the most incredible singing. The more the singing rose up to heaven, the greater the fire. And I said, "God are You burning this one down as well?' He said, "Look what I do." The roof of the church began to open. God's people had access into the very presence of God and back into the gathering. There was such an awesome presence of God that they were overwhelmed and the fire grew bigger. I said, "God what are you doing?" He said, "Go to the front door." I went to the front door and there was another splinter arrow and God said, "This one I have written with My own hand." He said, "What do you read?" I said, 'God, I read Revival.' He said, 'Do you know what revival is?' He said, 'Tell my people getting goose bumps the size of molehills, chills running down their spines, shaking hands and vibrations is not revival. That's my blessings. Revival is to purify and cleanse the temple that it may get ready for the glory of God. Revival is when God is in control." He said, "When My people allow me back into my sanctuary as God, My house will be purified, my house will become a house of praise. Then it will become a house of power. Then signs and wonders will once again occur and My Word shall become awesome in the gathering because they will use the name of Jesus which the modern church today hardly finds a place for." And I to tell you that when Almighty God hears the name of Jesus, heaven stands still. He says, "When My Son's name Jesus is once again spoken in the gatherings, when my people use the Word" the pure Word not all the infiltrations we've put into the Word, "I will hear." We've watered Gods Word down so that we don't know what God has said and what man has said. God said, "I am going to strip every tree that My Father has not planted. I am going to pluck them up." We've made God's Word virtually null and void. We've filled it with philosophies. We've filled it with man-made ideas. He said, that He's going strip all the compromises. It's going to be the power of His Word. The blood of the Lamb is going to cleanse God's people. The name of Jesus and the anointing of the Spirit is the signature to seal it all. They must get the glory, not us.

Then God said, "Tell My people I'm coming to visit them in a blanket form. My glory is going to descend into their midst. And if my people are not ready for My glory, Ananias and Sapphira will happen in the very presence of the gathering."

Then God said tell them, "I said to Moses, tell the Israelites I'm coming to visit." The Israelites were so excited. They said; "God's coming to visit." They had no idea who God was and I don't think the children of God today have a clear understanding of who God is. They treat Him too disrespectfully. But you know what those people had to do? They had to clean up! They had to be purified— their home, their lives, their clothes. That is why I believe God has sent us. We've come as a warning to the house of God which has gone into captivity. This nation that was born "In God We Trust" has turned from "In God We Trust" and they have elevated other things more than God. God said, "Tell them I'm coming to visit." Well when the children of Israel heard God was coming to visit they were so excited. But I tell you when God did visit they nearly died of fright. The Bible tells us the earth shook. There was a trumpet sound that was awesome. And God's people who a few days before were saying, "Hallelujah, He's coming," began to back off and got on their knees because you know when God's presence comes closer you start to see yourself as you really are. The camouflage falls off. The justification, falls by the wayside. The compromise no longer covers you. The fig leaves fall, and you are naked before God.

You know what He said? "I'm coming to visit my people and My glory is awesome." I said, "God, 'I don't understand your glory?" I have a grandson which I absolutely adore. He said, "What do you desire the most?" I said, "I want to love that grandson. I want to hold and kiss him and love him." "What if I told you that my glory was upon you and you couldn't even look at that grandson?" I said, "God that would be the cruelest thing you could ever do to me because I know I would forget. I would want to touch him and that child disintegrate in front of me." God says, "That's what my glory does to sin." God said, "Adam and Eve were in the garden, clothed with my glory. We communed face-to-face. When they sinned the glory fell and I wanted to embrace them but I didn't because my glory would consume them." So God the Father had to back off and Jesus became the way. Jesus stands between us and the Father.

You know, the sun shining down on this earth. It's got two deadly rays. If they weren't deflected by the earth's atmosphere we would be consumed. If Jesus didn't stand between us and the Father, we would be consumed. But you know what Jesus says? He says, "Bride, I'm getting you ready for glory! I've got to get you purified. I'm going to get you holy because I want to present you to My Father spotless, that He may touch you, that He may embrace you, that He may hold you to His bosom without you being consumed." Then God said, "Go to every place where I open the door to you in this country and tell them they have a choice- ICHABOD OR

REVIVAL." {www.mercygate.com/e107_plugins/content.
php?content.199}

CHAPTER TEN

CLIMATE CHANGE AND THE FUTURE

T o move into what will be our final chapter on climate change and what we come to is perhaps the most serious and important issue of all regarding it and that is the future. A future that unlike what science or Al Gore has to offer, thank Almighty God, is already written for us. It is without question one of the most glorious and exciting things of all about the religion of God and the bible. His Majesty actually looks to inform or rather wants to educate the children of men regarding the future:

> "I am God, and there is no other; I am God, and there is none like me. I make known the end from the beginning, from ancient times, what is still to come. I say: My purpose will stand and I will do all that I please." {Isaiah 46:9-10}

> "I have told you now before it happens, so that when it does happen you will believe." {John 14:29}

It is one of the most intriguing if not important of all subjects in the entire bible. A subject that unfortunately though is not without a great deal of difficulty for how exactly does one go about trying to interpret words that was written thousands of years ago? Just take what was given to Daniel as an example. No matter how much the angel Gabriel tried to explain to Daniel the visions which he was given Daniel was at a loss to understand it all. That is why Gabriel ultimately said to him to close up the words because it is for a distant time. {Daniel 8:27} Apparently such visions were only meant to be understood in their totality to those to whom it was to be given to know and that only at the appropriate times. Again the words of the angel Gabriel:

"He replied, 'Go your way Daniel, because the words are closed and sealed until the time of the end.'" {Daniel 12:9}

A message that interestingly enough wasn't given to just Daniel alone but as we see in the scriptures to a number of people the last of which was the apostle John. His book of Revelation is one astounding book- a message which we will try to decipher by paying attention more or less only to what it says regarding the weather. The interpretation will work by first rearranging the *seals*, *trumpets*, and *bowls* into an entirely different format. For it appears to this writer that the way it was originally written with the seven seals coming first and then the seven trumpet blasts and finally the seven bowls of God's anger is not chronologically sound. Rather, as we shall see there is, it appears, a connection between each of the events chronicled and perhaps the proper order is more in line with the opening of a seal to reveal the blowing of a trumpet and then to the pouring out of a bowl. It seems only logical for it to work this way seeing how each category has seven events following each other in succession as well as the weather itself. The underlined portions will work as a reference point for us towards this end and we will do this by going backwards through the scriptures beginning first with the seventh bowl, trumpet and seal.

7th Bowl {Rev. 16:17-21}
   "The seventh angel poured out his bowl into the air, and out of the temple came a loud voice from the throne, saying, 'IT IS DONE!' Then there came <u>flashes of lightning, rumblings, peals of thunder and a severe earthquake. No earthquake like it has ever occurred since man has been on earth, so tremendous was the quake.</u> The great city split into three parts, and the cities of the nations collapsed. God remem-

345

bered Babylon the Great and gave her the cup filled with the wine of the fury of His wrath. Every island fled away and the mountains could not be found. <u>From the sky huge hailstones of about a hundred pounds each fell upon men. And they cursed God on account of the plague of hail, because the plague was so terrible</u>."

7th Trumpet {Rev. 11:15-19}

"The seventh angel sounded his trumpet, and there were loud voices in heaven, which said: 'The kingdoms of the world has become the kingdom of our Lord and of His Christ, and He will reign for ever and ever.' And the twenty-four elders, who were seated on their thrones before God, fell on their faces and worshipped God, saying: 'We give thanks to you Lord God Almighty, the One who is and who was, because you have taken your power and have begun to reign. The nations were angry; and your wrath has come. The time has come for judging the dead, and for rewarding your servants the prophets and your saints and those who reverence your name, both small and great- and for destroying those who destroy the earth.' Then God's temple in heaven was opened, and within his temple was seen the Ark of the Covenant. And there came <u>flashes of lightning, rumblings, peals of thunder, an earthquake and a great hailstorm</u>."

7th Seal {Rev. 8:1-5}

"When he opened the seventh seal, there was silence in heaven for about half an hour. And I saw the seven angels who stand before God, and to them were given seven trumpets. Another angel, who had a golden censer, came and stood at the altar. He was given much incense to offer, with the prayers of all the saints, on the golden altar before the throne. The smoke of the incense, together with the prayers of the saints, went up before God from the angel's hand. Then the angel took the censer filled it with fire from the altar, and hurled it on the earth; and there <u>came rumblings, flashes of lightning and an earthquake</u>.

Job says to us regarding God's use of the weather:

"Have you entered the storehouses of the snow or seen the storehouses of the hail, which I reserve for times of trouble, for days of war and battle?" {Job 38:22}

It is hard to imagine one hundred pound hailstones falling out of the skies. For most people hailstones the size of baseballs are quite enough but can you imagine stones of ice weighing in at 100 pounds apiece? My word what kind of a people would provoke Almighty God into such actions? Then again perhaps a better question is, what kind of a people would presume to think that a God needed anyone to fight His battles for Him as the Moslems do their jihad? If His Majesty hasn't got the power requisite to do anything He wishes and if a people aren't going to become painfully aware of this in the future. In fact, if it wouldn't be of some interest and importance to mention here some rather odd weather phenomena that recently occurred over Edmonton, Canada. In a matter of hours the city and her streets were flooded with not only water but an enormous amount of hailstones. It was an event that grabbed everyone's attention but what was even more intriguing for this writer anyway was how this was repeated not long after in Houston, Texas. In just a matter of hours from this event over Edmonton the news of the day also surrounded talk of hailstones pummeling the city of Houston to the degree that windows in the cities skyscrapers were being blown out. Just a coincidence?! Not likely given these astonishing teachings of the bible and why if this was truly an explicit act of Almighty God would he do this? Well, can't help but wonder if it didn't have something to do with the oil industry for isn't oil the main business of both cities? Something apparently grabbed God's attention and what that could have possibly have been is of course for those within the boardrooms of those cities to ponder over and answer. Brings a whole new kind of clarity doesn't it to those words of His:

"It is a dreadful thing to fall into the hands of the living God." {Hebrews 10:31}

Imagine, and get this, science has trouble with 'certain abrupt meteorological events' that pop and now and then? Divine Communication folks! Divine Communication! It's as simple as that!

Now as for earthquakes well, here we find an event similar surely to the Sumatra Event except in this case it will all but end the human history of mankind. An earthquake dear reader is what ultimately is going to bring about the final end of all things. Almighty God will finally have had enough of mankind's sinful and wicked ways.

6th Bowl {Rev. 16:12-16}
"The sixth angel poured out his bowl on the great river Euphrates, and its water was dried up to prepare the way for the kings from the East. Then I saw three evil spirits that looked like frogs; they came out of the mouth of the dragon, out of the mouth of the beast and out of the mouth of the false prophet. They are spirits of demons performing miraculous signs, and they go out to the kings of the whole world, to gather

them for the battle on the great day of God Almighty. *'Behold, I come like a thief. Blessed is he who stays awake and keeps his clothes with him, so that he may not go naked and be shamefully exposed."*

Then they gathered the kings together to the place that in Hebrew is called Armageddon."

6th Trumpet {Rev. 9:13-21}
"The sixth angel sounded his trumpet, and I heard a voice coming from the horns of the golden altar that is before God. It said to the sixth angel who had the trumpet, 'Release the four angels who are bound at the great river Euphrates. And the four angels who had been kept ready for this very hour and day and month and year were released to kill a third of mankind. The number of the mounted troops was two hundred million. I heard their number. The horses and riders I saw in my vision looked like this: Their breastplates were fiery red, dark blue, and yellow as sulfur. The heads of the horses resembled the heads of lions, and out of their mouths came fire, smoke and sulfur. A third of mankind was killed by the three plagues of fire, sulfur that came out of their mouths. The power of the horses was in their mouths and in their tails; for their tails were like snakes, having heads with which they inflict injury. The rest of mankind that were not killed by these plagues still did not repent of the work of their hands; they did not stop worshipping demons, and idols of gold, silver, bronze, stone and wood-idols that cannot see or hear or walk. Nor did they repent of their murders, their magic arts, their sexual immorality or their thefts."

6th Seal {Rev. 6:12-17}
"I watched as he opened the sixth seal. <u>There was
a great earthquake. The sun turned black like sackcloth made of goat hair, the whole moon turned blood
red, and the stars in the sky fell to earth,</u> as late figs
drop from a fig tree when shaken by a strong wind.
The sky receded like a scroll, rolling up, and every
mountain and island was removed from its place.
Then the kings of the earth, the princes, the generals,
the rich, the mighty, and every slave and every free
man hid in caves and among the rocks of the mountains. 'They called to the mountains and the rocks,
Fall on us and hide us from the face of him who sits
on the throne and from the wrath of the Lamb! For
the great day of their wrath has come, and who can
stand?"

Now here again we find another earthquake, the same
one that we saw previously, and we can know this by way
of the sky receding like a scroll. Everything in both places
comes to a finality of human history with the most astonishing event here surely being the words of Christ. I mean
how odd to find in this portion of scripture both the Rapture
of the Church and the Battle of Armageddon taking place.
What are these two events doing being so closely related
to one another? Isn't the opinion by most that the Church
will have long since been raptured out by this time? That is
surely not the case here, however, for we see the scriptures
telling us that not until Armageddon begins will we see the
actual rapture of the church. Moreover a 200 hundred million
man army marching across the Euphrates alluvial plain?
Now what is this doing coming from the East? That is, from
the other side of the Euphrates River basin? Most if not all
biblical scholars you will find are of the opinion that this is
supposed to come from out of the land of the North? That

is from out of the land of Gog and Magog which is interpreted to be Russia and Germany? It appears that can't be, especially in view of how the scriptures teach that this 'Gog and Magog' will not try to attack the nation of Israel until after the one thousand year reign of Christ on this planet. Accordingly it is very, very doubtful therefore that Gog and Magog has anything whatsoever to do with either Russia or Germany. Two nations which are certainly not from the four corners of the earth as the scriptures also teach. {Rev. 20:7} An event of which actually occurs with the release of Satan from his prison. They go hand in hand with each other, and if that isn't something altogether significant. Makes for some serious questions doesn't it regarding many an interpretation of the end times? As for the earthquake, well given the 200 hundred million army moving across the land and that towards the city of Jerusalem and it will be as though God just took his hand and clenching it into a fist He will strike the earth once and for all! That is in the very heart of the city of Jerusalem as we saw under the seventh bowl.

5th Bowl {Rev. 16:10-11}
"The fifth angel poured out his bowl on the throne of the beast, and his kingdom was plunged into darkness. Men gnawed their tongues in agony and cursed the God of Heaven because of their pains and their sores, but they refused to repent of what they had done."

5th Trumpet {Rev. 9:1-12}
"The fifth angel sounded his trumpet, and I saw a star that had fallen from the sky to the earth. The star was given the key to the shaft of the Abyss. When he opened the Abyss, smoke arose from it like the smoke from a gigantic furnace. The sun and sky were darkened by the smoke from the abyss. And out of

the smoke locusts came down upon the earth and were given power like that of scorpions of the earth. They were told not to harm the grass of the earth or any plant or tree, but only those who did not have the seal of God on their foreheads. They were not given power to kill them but only to torture them for five months. And the agony they suffered was like that of the sting of a scorpion when it strikes a man. During those days men will seek death, but will not find it; they will long to die but death will elude them. The locusts looked like horses prepared for battle. On their heads they wore something like crowns of gold, and their faces resembled human faces. Their hair was like woman's hair, and their teeth were like lion's teeth. They had breastplates of iron, and the sound of their wings was like the thundering of many horses and chariots running into battle. They had tails and stings like scorpions, and in their tails they had power to torment people for five months. They had as king over them the angel of the Abyss, whose name in Hebrew is Abaddon, and in Greek, Apollon.

5th Seal {Rev. 6:9-11}
"When he opened the fifth seal, I saw under the altar the souls of those who had been slain because of the word of God and the testimony they had maintained. They called out in a loud voice, How long, Sovereign Lord, Holy and true, until you judge the inhabitants of the earth and avenge our blood?' Then each of them was given a white robe, and they were told to wait a little longer until the number of their fellow servants and brothers who were to be killed as they had been was completed."

Under these three events we find nothing regarding climate change except, that is, for some kind of smoke that will somehow darken the sun and sky. Other than that the only thing that would be of any significance here is if there are three voices that are crying out for vengeance it would have to be those three teenage girls who were beheaded at the hands of the Moslem jihadists in Indonesia. My word what a thing to do to some innocent children and how Almighty God must feel holding in his hands the slain souls of those children of His is something that should frighten every single person reading this book. This is not going to go over well at all, and to find and here that man Hasanuddins gloating that, "the girls heads were a present to Muslims for Idal Fitri "{the last day of the holy month of Ramadan} will surely be something that Almighty God will have him give account for. http://www.csmonitor.com/2007/0205/p07s02-woap.html

Bringing him as well as those murderers into His presence with those three girls standing there by His side, God will surely ask of them some serious questions. Moreover given the murders of that Protestant minister and the Bali bombing and one can't help but wonder if that earthquake that struck Indonesia didn't have something to do with that? Again it can't be a coincidence and to find another earthquake occurring March 28, 2005 and it makes for some serious reflection and consideration. For what we have here people is Christmas and Easter, and when you add to this other earthquakes like for example the Good Friday Earthquake of March 27, 1964 in Alaska and if the words 'El Nino' doesn't come to mind. Remember those fishermen from South America? So again Divine Communication folks, Divine Communication and look Indonesia we here and find actually gets hit with another earthquake and this on the very eve of the holy month of Ramadan{September 12, 2007}. Now if it that doesn't go to show and prove that God was and is being provoked. <u>This can't be just a coincidence!</u> <u>This can't be just a coincidence!</u> So my word and could there actually be more acts of terrorism and murdering being planned by these jihadists in Indonesia? Accordingly if people therefore shouldn't be on their knees crying, repenting and confessing for their sins and what not for you can be sure of this, no one wants to be looking to be punished by a kind that will be most excruciating. To be tortured by locusts {demons} and that for some five months is not where anyone wants to end up! So my word and look if truly the saying of what goes around comes around isn't most applicable here! Wow!

4th Bowl {Rev. 16:8-9}

"The fourth angel poured out his bowl on the sun, and <u>the sun was given power to scorch people with fire</u>. They were seared by the intense heat and they cursed the name of God, who had control over these plagues, but they refused to repent and glorify him."

4th Trumpet {Rev. 8:12-13}

The fourth angel sounded his trumpet, <u>and a third of the sun was struck, a third of the moon, and a third of the stars, so that a third of them turned dark. A third of the day was without light, and also a third of the night</u>. As I watched, I heard an eagle flying in midair call out in a loud voice: 'Woe! Woe! Woe to the inhabitants of the earth, because of the trumpet blasts about to be sounded by the other three angels."

4th Seal {Rev. 8:12-13}

"When the Lamb opened the fourth seal, I heard the voice of the fourth living creature say, "Come!" I looked, and there before me was a pale horse! Its rider was named Death, and Hades was following close behind him. They were given power over a fourth of the earth to kill by sword, famine and plague, and by the wild beasts of the earth.

Now in these next four episodes there is little resemblance between the seals to the trumpets and bowls. What we do see however, is that the trumpet blasts and pouring out of the bowls are speaking about events and matters that are essentially the same. Here we see that the sun is going to be stoked by Almighty God in such a way as to result in its possible implosion. Not only will it scorch people with fire but also one third of it will stop shining altogether. It brings well to mind some rather fascinating testimony from those who lived to experience that Tunguska meteorite in Siberia on June 30, 1908:

"Testimony of S. Semenov, as recorded by Leonid Kulik's expedition in 1930"

"At breakfast time I was sitting by the house at Vanavara trading post {65 kilometres |40 miles| south of the explosion}, facing North. |...| I suddenly saw that directly to the North, over Onkul's Tunguska road, the sky split in two and fire appeared high and wide over the forest {as Semenov showed, about 50° degrees up -expedition note}. The split in the sky grew larger, and the entire Northern side was covered with fire. At that moment I became so hot that I couldn't bear it, as if my shirt was on fire; from the northern side, where the fire was, came strong heat. I wanted to tear off my shirt and throw it down, but then the sky shut closed, and a strong thump sounded, and I was thrown a few yards. I lost my senses for a moment, but then my wife ran out and led me to the house. After that such noise came, as if rocks were falling or cannons were firing, the earth shook, and when I was on the ground, I pressed my head down, fearing rocks would smash it. When the sky opened up, hot wind raced between the houses, like from cannons, which left traces in the ground like pathways, and it damaged some crops. Later we saw that many windows were shattered, and in the barn a part of the iron lock snapped." www.answers.com/tunguska%20event

Now wow if this doesn't provide some great details and insight into what is going to be experienced by mankind in the future, and there are going to be people who are actually going to curse God because of it? Unbelievable!

Now as for the horse and rider, well it appears by way of this we will know when it will be making its rounds throughout the earth!

3rd Bowl {Rev. 16:4-7}

"The third angel poured out his bowl on the rivers and springs of water, and they became blood. Then I heard the angel in charge of the waters say: 'You are just in these judgments, you who are and who were, the Holy One, because you have so judged; for they have shed the blood of your saints and prophets, and you have given them blood to drink as they deserve.' And I heard the altar respond: 'Yes, Lord God Almighty, true and just are your judgments.'"

3rd Trumpet {Rev. 8:10-11}

"The third angel sounded his trumpet, and a great star, blazing like a torch, fell from the sky on a third of the rivers and on the springs of water- the name of the star is Wormwood. A third of the waters turned bitter, and many people died from the waters that had become bitter."

3rd Seal {Rev. 6:5-7}

"When the Lamb opened the third seal, I heard the third living creature say, "Come!" I looked, and there before me was a black horse! Its rider was holding a pair of scales in his hand. Then I heard what sounded like a voice among the four living creatures, saying, 'A quart of wheat for a day's wages, and three quarts of barley for a day's wages, and do not damage the oil and wine!'"

Under this third event we see how God will strike the rivers and springs with His judgment against a people for committing some terrible crimes against His people. What is there going to be more beheadings of teenage schoolgirls? Accordingly, is it any wonder then that under the seal we see hunger becoming rampant for people will have to ration what they have very carefully. Without water nothing lives, nothing survives and again if what goes around comes around isn't most applicable here!

2nd Bowl {Rev. 16:3}

"The second angel poured out his bowl on the sea, and it turned into blood like that of a dead man, and every living thing in the sea died."

2nd Trumpet {Rev. 8:8-9}

"The second angel sounded his trumpet, and something like a huge mountain, all ablaze, was thrown into the sea. A third of the sea turned into blood, a third of the living creatures in the sea died, and a third of the ships were destroyed."

2nd Seal {Rev. 6:3-4}

"When the Lamb opened the second seal, I heard the second living creature say, "Come!" Then another horse came out, a fiery red one. Its rider was given power to take peace from the earth and to make men slay each other. To him was given a large sword."

In the news recently there appeared a most astounding story:

'Terror as huge a meteor hits'
Wellington- "A search began yesterday for the remains of a large a meteor that exploded over New Zealand's North Island with enough force to shake buildings, leaving a plume of blue smoke that covered hundreds of square miles.

Falling debris from the meteor, which eyewitnesses said was as bright as the sun, was blamed for starting a forest fire near Napier, on the East Coast.

The spectacular explosion was seen by people on both sides of the North Island and from as far north as Auckland to Christchurch in the South Island. Witnesses said the fireball had a long, fiery tale. Airline pilots reported sightings and a meteor was picked up on radar by air traffic controllers.

Rodney Austin, information officer for the New Zealand Astronomical Society, said the meteor could have been as large as a railway locomotive. Phone lines to the emergency services were jammed by anxious callers. Jocelyn Nancarrow of Wanganui on the West Coast said: "It was like a huge, dynamite kind of explosion. The house shook, the ground shook. It appeared to be quite close. I was trembling with fear because I thought it was a plane that had exploded."

Another Napier witness, Tony Unsworth, said: "It was an amazing, bright, white ball heading down at about 45° degrees to the earth.

As it got further down, it just seemed to explode and bright blue smoke came after it."

Unsworth said the smoke covered the city of 60,000 people for at least an hour before sunset.

It is feared the remains could be difficult to find in New Zealand's rugged and sparsely populated landscape." {The Province Newspaper Thursday, July 8, 1999}

It appears that events on this world of ours are moving faster towards biblical prophecy and the end of human history than anyone could have ever imagined or thought? This can't be just another coincidence folks and to think that there are organizations like NASA and her scientists who talk about preventing and /or intercepting these meteorites with ICBM's? Unbelievable! Since when was the Creator of the Universe some kind of an absentee landlord over His creation? If nothing happens in ones own home without ones full knowledge you can be sure that nothing happens on God's planet without His full knowledge as well.

1st Bowl {Rev. 16:1-2}
"The first angel went and poured out his bowl on the land, and ugly and painful sores broke out on the people who had the mark of the beast and worshipped his image."

1st Trumpet {Rev. 8:7}
"The first angel sounded his trumpet, and there came hail and fire mixed with blood, and it was hurled down upon the earth. A third of the earth was burned up, a third of the trees were burned up, and all the green grass was burned up."

1st Seal {Rev. 6:1-2}

"I watched as the Lamb opened the first of the seven seals. Then I heard one of the four living creatures say in a voice like thunder, "Come!" I looked, and there before me was a white horse! Its rider held a bow, and he was given a crown, and he rode out as a conqueror bent on conquest."

Now under this last heading, or rather first heading of the trumpet and bowl, we see that a plague of blood and hail will be sent down upon the earth that will result in painful sores to break out upon people. A matter of which occurs ultimately because of the decision to take this mark of the beast {666} and to worship someone who considered itself to be God. Not only that, but one third of the earth's plant life will be burned up because mixed with the blood and hail will be fire. As for the seal, well what we have been shown here is our Lord and Savior Christ Jesus who as the supreme conqueror will ride out to begin the process of finally returning the world to His Authority, Dominion and Ruler-ship. A Kingship that was always His to begin with, but one in which mankind actually tried to rob Him of! This is confirmed by the words of St. John in chapter 19:11-21 and O what a great day that will finally be!

"I saw heaven standing open and there before me was a white horse, whose rider is called faithful and true. With justice, he judges and makes war. His eyes are like blazing fire, and on his head are many crowns. He has a name written on him that no one knows but he himself. He is dressed in a robe dipped in blood, and his name is the Word of God. The armies of heaven were following him, riding on white horses and dressed in fine linen, white and clean. Out of his mouth comes a sharp sword with

which to strike down the nations. He will rule them with an iron scepter. He treads the winepress of the fury of the wrath of God Almighty. On his robe and on his thigh he has this name written:
Kings of Kings and Lord of Lords.

And I saw an angel standing in the sun, who cried in a loud voice to all the birds flying in midair, 'Come, gather together for the great supper of God, so that you may eat the flesh of kings, generals, and mighty men, of horses and their riders, and the flesh of all people, free and slave, small and great.

Then I saw the beast and the kings of the earth and their armies gathered together to make war against the rider on the horse and his army. But the beast was captured, and with him the false prophet who had performed the miraculous signs on his behalf. With these signs he had deluded those who had received the mark of the beast and worshiped his image. The two of them were thrown alive into the fiery lake of burning sulfur. The rest of them were killed with the sword that came out of the mouth of the rider on the horse, and all the birds gorged themselves on their flesh." {Revelation 19:11- 21}

Not even a 200 hundred million man army is going to prevent the return of His world and creation back into His own hands. Wow, and imagine the likes of a General McArthur and those who follow in his train being reduced to nothing more than feed for the birds of the air. That is swallows, hummingbirds, seagulls, blackbirds, swans, loons, albatrosses, pelicans, cormorants, herons, wood storks, owls, eagles, falcons, and last but not least the vultures! Wow, beware people, the Christ of Almighty God! He is by no means someone to be reckoned with or ignored. Indeed for a King of His stature to have lowered himself to the degree of washing His servant's feet and then dying the way He did for us all is something that no one should overlook or dare reject. Get to know Him and get to know Him quickly and intimately for it appears to this writer that will be the only way to really survive what is about to come upon this planet of ours. Indeed if not especially so for women who are pregnant for as Christ warned:

"How dreadful it will be in those days for pregnant women and nursing mothers! Pray that your flight will not take place in winter or on the Sabbath. For there will be great distress, unequaled from the beginning of the world until now-and never to be equaled again." {Matthew 24:19}

For Him to mention this should not be taken lightly by anyone including those who think that they are going to be raptured out before any of this actually begins. It appears to this writer that is a wrong if not an altogether foolish an interpretation of the end times. Surely that this book proves out well enough and so in conclusion then there you have it an interpretation of a book that has for centuries been an enigma to understand and whether this is a correct interpretation of the book of Revelation or not is of course yet to be seen. The goal was to simply try and understand it from the perspective of what it has to say on climate change and it is believed by this writer that in the history of the Church no one has ever looked at it from this perspective. I certainly did not come up with it from reading any other book besides the bible itself and if it doesn't reveal for us that the chronology could in fact be far more correct with the opening of a seal to reveal the blowing of the trumpet and then to the pouring out of the bowl coming first. Personally I find it works well this way. Certainly no one can argue that the events chronicled do speak of events that are essentially the same. So climate change- it provides an interesting key, doesn't it, to unlocking much of the secrets of the bible? Now is there anything else that this book has to offer on the subject? Well it appears it most certainly does and that by way of those two witnesses of Almighty God who apparently are going to arrive in the city of Jerusalem sometime between these events of the seals, trumpets and bowls:

"I was given a reed like a measuring rod and was told, Go and measure the temple of God and the altar, and count the worshippers there. But exclude the outer court; do not measure it, because it has been given to the Gentiles. They will trample on the holy city for 42 months. And I will give power to my two witnesses, and they will prophesy for 1260 days clothed in sackcloth. These are the two olive trees and the two lamp stands that stand before the Lord of the earth. If anyone tries to harm them, fire comes from their mouths and devours their enemies. This is how anyone who wants to harm them must die. These men have the power to shut up the sky so that it will not rain during the time they are prophesying; and they have power to turn the waters into blood and to strike the earth with every kind of plague as often as they want."

"Now when they have finished their testimony, the beast that comes up from the Abyss will attack them, and kill them. Their bodies will lie in the street of the great city, which is figuratively called Sodom and Egypt, where also their Lord was crucified. For three and a half days men from every people, tribe, language and nation will gaze on their bodies and refuse them burial. The inhabitants of the earth will gloat over them and will celebrate by sending each other gifts, because these two prophets had tormented those who live on the earth."

"But after three and a half days a breath of life from God entered them, and they stood on their feet, and terror struck those who saw them. Then they heard a loud voice saying to them, Come up here. And they went up to heaven in a cloud, while their enemies looked on. *At that very hour there was a severe earthquake and a tenth of the city collapsed. Seven thousand people were killed in the earthquake, and the survivors were terrified and gave glory to the God of heaven."* {Revelation 11:1-13}

From the city of Jerusalem a rather phenomenal work of Almighty God is going to occur and why? Well it appears to have something to do with the temple of God and the Jewish people specifically. It goes back to that statement of St. Paul's wherein he said that the Jews always require a sign:

"Jews demand miraculous signs and Greeks look for wisdom." {1Corinthinas 1:22}

A sign that Almighty God will of course have to give to the Jewish people during this time because as we saw in chapter three their rejection of Christ Jesus as their Messiah is going to result in another king rising to power. A king who in the beginning will look genuine but will turn out to be an impostor and why the city of Jerusalem? Well because Jerusalem is where Almighty God placed His name originally. It is where the true religion of His Majesty comes from and where for all eternity His home will be. So it's only logical then that Satan will look to try and control the entire world from there. He wants to be and play god ultimately and what better place for that to occur than in that city and through the Jewish people. So with such a deception then Almighty God cannot and will not just stand by but will answer this and what better way for that to occur than through these two witnesses who will be given by Almighty God the kind of power to change the weather at will and inflict the world with any and all kinds of plagues. So one last and final time Almighty God will look to try and teach truth to the people of Jerusalem. It doesn't end very happily though for as we see an earthquake is going to strike Jerusalem killing some seven thousand people. Apparently instead of repenting the people are going to gloat over these two men's death by sending each other gifts? Jerusalem, Jerusalem? Unbelievable isn't it? Indeed and if you want or need the Old Testament reference to this you will find it in the words of the prophet Zechariah:

"Then I asked the angel, 'What are these two olive trees on the right and on the left of the lamp stand?'
Again I asked him, 'What are these two olive branches beside the two gold pipes that pour golden oil?'
He replied, 'Do you not know what these are?' 'No my lord,' I said.
So he said 'These are the two who are anointed to serve the Lord of all the earth.'" {Zechariah 4:11-14}

Interesting, isn't it? Whoever would have thought that something written some 600 years apart from each other are speaking of events that are again essentially the same? Only a God could be the author of something like this, and look if climate change doesn't prove that this will all happen exactly the way it is written. Surely no one can argue that given what we have seen in the histories of everything from Noah to Job, the history of Israel, the Moravians, the Methodists, and Oberlin. It all points in the direction of God and His Son Christ Jesus!!! When is all of this going to take place though that is the question? A question that could very well be answered shortly enough given what we see happening throughout the world especially with these crop circles which is just another form of Divine Communication. Remember those words of our Lord and Savior Christ Jesus:

"There will be great earthquakes, famines and pestilences in various places, and fearful events and great signs from heaven." {Luke 21:11}

Brings a whole new kind of emphasis doesn't it upon some interesting and none too important words from King Solomon:

"Remember your Creator in the days of your youth, before the days of trouble come and the years approach when you will say, I find no pleasure in them- before the sun and the light and the moon and the stars grow dark, and the clouds return after the rain." {Ecclesiastes 12:1-2}

Imagine the clouds our scientists are discovering are returning far too often after the rain. Why though has no one ever bothered to answer those questions posed to us from the book of Job?

"Does the rain have a Father? Who Fathers the drops of dew?" {Job 38:28}

Global warming people! Global warming!!!!

CONCLUSION

They say that the role of a minister is to raise the profound religious questions. That, and of course to comfort the afflicted and to afflict the comforted and to raise the question of how come you're suffering? Well if I have tired to do anything by the writing of this book on climate change it is exactly that! In fact astounded that no one has done so yet I find myself kind of blessed to be the first one to bring to the attention what the bible has to say on this important and timely subject. Do we ever need to get our heads out of the sand and start to pay far, far more attention to everything that the bible has to say? Industrial pollution, however it may aggravate the environment in which we live, is not the reason behind what is happening to our weather. Rather it is this other kind of pollution that the bible calls sin, which is disobedience to God's Laws and Commandments that is responsible for it all. This is the real issue and it is one that every single one of us had better start to look at and deal with far more seriously. In fact, if I wouldn't want to mention something that I came across just recently concerning this very matter. It occurred at work with some gossip about a girl in her mid-twenties who had apparently become pregnant by a 17 year old boy and the mother of the boy after looking into the whole predicament turned to her son and said to forget about the baby and the girl. Apparently after discovering that this girl already had two other children from two previous liaisons this mother balked at the very thought that her son's life was to be destroyed 'as it were' by ended up a husband and a father of not only their baby but that of the other two as well. I couldn't believe it. Imagine, I said to everyone, here you have a young girl in her early to mid-twenties with three children from three different fathers, all three of whom walked out on them all?! I couldn't believe it and after asking where this girl's own father and mother was I was informed that her father walked out on her and her mother many years earlier and was living in Winnipeg.

Flabbergasted by this I turned to the lady who had all the intimate details and shouted that when parents don't teach their children anything about sin, anything about God, anything about Christ, anything about the bible, what they inevitably are ending up doing is sending their children to hell and not only do they send their children to hell but they follow them there. Furthermore I countered it wasn't enough for Christ to die and pay for the sins of the human race but society is going to pay for the sins of its own as well! My word what is a nation ever going to look like or survive for that matter when its population is going to be reduced to nothing but wards of the state? This abandonment of children by their parents is something utterly and truly dreadful and if it doesn't bring well to mind those words of God from the prophet Malachi:

"He will turn the hearts of the fathers to their children, and the hearts of the children to their fathers, *or else I will come and strike the land with a curse.*" {Malachi 4:5-6}

Moreover if this one issue doesn't teach us about what religion, pure unadulterated religion really is and that is what? Well:

"Religion that God our Father accepts as pure and faultless is this: to look after orphans and widows and to keep oneself from being polluted by the world." {James 1:27}

At one time this came about as a result of misfortune and unfortunate circumstances. Today however this is the result of nothing more than ones own selfish wishes and desires. If there is one thing truly alarming about the way in which society is moving it is the creation now of widows and orphans by way of divorce and what not. This is not going to go over well. This is not going to go over well at all and if this illustration doesn't bring a whole new kind of truth to those words of Christ Jesus:

> *"Are you so dull? Don't you see that nothing that enters a man from the outside can make him unclean? For it doesn't go into his heart but into his stomach, and then out of his body. What comes out of a man is what makes him unclean. For from within, out of men's hearts, come evil thoughts, sexual immorality, theft, murder lust, adultery, greed, malice, deceit, lewdness, envy, slander, arrogance, and folly. All of these evils come from inside and make a man unclean.*
> {Mark 7: 18-23}

Mankind's sins and disobedience to God and His Laws are again reaching some truly unbelievable and bizarre forms. We, like Noah's generation, are again coming to that place where every imagination of the mind and heart is only evil all of the time. Pleasure seekers ultimately:

> "The Lord saw how great mankind's wickedness on the earth had become, and that every inclination of the thoughts of his heart was only evil all of the time." The Lord was grieved that he had made man on the earth, and his heart was filled with pain. So the Lord said, *I will wipe mankind, whom I have created, from the face of the earth-men and animals, and creatures that move along the ground, the birds of the air-for I am grieved that I have made them.* But Noah found favor in the eyes of the Lord." {Genesis 5: 5-8}

My word and a theocracy they say doesn't work? Really? If so then why is it that of all of the people we find asking if not pleading for prayer to be made for rain it would be the Prime Minister of Australia.

AUSSIES FEAR WORST DROUGHT

"Sydney- Prime Minister John Howard called yesterday on Australians to pray for drought breaking rain as the government dismissed reports it under-estimated water shortages in that country's main farming zone.

Howard last month warned that, without a significant downpour by June, irrigation to farming along southeastern Australia's Murray-Darling river system would be cut.

Although the area has had some rain since then, it remains firmly within the grasp of drought, with dam levels at less than six percent of capacity.

'This affects all of us, this drought, and I say without any hint of irony you should all continue to pray for more rain because we need it very, very badly,' Howard said. {Agence-France Preesse The Province Thrusday, May 17 2007}

Can't help but wonder if this goes out only to those who believe in God or whether this extends to everyone including those two men who are using parts of their anatomy for a circus show? Moreover does this include any kind of repentance and confession which ultimately is what is required before the ***Creator will change His policy on His planet!!!!***

Remember those words of King Solomon and with that we bring this to a conclusion:

"When the heavens are shut up and there is no rain because your people have sinned against you, and when they pray toward this place and confess your name and turn from their sin, because you have afflicted them, then hear from heaven and forgive the sin of your servants, your people Israel. Teach them the right way to live, and send rain on the land you gave your people for an inheritance.

When famine or plague comes to the land, or blight or mildew, locusts or grasshoppers, or when an enemy besieges them in any of their cities, whatever disaster or disease may come, and when a prayer or plea is made by any of your people Israel -each one aware of the afflictions of his own heart, and spreading out his hands toward this temple- then hear from heaven, your dwelling place. Forgive and act; deal with each man according to all that he does, since you know his heart {for you alone know the hearts of all men}, so that they will fear you all the time they live in the land you gave our fathers. {1 Kings 8: 35-40}

WORKS CITED

Aurant, P. {1980 &June 1981} More of Paul Harvey's the Rest of the Story. New York NY: Bantam Books

Bakker, J. {1996} I Was Wrong. Nashville, Tennessee: Thomas Nelson Publishers

Bradley, Raymond S. & Weiss, Harvey {26, January 2001} What Drives Societal Collapse. Pgs. 609-610 Science Magazine Volume 291

Canadian Press. {Sunday, June 30, 2004} Internet Service Providers face crackdown over child pornography, police warn The Vancouver Province Newspaper, Vancouver, British Columbia, Canada

Cantelon, W. {1973} The Day the Dollar Dies Plainfield, New Jersey: Logos International

Chernow, R. {August 1994} The Warburgs. New York & Toronto: Random House Inc.

Cho, P.Y. {1984} More Than Numbers. Milton Keynes, England: Word Publishing.

Curtis A K {1988} The Gallery Christian History Magazine Volume VII, Number 4, Issue #20

DesRoches, E. {October 6, 1997} Debit Cards Hit Small Business Bottom Line The Vancouver Sun Newspaper: Vancouver, British Columbia, Canada

Fisher M. {Wednesday, March 26, 2003 pg. A4} Bravo Company and an embedded army The Vancouver Sun, Vancouver, British Columbia, Canada

France Presse {December, 4, 2003} I prayed for us, then I ate him, cannibal tells court The Province Newspaper, Vancouver, British Columbia, Canada.

France Presse {February, 23, 2004} Climate Changes to Kill millions, Pentagon warns The Province Newspaper, Vancouver, British Columbia Canada

Greenfield, J.R. {Copyright 1928} Power From on High. Bethlehem, Pennslvannia

Harvey, E. & L. {1987} How They Prayed Vol. 2 Shoals, Indiana: Old Paths Tract Society

Hayley, M. {February, 26, 2005} End of Talmudic cycle sparks International Party The Vancouver Sun Newspaper Vancouver, British Columbia, Canada

Hellyer, P. {1997} The Evil Empire Globalizations Darker Side. Toronto, Ontario: Chimo Media Limited 99 Atlantic Ave. Suite 302 Toronto, Ont. M6K 3J8

Highfield, R. {April 14, 2003} Deity Discredited National Post Newspaper Vancouver, British Columbia, Canada

J. Brendan Murphy, Gabriel Gutierrez-Alonso, R. Damian Nance, Javier Fernandez-Suarez, J. Duncan Keppie, Cecilio Quesada, Rob A Strachan, Jarda Dostal{May 2006}Origin of the Rheic Ocean: Rifting along a Neoproterozoic suture Geology Magazine Volume 34 Number 5

Keel, J.A. {1975} The Mothman Prophecies New York, NY 10010: Tom Doherty Associates, LLC

Lenoir, F. Belgian Pedophile gets life in Prison Reuters with files from the Daily Telegraph The Vancouver Sun Newspaper, Vancouver, British Columbia, Canada

R. M. Riss. {1988} Dictionary of Pentecostal and Charismatic Movements, Gran Rapids, Michigan: Zondervan Publishing house

McCasland, D. {1993} Oswald Chambers Abandoned to God Grand Rapids, Michigan: Oswald Chambers Publications Association Ltd. Discovery House

Miller, B. {MCMXLI} Charles Finney. Minneapolis, Minnesota: Zondervan Publishing House

Reinhard, J. {Volume 196, no5} At 22,000 Feet Children of an Inca Sacrifice found Frozen in time. National Geographic, pg. 36-35

Relfe, S. M. {1998} Cure of all Ills Montgomery, Alabama: League of Prayer

Sagan, C. {1994} Pale Blue Dot A Vision of the Human Future in Space New York: Random House

Schaff, Phillip. History of the Christian Church WM. B. Eerdmans Publishing Co. Grand Rapids 1980

Sherdan, W. A. The Fortune Sellers The Big Business of Buying and Selling Predictions, New York NY: John Wiley & Sons

Wallis, A. {1979} Revival the Rain from Heaven. Old Tappan, New Jersy: Originally published by Hodder & Stoughton Limited

Watson, R. {1982} The Moravians and John Wesley. Christian History Magazine pg. 30

Wesley, J. The Journal of John Wesley

Printed in the United States
124990LV00003B/1-9/P

9 781606 478134